# EDWARDIAN SHAW

*Also by Leon Hugo*

BERNARD SHAW: Playwright and Preacher

# Edwardian Shaw

## The Writer and his Age

Leon Hugo

First published in Great Britain 1999 by
**MACMILLAN PRESS LTD**
Houndmills, Basingstoke, Hampshire RG21 6XS and London
Companies and representatives throughout the world

A catalogue record for this book is available from the British Library.

ISBN 0–333–73355–X

First published in the United States of America 1999 by
**ST. MARTIN'S PRESS, INC.,**
Scholarly and Reference Division,
175 Fifth Avenue, New York, N.Y. 10010

ISBN 0–312–21796–X

Library of Congress Cataloging-in-Publication Data
Hugo, Leon.
Edwardian Shaw : the writer and his age / Leon Hugo.
p.   cm.
Includes bibliographical references and index.
ISBN 0–312–21796–X
1. Shaw, Bernard, 1856–1950.   2. Shaw, Bernard, 1856–1950–
–Contemporary Great Britain.   3. Great Britain—History—Edward VII,
1901–1910.   4. Dramatists, Irish—20th century—Biography.
I. Title.
PR5366.H84   1998
822'.912—dc21                                                                98–24312
                                                                                          CIP

This book is printed on paper suitable for recycling and made from fully managed and
sustained forest sources.

10   9   8   7   6   5   4   3   2   1
08   07   06   05   04   03   02   01   00   99

Printed and bound in Great Britain by
Antony Rowe Ltd, Chippenham, Wiltshire

# Contents

# Preface

Three weeks after the turn of the century, on 22 January 1901, Queen Victoria died and the age for which she was eponymous passed into history. Her eldest son Albert Edward – Edward VII – succeeded her; the Edwardian Age was born. And Bernard Shaw, 44 years old, faced the most critical period of his career.

Behind him lay some twenty years as a novelist, art, music and drama critic, Fabian activist and playwright. He was known but scarcely famous; he had a reputation, but its concomitant, recognition, amounted to very little in the broad arena of public affairs. He scarcely counted as a playwright. One limited success in London and America with *Arms and the Man*, considerably greater success, again in America, with *The Devil's Disciple*; for the rest, and by this time he had written ten plays, almost complete failure, particularly where it mattered most to him, in the theatrical capital of the world, London. Most, if not all, of the plays of the 1890s would survive to become standard works in the theatrical repertoire, but it is in the nature of the occupation that if a playwright amounts to nothing in the eyes of his contemporaries, he does not exist. This was Shaw in January 1901, a non-existent playwright; in his friend William Archer's opinion no more than a footnote in literary history designating him a literary eccentric. Shaw would have known that in the next few years he would have to leap from the footnote into the main text; that these years would either make or break him.

They made him, of course: effectually a Nobody in 1901, he was emphatically a Somebody in 1910. It was a remarkable transformation, and this study is an attempt to depict it; to depict Shaw the Fabian, the revolutionary public man, the subversive playwright, the controversialist, the wit – the entity that can be described only as the Shavian phenomenon – confronting a deeply entrenched conservative age, trying to mould it into his likeness and being, and winning his way to become the dominant radical voice of the age. It was no easy rite of passage. There were triumphs, there were setbacks; success and crashing failure. By 1910, when there could be no gainsaying the irresistible force of his personality and his works, there were many who continued to resist him. This is paradox, but Shaw and paradox were synonymous.

It is not usual to take up a life *in medias res* and drop it ten years later, a life not even as full as Shaw's. Precedent for this kind of treatment may be found in Stanley Weintraub's *Journey to Heartbreak*, which focuses on Shaw during the First World War; justification for the exercise lying in the contained nature of the Edwardian years, which lend themselves to similar treatment. This said, it has to be emphasized that the present work is not a biography in the usual sense of the word. The Shaw of these pages is the public Shaw making himself heard in the public arena of the Edwardian world, and there is no pretence at superseding any standard biographies of the subject; little attempt to scratch beneath the public surface of the personality.

The 'Age' denoted in this study is the duration of Edward's reign, 1901 to 1910. This is not usual practice, which extends the period to the outbreak of the First World War in 1914. Edward died at an inconvenient time. A reign that began amid auguries of continued prosperity and stability at home and in an Empire on which the sun never set soon found itself caught up in domestic and foreign turmoil which refused to be settled and continued to mount in intensity until by 1914, all control having been surrendered, the nation lurched into war. Then everything 'Edwardian' withered and died. However, the year of Edward's death, 1910, marks a climactic moment and a pivotal point in Shaw's career. Climactic because Shaw's series of confrontations with the Examiner of Plays and the Joint Select Committee appointed to look into stage censorship had taken place not many months before; also because his play *Misalliance*, the most 'modern' of his plays to date, failed. Pivotal because this failure seems to have induced him to take stock of his career. These reasons apply to Shaw; there are other more general ones: the first Post-Impressionist exhibition in London in 1910, Richard Strauss's *Elektra* at Covent Garden in the same year, Stravinsky's *Fire Bird*. These and similar occurrences in the arts other than drama announced a cultural break with the past of decisive importance. And a year later, famously, as though to endorse this break, human nature changed. At least, Virginia Woolf said it did. These reasons are substantial enough to allow the literal reading of 'Edwardian' to be applied to this study.

The Shaw of these pages, the public Shaw, was interested in and wrote on so many topics and issues that it would take a study of considerably greater amplitude than this to cover everything that engaged his attention. Selection has been inevitable, the topics presented in loose chronology and based on what contemporary documents show to have been among Shaw's principal concerns at given times: his declarations of purpose when the new century dawned, his self-promotion campaign in the early months of the century, his campaign against medical authority during the small-pox scare of 1901–2, his campaigns for the Fabian cause in these early years, and so on.

It is Shaw the playwright as distinct from the reformer that occupies centre stage in this account. It is for this reason that those legendary seasons at the Royal Court Theatre under John E. Vedrenne and Harley Granville Barker are a central consideration. Here, from 1904 to 1907, Shaw confronted and confounded the Edwardian world with his subversive brand of dramaturgy, and the Edwardian world in turn, in the persons of its theatre critics, resented and resisted him. This is the focus of the study, rather than a consideration of the plays as dramatic literature; this the measuring rod against Shaw's rise to dominance of the theatre.

Successful though the seasons at the Court had been, he was a long way from achieving general recognition. Critical antipathy remained and intensified after 1907, while other confrontations, principally those with the Examiner of Plays and with the Joint Parliamentary Sub-Committee appointed to look into stage censorship, reinforce an impression of almost total rejection. The rebuffs and put-downs, the hostility to him and what he represented seemed never-ending. Yet somehow he won through.

'The Glass Case Age' – this was Lytton Strachey's description of the late-Victorian period. Shaw is unlikely to have come across Strachey's coinage and yet, inspired by a similar radical mind-set, he enhanced the image by putting Strachey's glass-encased Victorian-Edwardians into a glass house. People who lived in glass houses did not, would not dare to, throw stones. Thrown stones would smash the verities on which they based their lives. Stone-throwing was therefore immoral. Shaw was a champion stone-thrower, he dedicated his life to perfecting the art; he was immoral and heretical in the highest degree. The walls of the English home, though made of glass, were thick and tough and Shaw's stone-throwing was rather like Captain Bluntschli's description of a cavalry charge in *Arms and the Man*: peas flung against a window pane. But he was audible – how audible he was! – and he never let up and his fusillades of flinty pebbles did not stop rattling, not for a second in those years, on glass-house panes. He frequently succeeded in cracking them, more than once of smashing a few – of smashing as well Strachey's glass-casings within the glass house – thereby allowing immoral Shavian air to gust into the dwelling and swirl uncomfortably and coldly round its inhabitants – until in 1910 in *Misalliance*, his patience apparently exhausted, he completed his demolition of the age by having his symbol of the future, an aeroplane, crash into his symbol of the past, the glass house. His reward was predictable: suspicion, apprehension, resistance, hostility, all held more or less in check because the object of these sentiments was endlessly witty and entertaining, therefore perhaps not quite as wicked and dangerously destructive as his behaviour led his contemporaries to fear. Conflict – confrontation – between him and the age was inevitable: confrontation between the New Morality as embodied in him, the most eloquent radical reformer of the day, and the Old Morality, as embodied in the established order of institutions.

These pages seek to resuscitate Edwardian Shaw, consequently contemporary documents have been used virtually throughout, the aim being to go back to primary sources the better to reflect Shaw's impact on the Edwardian world. This may create the impression that the work exists in a critical vacuum, rising spontaneously from the miasmal mists of ninety years ago. Nothing could be further from the truth, and it becomes both a duty and a pleasure to acknowledge predecessors and contemporaries and the work they have done – bibliographical, biographical, expository, explanatory, analytic, deconstructive and what you will.

Bibliographical assistance begins and ends in the two-volume *Bernard Shaw: A Bibliography* (Laurence, 1983). That this is the cornerstone of primary research into Shaw is to say the obvious; that it is a presence, though unstated, on every page of the present study needs to be said. Another immense bibliographical undertaking is the three-volume *G. B. Shaw: An Annotated Bibliography of Writings About Him* (Habermann, Wearing and Adams, 1987), without which, as guide and pointer, sections of the present study would not have been possible. Yet another helpful source-book is *Bernard Shaw: A Guide to Research* (Weintraub, 1992).

As for the letters, the obvious starting point is the four-volume *Collected Letters* (Laurence, 1965 through to 1988) without which any commentator would have to look at the Shavian world as through a glass darkly. There is of course considerable supplementary material in sundry older collections such as the Shaw–Terry (St John) and the Shaw–Campbell (Dent) letters, Shaw's letters to

Granville Barker (Purdom) and, to move to more recent times, *Granville Barker and His Correspondents* (Salmon, 1986) and *Shaw, Lady Gregory and the Abbey: A Correspondence and a Record* (Laurence and Grene, 1993). The 'Selected Correspondence', currently being brought out by the University of Toronto Press, has *Theatrics* (Laurence, 1995), *Bernard Shaw and H. G. Wells* (Percy Smith, 1995) and *Bernard Shaw and Gabriel Pascal* (Dukore, 1996) as its first three volumes.

Many of the documents cited in these pages have been taken up in collections, sometimes by the authors themselves, as in Max Beerbohm's *Around Theatres*, sometimes by other compilers, as with T. F. Evans's *Shaw: the Critical Heritage*. Shaw himself, or rather those bits and pieces of himself that he did not include in his Collected Works, has been collected in many disparate volumes by many dedicated editors. Thus Shaw on theatre (West), on religion (Smith), on platform and in pulpit (Laurence), on language (Tauber), on politics (Hubenka), to cite a few of the many. More recent compilations include *Bernard Shaw and the London Art Scene* (Weintraub, 1989), *Bernard Shaw on Photography* (Jay and Moore, 1989), *Shaw: Interviews and Recollections* (Gibbs, 1991) and *Bernard Shaw's Book Reviews Originally Published in the 'Pall Mall Gazette' from 1885 to 1888* (1991), now supplemented by *Bernard Shaw's Book Reviews, 1884–1950* (both by Tyson, 1996). Such sources, when used, have generally not been cited, but their usefulness in filling gaps has been immense.

Shaw spoke of himself as being in an 'apostolic' literary succession. There is surely an 'apostolic' succession of critical works about Shaw – of articles, essays and monographs on him which, starting in about 1904, continued throughout his life and on to the present day. Chapter 15 of this work contains an account of the beginning of this criticism, when a few first-generation Shavians established this critical 'succession' in attempts to get to grips with their challenging subject. It was from the comparatively small beginning in the Edwardian years that the avalanche developed – the avalanche of the Bernard Shaw industry, certainly one of the major secondary literary industries of the century. All this is a measure of Shaw's impact on the age – a measure and a salute, because none of this criticism, not even the most wrong-headed and prejudiced, of which there is plenty, attempts to deny that he was an eminent contemporary. There is all this in the past informing the present, and of more recent works this writer can do no more than point to a selection as denoting scholarship's continuing urge to perpetuate the apostolic succession of criticism.

One begins with biography where Michael Holroyd's three-volume Life – _The Search for Love, The Pursuit of Power_ and _The Lure of Fantasy_ and the fourth-volume addendum, _The Last Laugh_ – takes pride of place as the most complete biography yet written. The best supplement to date is Stanley Weintraub's _Shaw's People: From Victoria to Churchill_ (1996), which fills in some gaps in Holroyd's work by adding insights into aspects of Shaw's relations with notable contemporaries. Another biographical work is Sally Peters's _Bernard Shaw: The Ascent of the Superman_ (1996), which attempts to go beyond Holroyd in depicting Shaw's 'secret' self as a never-confessed homosexual.

As for critical work on the plays and other writings by Shaw, and to retrieve no more than a selection from the past ten years, there is _Shaw's Sense of History_ (Wisenthal, 1988), _Bernard Shaw and the Comic Sublime_ (Gordon, 1990), _The Playwrighting Self of Bernard Shaw_ (Bertolini, 1991), _George Bernard Shaw and Christopher Newton: Explorations of Shavian Theatre_ (Garebian, 1992), _Heartbreak House: Preludes of Apocalypse_ (Gibbs, 1994), _Bernard Shaw and the Socialist Theatre_ (Davis, 1994), _Shaw and Joyce: 'The Last Word in Stolentelling'_ (Black, 1995) and _Bernard Shaw's Novels: Portraits of the Artist as Man and Superman_ (Dietrich, 1996).

Shaw was no mean compiler and editor and all that he wished to retain of his work he included in the Standard Edition, published by Constable of London in 1931, continuing to 1951. Several of those volumes, the non-dramatic works in particular, have never been republished, either by Constable, whose contract with Shaw lapsed with his death, or, if republished by another house, have not gained the accessibility of the Standard Edition, the 37 volumes of which probably reside in more libraries throughout the world than the sum of subsequent disparate editions. For this reason, and unless otherwise stated, the Standard Edition, elderly though it now is, superseded though it has been in many instances, has been used as the basic Shavian reference.

It is pleasant to record thanks and appreciation to the following institutions and individuals:

- to the Humanities Research Centre of South Africa and the University of South Africa for financial assistance;

- to the Society of Authors on behalf of the Bernard Shaw Estate;
- to fellow Shavian scholars in the USA and the UK, particularly Dan H. Laurence, Stanley Weintraub and Fred D. Crawford in the United States and Tom Evans in the United Kingdom, without whose guidance, practical assistance and support, always generously given, this book would not have been possible;
- to the following institutions and the staff associated with them: the British Library, especially the Newspaper Library at Colindale; the Enthoven Collection (now incorporated in the British Theatre Museum) and the help offered by Ms Claire Hudson; the Harry Ransome Humanities Research Center, University of Texas at Austin, Texas; the inter-library-loan department of the library of the University of South Africa; the Dan H. Laurence Archive, University of Guelph;
- to editors Fred D. Crawford and John Bertolini and the Pennsylvania State University Press for permission to reproduce material contained in Chapter 7, originally published in the *Annual of Bernard Shaw Studies*, 1992;
- to associates and friends named above, my warmest thanks; and to my wife Betty, to whom I owe so much, this book is dedicated.

Leon Hugo

# Introduction:
# G.B.S. in the 1890s

The verdict of history is that it was in the 1890s that Shaw vanquished the demon failure and came into his own as the dominant personality of his age. Twelve volumes of the Standard Edition of the Works are there to prove it, or so they seem massively to aver. Four volumes of music criticism, which retain to this day a freshness and relevance that mark the author as quite the equal of Berlioz in the nineteenth century and a model for all those who followed in the twentieth – Newman, Tovey, and scores of lesser fry whose indebtedness to G.B.S.'s flair for the musical *mot juste* is greater than they will ever confess. Three volumes of drama criticism, which mark G.B.S. in a period which boasted uncommonly able drama critics, as at least their equal in dedication and everyone's superior, then and since, as a crusader, trumpet-tongued, enduringly witty, for a more exalted and challenging kind of drama than was being purveyed in the theatres of the time. One volume on Fabian Socialism,[1] and another containing what Shaw described as his Major Critical Essays – one on Ibsen, another on Wagner and a third a defence of the 'sanity' of modern art. All this, and also some plays – three volumes of these, ten plays, all of which remain on permanent stand-by in the theatrical repertoire of the world and at least six which are established classics, continually produced, regularly reprinted, world-wide.

This, says history, is the Shavian legacy of the 1890s. An impressive record, a handsome bequest. Yes, but.

History has the habit of looking at the past through the wrong end of the telescope; it sees the trees but not the wood, a necessary exercise if we are to make sense of the past, but over-simplifying perspectives in that it takes little or no account of contemporary attitudes; all the 'wood' in fact which kept Shaw down during the 1890s and nearly succeeded in permanently stunting his growth. The truth is, by the end of the decade Shaw was still, if not the failure he had been at the end of the 1880s, not remotely a success as a social or moral revolutionist or as a playwright, least of all by his high standards.

1

All that splendid work, yet a comparative failure. This was not merely because his contemporaries refused to recognize his genius, although this had something to do with it; neither because Shaw was too advanced for his time, although there was something in this as well; nor because he adopted a remote, unreadable style: his arena, on the contrary, was the popular press, the popular platform and the popular stage and he addressed his audiences in prose or dialogue of crystalline clarity. He made a name for himself, or rather he made a name for the subversive, confrontational entity that went under the initials of 'G.B.S.' There is a paradox here. His failure, then, was of a special kind which requires assessment if we are to arrive at a just estimate of his Edwardian achievement.

At the end of the 1880s Shaw could look back on a daunting record of failure. His five novels, at which he had methodically laboured during his twenties and on into his early thirties, had been rejected by leading London publishers and, although three of them eventually found their way into print in low-circulation Socialist magazines in the mid- to late-1880s (followed by limited publication in book form of *Cashel Byron's Profession* and *An Unsocial Socialist*), they made it abundantly clear to their author that the novel was not his medium for getting to and at people. If he was going to do this, it would have to be by some other means. He had no thought, no real thought, in spite of the abortive collaboration with Archer in 1885, of writing plays. The Fabian Society was claiming most of his time, but it was not taking his voice where Shaw wanted it to be heard, into the living rooms of middle-class London, and it was not earning him a living. He had to earn a living.

Journalism was the only option available to him, and this is what he became – a reviewer, first of books, then of the London art scene, then more decisively music critic for the *Star* from 1888 to 1889 (as 'Corno di Bassetto'), then for the *World* from 1890 to 1894 (as 'G.B.S.'), then of drama for the *Saturday Review* from 1895 to 1898 (still as 'G.B.S.'). These three positions gave him a regular income and, no less important, a regular column in which he could establish his voice. It was no mean voice. As the century moved through its last decade, Shaw – 'G.B.S.' – came into his own as a critic of formidable ability.

There is no need to develop this: seven of the 12 volumes referred to above testify to his developing mastery. They also testify to the highly subversive stance he adopted as a critic, subversive in

that he espoused and campaigned on behalf of causes that seemed
to go against everything his contemporaries held to be valid, incon-
trovertible and true. It was the revolutionist Wagner in music, the
immoral Ibsen in the drama – and as though this was not enough
in itself there was always the cause of the revolutionist, immoral
G.B.S. himself.

One may wonder what his readers – his settled, sober, middle-
class, intelligent, nominally liberal-minded readers – thought of
this assertive presence at their breakfast tables. There could be no
denying his self-assurance; also his joshing, rather familiar style of
address, which could be refreshing in small doses, except that the
doses G.B.S. doled out tended to come in table, not teaspoons.
Mock modesty was not an apparent failing and, in fact, he was not
at all backward in telling the world that he thought a devil of a lot
of himself. He was undeniably amusing; he certainly knew his
music, he knew his plays, and he could speak with compelling
authority on those subjects. But how real was the call for the new-
fangled, to say nothing of the repudiation of the comfortably
established, when made in such strenuously personal terms? Could
one take such a personality seriously?

The plain answer was no. A brilliant witty fellow, absolutely; but
too subversive and radical – too uncomfortable.

His contrariness was put on display in practically every notice he
wrote, but nowhere was it more breathtaking, one could say inso-
lent, than in his periodic attacks on Shakespeare. These were
designed to test the tolerance of the tolerant, the blood pressure of
the bellicose. 'With the single exception of Homer,' G.B.S. declared
one memorable Saturday morning, in the course of a review of
*Cymbeline*, 'there is no eminent writer, not even Sir Walter Scott,
whom I despise so entirely as I despise Shakespear when I measure
my mind against his.' His impatience had reached such a pitch of
intensity that it would be a relief to dig him up and throw stones at
him. 'To read Cymbeline and to think of Goethe, of Wagner, of
Ibsen, is, for me, to imperil the habit of studied moderation of statement which years of public responsibility as a journalist have made
almost second nature to me.'[2] Even his growing coterie of admirers
must have blanched, and so great was the sense of outrage no one
saw this for what it was: a studied piece of *im*moderation aimed at
ridiculing the mutilated Shakespeare the great Irving produced
and the witlessly 'bardolatrous' response of audiences to such
offerings.

It was by such too-clever-by-half tactics that Shaw undermined his mission.

We are now able to see that G.B.S. was a deliberately cultivated public image. It was as far from the real Shaw, as Shaw himself eventually admitted, as to be his most successful work of fiction, carrying about in his battery of words the biggest joke of all, that he was serious and wanted to be taken seriously. One cannot fault the 1890s for failing to see this. A revisionist by necessity in the Fabian Socialist cause, Shaw abjured revisionism in the cultural cause and went for the kill without so much as a gesture of apology. As that early Shavian, Holbrook Jackson, put it: '[I]t took even "the intellectuals," whose high priest [G.B.S.] became, twenty years to realise that he was in earnest and a genius.'[3] If it took the 'intellectuals' this long, how much longer, then, for the ordinary Victorian gentleman and his good lady to concede more than mere 'cynicism' to this firebrand? Twenty years and many many months.

This was Shaw the journalist in the 1890s. Shaw the playwright was miles behind his ferocious *alter ego*. In January 1901, on the sixth day of the new century when retrospection and introspection were being indulged at global and personal levels, Shaw admitted as much. It was in a letter to the actor Frederick Kerr:

> [F]or the last eight or nine years, I have written a play whenever anyone asked me to – ten in all. Not one of these plays has been produced by the people for whom they were written; in fact, except for a few scratch matinees, a provincial tour which had to take a play of mine because it could get nothing else, a flutter at a suburban theatre, and the shows of forlorn hopes like the Independent Theatre &c &c, they have not been produced at all. Nobody was to blame; but the fact remains that nothing ever came off. Managers very seldom know what they want. They sometimes thought they wanted a play by me until they saw the prompt book; and then they knew well enough that they didnt want *that*. So I published the plays, and gave up the theatre as a bad job.[4]

It was a bleak retrospect, which a more detailed assay does little to ameliorate.

The reception afforded his first play, *Widowers' Houses*, plainly gave Shaw sufficient encouragement for him to pursue his newly discovered avocation as a playwright. Put on by Grein's

Independent Theatre Society at the Royalty for two performances (in the evening of 9 December 1892, followed by a matinee on 13 December), the play elicited a response out of proportion to its modest presentation. Shaw's burgeoning reputation as an out-spoken Fabian Socialist and music critic contributed to the interest, as did the controversial theme of the play, about 'house- knacking' or in more modern parlance 'rack-rent'. His appearance after the performance, not to take a modest bow but to make a speech further denouncing the social evil the play depicted, added to the furore. He was met by cheers and jeers. '[A]n admirable speaker – and a detestable dramatist,' said A. B. Walkley in the *Star*.[5]

Quite a hubbub followed. The *Era* of 24 December reported:

> Hardly any recent play has provoked so much newspaper and other controversy … At least two of the daily papers, on the day after its production, devoted leading articles to its consideration, besides special criticisms of almost unprecedented length … Then all last week a controversy on its merits and demerits raged in a morning paper …'

Shaw enjoyed the publicity enormously and contributed to it by responding at length in the *Star* on 19 December. Most of his letter is devoted to re-expounding the sociological issue raised by the play and criticizing the critics for their ignorance of these issues. But he finds time to comment on the critical reaction to his debut. He is forbearing and perhaps a little relieved:

> I think it is now clear that the 'new drama' has no malice to fear from the serious critics … the influential critics have, it seems to me, been not merely fair, but generous in their attitude … I have had fair play from my opponents, and considerably more than that from my partisans; and if this is how I fare, I do not see that anybody else need fear.

Shaw's sensitivity to critical reception and his proneness to retaliate emerges here. This would be a constant of his playwriting career for the next twenty years and more; it will be a recurring theme in this study of his Edwardian years. Here on this first occasion he is almost friendly. It would be the last time, as it turned out, that he would apply such terms as 'no malice', 'fair play' and 'generous' to the London critics.

Not many months later, when Grein published *Widowers' Houses* as the first of the 'Independent Theatre Series', Shaw had already found considerably less cause for forbearance and in an Appendix to the text of the play he presented readers with excerpts from critical notices to demonstrate how singularly dull the critics had been.[6] He makes no attempt to hide his disdain: if the critics were intent on misunderstanding and condemning him, he would jolly well fight back. So the battle lines were drawn from the beginning, with Shaw alone on one side confronting the London critics *en masse*. A long, hard war lay ahead.

It was a similar story, with a few variations, with the second play to reach the London stage, *Arms and the Man*, produced at the Avenue Theatre on 21 April 1894. The high-minded umbrage taken by critics at *Widowers' Houses* was changed to supercilious, if amused, incredulity. 'Some offence was bred,' said Joseph Knight in the *Athenaeum*, '... and the whole is idle, brilliant and fantastic.'[7] Archer described it as quite as funny as *Charley's Aunt* but warned his readers not to look for a conventional depiction of life, but rather 'a fantastic, psychological extravaganza, in which drama, farce, and Gilbertian irony keep flashing past the bewildered eye, as in a sort of merry-go-round'.[8] The Prince of Wales, who attended a performance, may or may not have spoilt subsequent box-office takings by pronouncing the aspirant playwright to be mad. Only one critic, Walkley, saw that Shaw, so far from being cynical, had written a play that 'presents us with a criticism of conduct, a theory of life',[9] for which insight G.B.S. thanked him when, true to form, he came out in defence of the play in the *New Review* of July 1894. A good deal of what he said about, among other things, Bluntschli's predilection for chocolates, was taken up in the Preface to *Plays Pleasant*: the characters and the theme – love and war – were drawn from 'real life' while many of his critics had drawn their responses from 'stage life'. Turning on the critics:

> I demand ... that when I deal with facts into which the critic has never enquired, and of which he has had no personal experience, he shall not make his own vain imaginings the criterion of my accuracy. I really cannot undertake, every time I write a play, to follow it up by a text-book ... When I have written a play the whole novelty of which lies in the fact that it is void of malice ... and laboriously exact as to all essential facts, I object to being complimented on my 'brilliancy' as a fabricator of cynical extravagances.

No critic, we may be sure, took kindly to this lofty demand.

*Arms and the Man* had a fairly good run of fifty performances and earned Shaw in the region of £25 a week, but the production lost money. Shaw would have been encouraged, however. He had found his strength in comedy; success seemed within his grasp, particularly when the American actor-manager Richard Mansfield took *Arms and the Man* in 1894 and made a small success of it, enough of one, as Shaw told him, to keep him in pocket for six months. This was a flash in the pan. Shaw's career as a playwright from then on until 1904 amounted, with one exception, to failure as total and very nearly as defeating as his career as a novelist had been. Plays came from his pen in rapid succession and managers in London and the United States made it clear, precisely as Shaw told Kerr in the letter cited above, that they were not prepared to accept them. Grein refused both *The Philanderer* and *Mrs Warren's Profession* for the Independent Theatre. Mansfield in America accepted *Candida*, then changed his mind. Irving at the Lyceum gave every appearance of wanting to include *The Man of Destiny* in his repertoire, then shelved it. Terriss at the Adelphi invited Shaw to write a melodrama and, when Shaw obliged with *The Devil's Disciple*, lost interest. Cyril Maude at the Haymarket accepted *You Never Can Tell*, then rejected it, or rather Shaw insisted that it be withdrawn when it became clear in rehearsal that the cast could not make head or tail of their parts.

It was a disconsolate but determined Shaw who, viewing these unending failures, wrote to Ellen Terry: 'I must try again & again & again. I always said I should have to write twenty bad plays before I could write one good one.'[10] For once the chirpily confident G.B.S. is absent.

It was also in the midst of these failures that Shaw wrote to the publisher, Grant Richards: 'As far as I have been able to ascertain ... the public does not read plays ... Have you any reason to suppose that it has changed its habits?'[11] Richards courageously supposed that the public could well be persuaded to change its habits and published *Plays Pleasant and Unpleasant* in April 1898, the acting texts fleshed out by Shaw with descriptions to meet the needs of a readers' market. Stone (New York and Chicago) brought out an American edition at the same time.

Such hope as Shaw may have nurtured in making a success of publication was soon dashed. No one was impressed. The New York *Critic* spoke for the few who noticed the publication in a sneering review. *Widowers' Houses* and *Mrs Warren's Profession* had strength and would survive, the reviewer said, but:

> In printing his plays ... Mr Bernard Shaw, in his ingeniously egotistical manner, ... freely admits that the want of money has been his chief motive ... [and] has been induced to try to provide for the future by making over his old work into books. It is, we fear, a treacherous staff to lean upon, but judging from the ability which he displays in his preface, in drawing attention to the wares in the body of his book, he might, if he can bring his talents to bear upon others' works, make a fortune in a few years as a publisher's reviewer.[12]

Then Mansfield decided that *The Devil's Disciple* had possibilities. He gave the play its world première in Alabama, NY on 1 October 1897, then took it to the Fifth Avenue Theatre in New York, where it opened to enthusiastic reviews on 4 October. *The New York Times* had announced the pending production as by 'that distinguished Irish wit, cynic, vegetarian, and dress reformer ... a writer ... consistently odd and methodically unusual',[13] terms which testify to the success with which the G.B.S. persona had impinged on the United States; but after the performance the paper ungrudgingly conceded that Shaw's talent went well beyond the much-publicized fads: 'Bernard Shaw's play reveals him as a dramatist, a real dramatist, as well as a wit with a fondness for irony and paradox.'[14] After New York Mansfield took *The Devil's Disciple* on a successful tour and substantial royalties began to come Shaw's way at last. This saved his career. He had worked himself to the verge of a complete breakdown; illness and exhaustion obliged him to relinquish his post as drama critic for the *Saturday Review* in May 1898; he was in grave danger of extinguishing himself completely. *The Devil's Disciple* helped him to move out of employeeship and swept aside his specious scruples about marrying Charlotte Payne-Townshend. Although lean years still lay ahead, he would henceforth never be other than self-employed.

Some small ripples of the American success slowly reached England: *The Devil's Disciple* and *You Never Can Tell* were produced during 1899–1900; *You Never Can Tell* became Shaw's third West End production when put on by the Stage Society at the Strand on 2 May 1900. It did not take the city by storm; at the same time, it contributed, as did the other productions in the provinces and outer London, to a climate of qualified tolerance, an advance on the indifference of the previous eight years.

The second half of 1900 provided a great opportunity for journalists with a bent for instant history to survey the scene and round off the year, the decade, the century. Plays and playwrights were assessed along with everything else. Shaw was included in the reckoning, not as a major force in the theatrical world, but at least as a name to be mentioned in passing. One such assessment, 'English Dramatists of To-day' by W. K. Tarpay, appeared in the *Critic* in August. Pinero is rated 'foremost among living English dramatists', Jones 'an easy second', and in a more or less parenthetical subsection, 'writers of a newer reputation', Shaw's name crops up along with such forgotten luminaries as John Oliver Hobbes (Mrs Craigie) and H. V. Esmond. His is 'undoubtedly the most brilliant all round intellect' writing for the English stage, but he has not joined the ranks of the regular playwrights: '[I]ndeed, it is difficult to think of Mr Shaw as in any sense a "regular", or as joining any ranks whatsoever.' He is a 'moral force', possesses a 'cleverness that is amazing' and once, in one play, he has 'transcended cleverness, and touched the borders of the fairyland of genius ... I am tempted to say that there is in *Candida* a germ of immortality.'

The London performance of *You Never Can Tell* encouraged one English critic, G. S. Street, to write about Shaw as though he was more than a passing gadfly and possibly, if Shaw corrected the error of his ways, the playwright of the twentieth century. Street's article 'Sheridan and Mr Shaw' appeared in *Blackwood's Magazine* in June 1900, a significant event in itself because this was the first time that bastion of northern conservatism deigned to notice Shaw and, what was more, to notice him indulgently. It would take inordinate pains in future years to correct this lapse.

'[T]he least return one can make for the hearty laughter afforded one by Mr Shaw is to take him seriously,' says Street, scoring what may well be a first among critics for daring to say this. But he comes to the regretful conclusion that Shaw is not a playwright: his weakness is a superabundance of ideas which 'have to come in at all cost, and character and experience can go hang'. This has two bad effects, the first that one seems to be listening to a witty lecture, not a play, the second that it 'causes Mr Shaw to use his actors worse than dogs'. However, Street adds, the superabundance of ideas is the great attraction of the plays. 'If Mr Shaw were to repeat *You*

*Never Can Tell* for ever, I would go to see it in its latest form whenever it appeared ... Let Mr Shaw go on and prosper. Prosper? The audience at *You Never Can Tell* shouted with laughter all the time ...'

Tarpay consigns Shaw to a corner of his article, then worries over him like a dog with a bone. Street, having spelled out Shaw's shortcomings, executes a *volte face*. Both critics feel duty bound to find fundamental fault, yet neither can shrug off the fascination that Shavian drama exerts over him. Such gymnastics would become a regular feature of critical responses in the years ahead.

By 1900 Shaw was no longer the nonentity he had been ten years before. He had made something of a reputation for himself. A comparatively limited reputation, however, where the Fabian Society, which numbered no more than 800 members at the turn of the century, was still an infant in English political life, where his books reached a few hundred readers at most, and his music and drama criticism had tended to promote the outrageous G.B.S. persona rather than the serious-minded world-betterer, and where his plays – all but one, and that far from home – had failed to impinge on his contemporaries as the products of genius.

Failure had persisted. The turn of the century would have prompted him to take stock of himself and his career. He would have realized that the next ten years would make or break him. Being Shaw, he could have had no doubt that they would make him. His belief in himself and his will to succeed would not be allowed to falter. He told Archer at the time: 'As a matter of fact I am by a very great deal the best English-language playwright since Shakespear, and considerably his superior on a good many points.'[15] His immediate task was to convince his contemporaries that this was so.

# 1901–1904
# Educate, Agitate

# 1

# January–May 1901: A Natural-Born Mountebank

I

January 1901 was a busy month for the world at large, busier for Britain, excessively busy for the newspaper editors of that country.

It began busily on the first day of the month, for no less an authority than the Astronomer Royal had decreed this day the first of the new century and this invited stock-taking on a grand scale. *Fin de siècle* had been the mood of the 1890s, now on 1 January 1901 the mood swung away to encompass the wider fresher vistas of the future. Everyone was caught up in the mystique of the occasion and indulged himself or herself in reveries that encompassed past endeavours, present hopes and future challenges. Every newspaper editor in the country knew this and each, in his different voice, said it. Ponderous platitudes abounded, nowhere more sonorously than in *The Times*. This paper, aware as always that its was the top voice for the top people and would dominate the yapping of its lesser contemporaries, declared firmly and unfrivolously that 'An irresistible interest impels all but the most frivolous to look before and after as we enter on the new stage in the immeasurable process of the suns which begins to-day'.[1] It looked after by printing a survey of the past century, year by year, on 31 December and 1 January, to which Kipling's flair and Alfred Austen's less obvious talent lent poetic cadence,[2] and it looked before in a leading article of more than usual sententiousness.

Patriotism, imperial pride and the certainty of Britain's continuing greatness were unfurled to the muted beat of verbal drums. 'Shall we', the leader asked,

be able to hold our own amongst [new forces and new ambitions] and to vindicate for the next hundred years the unexampled position we have achieved in the last hundred ...? The auguries are not unpropitious. We enter upon the new century with a heritage of achievement and of glory older, more continuous, and not less splendid than that of any other nation in the world.

It was not deemed necessary, except in a passing phrase about British virility and doggedness being put to the proof of war, to mention the Boer War, then in its second year, least of all as cause for uneasy reflection, even although the same issue of the paper contained a report on the Boer Commando leader De Wet's 'invasion' of the Cape Colony. This was a minor irritation. The major point was that Great Britain was truly great and change of any kind would be unnecessary, undesirable and unpatriotic.

The nation had barely recovered from this self-congratulatory orgy when it was called on to perform another, a more solemn rite. Queen Victoria died on 22 January. *The Times* summoned the Poet Laureate to lead the Empire in its woe and Austen obliged with an elegy of notable ineptitude. 'Dead!' he cried, 'and the world seems widowéd!'[3] Some 3000 more elegies by as many versifiers were printed in the British press in the month that followed, none markedly better than the Laureate's lament.

The national outpouring of grief went on for some time; one does not dismiss 64 glorious years in a day or even a week. John Galsworthy captured the national sentiment in the second book of *The Forsyte Saga, In Chancery*, when Soames Forsyte and his brand-new wife Annette are part of the crowd lining the streets of London on the day of the funeral:

> Slow came the music and the march, till, in silence, the long line wound in through the Park gate. He heard Annette whisper, 'How sad it is and beautiful!' felt the clutch of her hand as she stood up on tiptoe; and the crowd's emotion gripped him. There it was – the bier of the Queen, coffin of the Age slow passing! And as it went by there came a murmuring groan from the long line of those who watched, a sound such as Soames had never heard, so unconscious, primitive, deep and wild, that neither he nor any knew whether they had joined in uttering it. Strange sound, indeed! Tribute of an Age to its own death ... Ah! Ah! ... The hold on life had slipped. That which had seemed eternal had gone! The Queen – God bless her.

It moved on with the bier, that travelling groan, as a fire moves over grass in a thin line; it kept step, and marched alongside down the crowds mile after mile. It was a human sound, and yet inhuman, pushed out by animal sub-consciousness, by intimate knowledge of universal death and change. None of us – none of us can hold on for ever!

Understandably, there was unwillingness to turn to Edward as the new king. *The Times*, while observing due process loyally enough, seemed unwilling to turn to him, remarking somewhat gratuitously that there were aspects of his career, now that he was about to become king, that one would have wished otherwise. Even so, the reluctance seemed due less to reservations about his peccable past than to an unreadiness to turn away from the age Victoria had embodied. The Queen was dead but no one wanted to shout 'Long live the King!' – because she was not dead, not really, to most Englishmen and women, and she would remain a presence in their living rooms and in their emotional lives for years to come.

A new century, a new King, but no desire to change the status quo, no intimation that things were perhaps not as good as they should have been, no inkling that forces were at work aimed at galvanizing the country into awareness of the need to bring its institutions, its systems, its way of thinking up to date, the better to cope with the new age. Industrial unrest, a ferment of new ideas, economic, political, social and cultural change – these were all very well on the Continent, but had England not withstood invasion before? Revolution, no matter of what kind, would be stoutly resisted on this isle.

## II

Shaw was also very busy in January 1901, endeavouring from day one to change the status quo.

He also took stock, also delivered judgment on the state of the nation, giving the *Morning Leader* of 1 January the benefit of his opinion in a column headed 'Respice, Aspice, Prospice':

I warn you that in a hundred years we shall all be dead. I encourage you with the reflection that we shall none of us be missed. I forecast the Twentieth Century as a series of experimental proofs that the sort of man our civilization produces is incapable of politically organising that civilization. The chief events of the century as far as the British Empire is concerned, will be the removal of the Imperial Government from England to one of the larger provinces, our island being reduced to the status of a Crown Colony, under a Commissioner of the Milner school ...

This not wholly flippant concoction was as unlike the complacent intonations of *The Times* as G.B.S. was unlike Robert Browning; and it avoided the clichés.

Then on 6 January Shaw allowed himself his moment of introspection in the letter to Frederick Kerr cited in the Introduction. *Fin de siècle* had not done his cause any good; on the contrary it had held his progressive views and his progressive plays back and now, in the dawning of the new century, he admitted to having given the theatre up in disgust and publishing his plays instead. Publication of this kind was on his mind at this time, as we shall see. But abandoning the theatre? Not really, and if the next three years continued to provide no more than crumbs from the theatrical table, opportunity would arise and he would be ready to scoop it up.

Queen Victoria's death invited him to participate in the general lamentation in his own way. He wrote to the *Morning Leader* deploring 'the rapture of mourning in which the nation [was] ... enjoying its favourite festival – a funeral'. The total suspension of common sense and sincere human feeling called for 'vigorous remonstrance'. It was the insanitary and superstitious procedure surrounding the obsequies that appalled him. The Queen's remains should have been cremated at once or buried in a perishable coffin in a shallow grave. 'The example set by such a course would have been socially invaluable. The example set by the present procedure is socially deplorable.'

The editor, Parke, rejected the letter. 'I do not mind fighting the war policy of the nation ...,' he told Shaw, 'but I am not anxious to run counter to its loyalty in its most solemn expression. (Cheers.)'[4] Shaw's penchant for saying the right thing at the wrong time was wisely, if sardonically, held in check on this occasion.

One wonders whether he was part of the crowd that watched the funeral cortège and joined in that groan of travail. Not likely.

A considerably more important and substantial statement came from his pen that month: 'Civilization and the Soldier', published in the *Humane Review*. This *Review*, begun in April 1900 with the purpose, as the editorial preamble to the first number put it, of devoting itself to 'the ethics of humaneness', featured Shaw prominently in its first issue with an essay on an already familiar Shavian topic, 'The Conflict between Science and Common Sense', in which he advertised himself as one of the most advanced men of the age. Here, now, in 'Civilization and the Soldier',[5] this most advanced man of the age considers the auguries rather more seriously than he had in his observations in the *Morning Leader* of 1 January and, one may add, more acutely than *The Times* had done in its leader of 1 January.

The essay was prompted by *Fabianism and the Empire*, published in October 1900. Though drafted and redrafted by Shaw, the pamphlet expressed collective Fabian opinion. 'Civilization and the Soldier', on the other hand, is an individual opinion, a characteristically Shavian development of the ideas contained in the earlier document – a 'Shavianism and the Empire', in which Shaw considers the implications of an imperial policy bolstered by force of arms. This is the starting point of 'Civilization and the Soldier': a war was being fought in the name of 'Empire' in South Africa; the soldier was the instrument of Empire. Given this situation, in what ways, if at all, was 'civilization' being consolidated?

It is the most forceful essay Shaw penned on the subject and surprising that he did not include it among his collected works.[6] He assumes the role of sage and prophet of global vision possibly for the first time; and he finds nothing propitious in the auguries, nothing to warrant the optimism of *The Times*, or, for that matter, the optimism of the country as a whole.

This is particularly true of the preamble, an expertly paced consideration of 'the Englishman' as Shaw observed him during the Mediterranean cruise he and his wife Charlotte went on in 1899, shortly before the outbreak of the Boer War. The scene is the cruise ship on the 'bosom, gently heaving of the Ionian sea,... the cradle and grave of many civilizations'. Here his fellow passengers pass their days secure in the belief 'that England must be greater than any other country because they were born in it'. Ordinarily this would not seem ridiculous; but here, 'on the bosom, gently heaving, which makes so light of us, our absurd ephemerality will not hide itself decently'. He adds, 'We are ploughing the fields of Neptune from tomb to tomb of perished civilizations ...'

Why, he asks, did these people perish? 'The answer is simple: they were not English.'

Yet to him, an Irishman, 'Nothing is more clear to me than that English civilization is at the end of its tether and that the tether can only be lengthened by the substitution for these artless grown-up children of a quite different sort of Englishman.'

He grants to the Ionian Neptune the conceit, foolishness and folly of the English and of all nations, grants as well that 'history cannot show us a single civilization that has survived the imperialist stage of democratic capitalism'. He sees 'that the fatal hour is at hand for England', that the ship 'sails through a deadly mist of illusion', that history is repeating itself, that 'the mortal diseases of the bygone civilizations reappear with deadly punctuality as the day draws nigh in which we must in our turn go under …'

But he refuses to submit. 'Demonstrate to me that life is religiously, morally, scientifically, politically, philosophically and practically not worth going on with, and I must reply, So much the worse, not for life, but for what you call religion, science, politics, philosophy, and the current practice of the art of living.'

> I am a great believer in life … Let the … respectable nations perish: the race is imperishable … And so, on the bosom, gently heaving, I salute the survivors of civilizations, the kindreds of Prometheus, the defiers of prohibitions, the thought-free, the self-respecters, the critics of the gods.

The oracular stance and the rhetoric set this preamble apart from the essay as a whole and from the polemical Shaw of the 1890s. *Man and Superman*, together with Tanner's 'Revolutionist's Handbook', and the imperative of that work, that political man, if he wished to survive, had to breed, not merely a 'different' being, but an altogether superior political one, capable of managing the nations of the world in its progress into the new century, is in embryo here. Not surprisingly, Shaw began work in earnest on *Man and Superman* during the course of the year. One can also detect in seminal form the thought that would lead to Creative Evolution and its exposition in *Back to Methuselah* more than twenty years later.

The remainder of 'Civilization and the Soldier' focuses on the soldier in his maintenance of British Imperial policy. Here Shaw is more recognizably the polemicist of the 1890s, demolishing shibboleths with practised ease:

> Empire is upon England now, and England has not got the nerve

for it. Her old Promethean fire is burnt out; and she grovels before all the idols and all the institutions. Grovels flattest, too, before that woodenest of all idols, the soldier, and that most foolish of all institutions, the army.

The dissection of imperial policy that follows leads to the expected Shavian conclusion, that 'What will win the race for Empire is the courage to look realities in the face and the energy to adapt social organisation to the needs of the modern conscience …' Britain should not abandon Empire. Far from it: the 'race for Empire' was on and Britain had to compete. But that Britain should employ the soldier, whose occupation it was to destroy and kill, as the prop of Empire was criminal folly. The soldier had to be substituted by a more enlightened agent if Empire was to succeed – by a Socialist dispensation. So Shaw ends by re-affirming Fabian policy.

The mocking but weirdly prophetic conclusion encapsulates the sentiments of a man who, though himself committed to life, has little hope of exacting the same commitment from his contemporaries:

Yes: there is no denying it: the evidence goes to prove, so far, that this island is done for as the centre of Empire … In a few centuries, the Ionian sea will still laugh in the southern sun; and on its bosom, gently heaving, the shadows of airships (of Chinese manufacture, run by international Federations as State lines) will flit towards the white cliffed island where a once famous nation will live by letting lodgings.

'Civilization and the Soldier' is Shaw's declaration of intent for the new century: that he intended to continue his campaign to reform England; more, that he intended to increase the intensity of his attacks on what he saw as outworn, corrupt institutions and habits of mind; still more, of extending his vision beyond the white cliffs of Dover to take in what lay beyond. Edwardian England may have preferred to linger in the shadow of Victorian England, but not Edwardian Shaw.

As if to emphasize this – and to cap this auspicious month – he published *Three Plays for Puritans* on 15 January, a week before Victoria's death.[7] A fortuitous date, but emblematic in retrospect as denoting his unregretting epitaph on Victorianism. Also emblematic in declaring his intention to refurbish his public image, neglected since his marriage and illness, and to thrust it anew into the consciousness of the age.

## III

The plays in *Three Plays for Puritans* – *The Devil's Disciple, Captain Brassbound's Conversion* and *Caesar and Cleopatra* – were of the 1890s, but the Preface was not. Shaw wrote it in 1900; it was a sounding-off in anticipation of the new century, its composition predating 'Civilization and the Soldier' by some months. Ever aware of the significance of the moment, he used the Preface to look back, the more effectively to define his position in the present, and to establish his role for the future. It is a traditional 'defence' or 'apology' in many respects, expressed, however, in Shaw's unapologetic way. As such, it shows him testing his public relations techniques to the full, performing a vigorous exercise in self-advertisement in the process. A later age would have described it as a 'hard sell'.

Why, he asks, should he get another man to praise him when he can do it himself? He can out-criticize the ablest critic, out-philosophize him as well. He is a charlatan – not by necessity but by vocation – and a natural-born mountebank. He really cannot subscribe to the demand for mock modesty and is ashamed neither of his work nor of the way it is done. 'I leave', he says, 'the delicacies of retirement to those who are gentlemen first and literary workmen afterwards. The cart and trumpet for me.' In sum, because in England and elsewhere genius, needing bread, is rewarded with a stone after death, he has resorted to the only remedy that will ensure him his supper – 'sedulous advertisement'.[8] At one point, Shaw blames 'G.B.S. the journalist' for public misunderstanding of 'Shaw the dramatist'. It is not a distinction he is inclined to maintain in the Preface as a whole. 'G.B.S. the journalist' pops up wherever and whenever Shaw needs him; he is the licensed fool who, in tandem with 'Shaw the dramatist', flaunts his shamelessness for all he is worth.

Taken as a whole and in the context of his career, the Preface is as brilliant as anything Shaw wrote at the time. Perhaps too brilliant, too much of a G.B.S. showpiece, a reversion to the 1890's persona. It is as though the reader is frog-marched through the paragraphs by a hectoring sergeant-major and told to take it or leave it. Most would have chosen to leave it. The young Arnold

Bennett placed the Shaw of this Preface to a nicety: 'Mr Shaw's words ... are as cold as steel and they cut ... He has developed into a sort of intellectual bravo ... He has the arrogance which usually accompanies abnormal intellect' and being arrogant, Shaw treats readers of his Preface as if they were feeble-minded.[9] That this arrogance was caused by Shaw's frustration at not getting the recognition he believed he deserved was – to the public at large – neither here nor there.

The self-advertisement is so immoderate that most readers would have missed the typically Shavian anti-thesis, that the voracious, reputation-hungry, almost excessively self-aware G.B.S. is due for relegation to a minor role in future campaigns, particularly as far as Shaw the dramatist is concerned. Shaw the dramatist is comparatively modest about himself: he is technically no 'original' but a very old-fashioned playwright; his diabolonianism, so far from being inspired by devilish perversion, is as old as a sane morality; and he is not a 'greater' playwright than Shakespeare, merely an apostle of a more modern, therefore more relevant, system of human conduct, and a very minor apostle at that. By the end of the Preface Shaw the dramatist is plainly in control of the cart, the disreputable fellow with the trumpet having been bundled off into the dust. At most, Shaw the dramatist says, if he can persuade his audiences to accept his view of life, he will perhaps 'enjoy a few years of immortality'. As for the future: '... the whirligig of time will soon bring my audiences to my own point of view; and then the next Shakespear that comes along will turn these petty tentatives of mine into masterpieces final for their epoch ...'[10] He does not exclude the possibility that, given time, he would become the age's Shakespeare, an option he would want to leave open for himself.

Having launched himself so spectacularly during January, Shaw did not let up. His star, rising from the ashes of the 1890s, had to be seen to be dancing brightly in the firmament. So not long afterwards he went 'popular', featuring himself in two self-drafted interviews in the *Daily Mail*.

The first of these appeared under the headline, 'The Robing of G.B.S.'[11] The robes in question were civic ones which he, as a councillor of the newly formed borough of St Pancras, was required to wear, much against his will. 'When [the robes] were suggested in committee I made a long and excellent speech – my speeches are always excellent – against them.' In vain. 'The councillors ... told me that I should be the last man to object to wear the robes, as they would cover up my disgraceful clothes. I then said that I would rather look disgraceful than ridiculous.' He was obliged to try his robes on, 'and all the councillors shrieked with laughter for about ten minutes.'

The report contains more than the announcement that G.B.S. was now a borough councillor, robes and all, although the additional item of news comes a poor second. It concerned the council's decision to have a mace – 'a very serious matter', says Shaw, abruptly becoming a disciple of the William Morris school of aesthetics. A prize was being offered at the Central School of Arts and Crafts for the best design. Shaw thought that other councillors should consult this school, but being all so horribly ignorant they would probably call in at the nearest jeweller's and say, 'I want a mace, just send one home, please.'

This slight piece has a more than personal angle to it. The same cannot be said of the next 'interview', 'G.B.S. Confesses', which the same paper, the *Daily Mail*, carried two months later.[12] A 'Shaw clock', four columns wide, dominates the page, dwarfing the commercial advertisements. This clock depicts Shaw at breakfast, at 'literary work', greeting an interviewer, at a borough council meeting, addressing a Socialist gathering, and so on. The eye-catching centrepiece of the clock is a pen and ink sketch of Shaw. The hours depict Shaw eleven times, the centrepiece making it a dozen. The caption reads: 'Once round the clock with Mr George Bernard Shaw, the well-known novelist, playwright, critic and socialist.'

The 'interview' itself, a little under 1000 words, has Shaw outlining his day, beginning effectively at 9.00 a.m. ('Dash out of bed. Air bath. Exercise. Cold-water bath. Looking glass (twenty minutes). Down to breakfast') and continuing for anything up to 15 or more hours ('Bed. Broken slumber and whitening hair'). The day overflows with a stream of interviews, a borough council meeting, alternatively a Fabian committee meeting followed by a public meeting. Entries include the following witticisms:

11.30. *Daily Mail* interviewer. Trade Union question. What are my views?

11.45. American interviewer. Local government of America; wants to know what I meant last time.

12.00. Another Yankee interviewer. Shakespeare: wants to

know whether I think 'As you Like It' or 'School for Scandal' his best play.

12.15. Another American interviewer. Will I give him a few thousand words on my private opinion of Edward VII?

12.30. Local politician …

'G.B.S. Confesses' is a slight but skilful propaganda piece which as much as shouts that he is a remarkably busy and versatile man of affairs. Those 'interviews' during the course of the day (in themselves a broad hint that the world's newspapermen are beating a road to his door) place him as a sought-after authority on trade unions, local government, drama criticism and contemporary affairs. To this is added the visit of a 'local politician' who wants him to contest the parliamentary seat of his district at the next election. A rising politician as well, we see. And, to judge from the final comment, there is a veritable clamour of voices demanding to know when his next play will be completed.

'G.B.S. Confesses' obviously enjoyed the willing assistance of a competent artist and the support of the editor: Shaw was plainly making himself worth this striking, and in newspaper terms expensive, kind of feature. Ephemeral though it was, it would live in memory as an engaging 'puff direct'.

There was to be no let up: Shaw's personal iron had to be struck, and struck again, to keep it hot, and so 'Who I am, and What I Think' followed hard on the heels of 'G.B.S. Confesses' in Frank Harris's short-lived *The Candid Friend*.[13] Shaw resurrected the 'catechism', as he called it, as 'Mainly About Myself' in *Shaw Gives Himself Away*[14] in 1939 and again in *Sixteen Self-Sketches*[15] in 1949, reverting to the original title and implying by this that the text was identical to the original. This is not so; it has been revised, and it is worth briefly checking these revisions for the light they throw on Edwardian Shaw.

He was an inveterate reviser. Like other men of letters, he wanted to preserve the best possible version of his work and his personal image for posterity. Scholarship has been arguing the validity of the 'final version' for some time without reaching agreement. Shaw's 'final versions' (in his play texts) are generally accepted as authoritative and here with 'Who I Am and What I Think' the revision is harmless enough. Comparing and contrasting the 1901 original with the 1949 revision, one discovers departures from the original text but no real attempt to 'cheat' posterity. There is, for example, the excision of sections of the original that would have amounted to overlapping in the pages of *Sixteen Self-Sketches*, and there is some revision and excision of sections that the older Shaw would have regarded as dated and irrelevant. Occasionally, however, one sees the older Shaw appraising G.B.S. of fifty years before and touching him up. These 'redefinitions' occur most markedly and revealingly in Shaw's responses to questions about money and sex. In 1901 the question, 'Do you think that poverty stands in the way of success or that it rather acts as an incentive to it?' seems to touch G.B.S. of 1901 on a raw spot and he launches into a wide-ranging attack on aspects of poverty, 'genteel' poverty in particular. Shaw of 1949 eliminates most of the fury while retaining the essence of the response. Here more than elsewhere excision has the effect of presenting a considerably less thwarted personality than existed in 1901. After half a century of unparalleled success Shaw of 1949 could not have wished it otherwise. When it comes to sex the older Shaw, living in a vastly more permissive era, feels free to add some comments about his 'crudely erotic' imagined life as a youngster but then, perplexingly, inveighs against Freud for having been 'utterly void of delicacy' and wonders that the ban on Havelock Ellis's 'ponderous sex-treatises' had been lifted. The contradictions cannot be reconciled and point to anomalies in Shaw's mental and emotional approach to the matter, even when he was in his nineties. That these anomalies were the web and woof of Victorian mores may explain them in Shaw, but they do not resolve them.

One notes throughout the 1949 revision how much the older Shaw whittles away at Edwardian Shaw's turn of phrase, reducing a tempest of words to a breeze. Overall, there is no attempt to 'destroy the evidence', but the general effect is to reduce the sense of pressure under which G.B.S. wrote and to render the persona in a less vigorous and interesting light. The result is a muted portrait. Emotion corrected in tranquillity fifty years after does not automatically sharpen the image.

This piece ended Shaw's publicity campaign for the year. Not only for the year but, in certain respects, his entire career. Shaw would not ever stop talking about himself, and his highly personal manner would always be a presence in his writing; this was his style. But the bald-faced projection of 'brilliance', 'shamelessness', 'brazenness' and so on as attributes of a unique and priceless individual fell away. G.B.S. was not abandoned, but he was moved to a

markedly subordinate niche in the Shavian pantheon and henceforth made to serve issues greater than himself – greater, Shaw
believed, than Shaw himself.

There was a rationale in all this self-promotion, of course, the first
and most obvious being that, deprived of his weekly feuilletons,
Shaw decided to put his name back into circulation.[16] Many people
then and now see this as the only motive – a spontaneous compul-
sion to promote himself, to keep in the public eye, to be discussed,
spoken about, laughed at, dismissed as a crank: no matter what the
response, the puffing had to continue, the publicity had to be kept
going. Archer told Shaw that he was little more than one of the
current literary notabilities on whom the halfpenny reporters could
rely for a comic interview.[17] There may be an element of truth in
this, but it is a small part of the whole.

For all his assertions to the contrary, Shaw would have known
better than anyone that he had not arrived on the scene, not with
anything that his contemporaries would hail as a work or works of
substance and significance. Yet he also knew better than anyone
that he had produced works of genuine substance. Therefore,
knowing better than anyone that worth is worthless unless it is
kept in the public eye, he determined to assert his worth by publi-
cizing himself and his products. It was a simple rationale based on
the time-honoured principle that in show business one could not
afford to be backward in hawking one's wares.

A third consideration comprehends the foregoing. This is that he
saw himself as a man with a mission. He would write the Preface to
*Man and Superman* three years later, but the well-known credo of
that piece would certainly have been informing his every action in
1901: 'This is the true joy in life, the being used for a purpose recognized by yourself as a mighty one; the being thoroughly worn out
before you are thrown on the scrap heap; the being a force of
Nature ...'[18] Conceiving himself in these terms, and dedicated to
overhauling and reshaping individual and communal life no less,
he would have known that he had to function not merely
adequately but supremely well, using his gifts – using, that is to say,
his mastery of words and his flair for comedy *and* his aptitude for
strutting about the public stage – in the cause of the mighty
purpose.

This combination of elements seems as unlikely today as it did a
hundred years ago: a would-be sage and world-betterer behaving
like a clown. It is the paradox of Shaw's career, and it is

compounded by the fact that he chose to convey the essence of his gospel in plays. As practically every Edwardian would have told him, the play was an entertainment, not the medium for messiahs, least of all jokey ones. Salvation was a serious, a solemn, business. His refusal to heed such critics but to persist in his chosen way puzzled, dismayed and offended. The elements seemed irreconcilable, to point to a divided self and a fatal flaw in his artistic make-up. As B. Ifor Evans remarked, pointing to the alleged flaw and by implication to a failed career, 'Our age needed a Thomas Aquinas, and we were given G. B. Shaw.'[19]

Shaw spent a good deal of time arguing away the paradox, pointing to Molière and Heine, among others, as precedents. But he knew that argument alone would not win the battle for him. This could be won only by the assertion of his will over that of the age – only, therefore, in drawing an audience, the bigger the better, and when drawing it, in making it listen and, in making it listen, converting it to his way of thinking. He had to sell himself and he had to sell his mission. They were one and indivisible.

This was the more complex rationale behind and within the publicity stunts and his apparently insatiable urge to declare his worth. Would Thomas Aquinas have found an audience in Edwardian England? Certainly not, and perhaps the mighty purpose that shuffles and deals the cards for this planet knew better than Shaw's critics what the Edwardian world needed.

# 2

# 1901–1902: Pathological Effusions

'I must educate a new generation with my pen from childhood up.'[1] Thus Shaw to Ellen Terry, in the wake of her 'rejection' of *Captain Brassbound's Conversion*. He was disappointed, he was bitter, he was in deadly earnest. 'Educate' was a Fabian slogan together with 'Agitate' and Shaw had no hesitation in stitching them to his banner. As for the third Fabian imperative, 'Organize', he was happy to leave that to the Webbs, preferring 'Confront' or 'Subvert' to round off his personal Trinity. Everything he wrote from then on – virtually everything he had ever written – took its cue from these three entities. His more permanent publications of the time – the Preface to *Three Plays for Puritans*, the Preface to the 1902 publication of *Mrs Warren's Profession*, the Preface to *Man and Superman* – are singly and cumulatively a furious attempt to educate the public in Shavian thinking and playwriting, the necessary Shavian corollaries being to agitate and confront his readers to the *n*th degree while doing so, the better to make them think.

But publications such as these, together with the plays they supported, reached only a very small audience. In themselves they were ineffectual and could be discounted as significant features of his educational programme, particularly when the plays remained unperformed. The *Bibliography* for the years 1901 to 1904 points to Shaw's dilemma; to a Shaw who, aware of this cul-de-sac in his career, decided to make a virtue of necessity and secure a more immediate and accessible platform for his campaigns. We recall his remark about having given the theatre up in disgust and for a while it may have seemed that this was so. It was not so, in fact: the Stage Society in London, Arnold Daly in the United States, the entry into his life of his Austrian translator, Siegfried Trebitsch, and the writing of *Man and Superman* enabled him to retain his profession as a practising playwright. But there is a discernible shift of immediate focus towards a medium with the power and reach to take his

27

name into every home in, if not the land, metropolitan London at least. A shift towards the press. If a new generation had to be educated, if his creeds had imperatively to go forth for the greater enlightenment of the age, then this was the obvious substitute for unacted, unread plays.

It was no neophyte who launched himself on to this platform in 1901. A hardened music and drama critic, already past his apprenticeship in newspaper controversy during the 1890s, he could command the press with practised ease. It was there beckoning him, about to enter upon its own 'Golden Age', and marvellously accessible. He grabbed it with both hands. It was his rod and his staff and with these weapons he intended greatly to discomfit his contemporaries. A happy convergence, the broad river of a mighty press only too glad to have someone of Shaw's unsettling calibre to provide it with material, and the entry into this of the turbulent tributary that was Shaw, himself only too glad to wage war on the age through its hospitable pages.

In a later chapter, 'Transformation', the range and extent of Shaw's 'takeover' of the London press during the Edwardian years will be considered. Here it is necessary to look at an issue which he made his own in the early years of the century, about which the British public had need of fundamental instruction: vaccination. There are other issues that could be considered. His first sounding-off on the subject of a revised orthography occurs in 1901 and recurs sporadically throughout the Edwardian years. It was a lifelong cause which would enjoy huge publicity after his death when he bequested his residuary estate to the promotion and establishment of a new English phonetic alphabet. There are articles and letters on Fabian policy regarding the Boer War, which entered its third year in 1901; on photography, on making plays readable and – in short – on topics which demonstrate Shaw's wide-ranging entry into the affairs of the moment. But the vaccination controversy dominates his programme. It is, on the face of it, rather a dull subject, except that Shaw had no difficulty turning it into vividly rendered and far from dull controversy.

There is another reason for considering it: the campaign he conducted is a model of the polemical method Shaw made his own, as contained in the principle that: '... the way to get at the merits of a case is not to listen to the fool who imagines himself impartial, but to get it argued with reckless bias for and against. To understand a saint, you must hear the devil's advocate ...'[2] Any examination of

Shaw's smallpox and vaccination campaign, for that matter most of the campaigns he conducted, should be understood in these terms, that he made an impartial point of being recklessly partial in debating the issue at hand.

This 'reckless bias' may explain why biographers have tended to make a somewhat embarrassed point of skirting round the campaigns Shaw conducted against orthodox opinion regarding smallpox and vaccination. Their assessment seems to be that Shaw, contracting smallpox during the epidemic in London in 1881 in spite of having been vaccinated against the disease when a child, thereafter vented a lifelong personal grievance in being stridently anti-vaccinationist, crankily refusing to acknowledge the sanity of the measure. This is not an accurate reflection of what Shaw said about smallpox and vaccination and what he tried to achieve during his 1901–2 campaign, even when the reckless bias is discounted. Some correction of the prevailing interpretation is called for.

Some indication of the basis of Shaw's scepticism is also necessary, because, for all the individuality of his voice, he did not speak spontaneously and indeed could claim authority of a kind for his stance. Leaving aside his personal history, to say nothing of the epidemics of 1871 (one of the worst ever) and the less damaging but still serious one of 1881, he found endorsement for his scepticism in no less a publication than that depository of orthodox doctrine, the *Encyclopaedia Britannica*. It is in the Ninth Edition of 1888, in the entry under 'Vaccination' written by an anonymous 'C.C.', that one sees a reaction against the high hopes held out for Jennerian vaccination – a reaction that anticipates Shaw's campaign in the early 1900s quite strikingly. C.C. declares his independence of officially sanctioned opinion, is sceptical of the claims made by the pro-vaccinationists and argues, much as Shaw would, that the disease, while tending like all pestilences to advance and retreat in accordance with its own inscrutable laws, finds its readiest breeding ground in the filth and squalor of slum dwellings, no matter how assiduously vaccination programmes may be carried out. C.C. relies as far as he is able on statistical evidence, of which there was a glaring paucity at the time; and Shaw, taking the issue further in 1902, would call repeatedly for scientifically verifiable figures and, all in all, for reliable statistical tables, of which there continued to be a paucity. There is no means of knowing whether Shaw ever consulted C.C's article and one cannot press the point too closely;

however, habitué of the British Museum Reading Room that Shaw was, the likelihood is that he read him or someone of like persuasion. By 1902, with the appearance of the tenth edition of the *Britannica*, C.C. had been swept unceremoniously aside by a resurgence of pro-vaccination orthodoxy, yet Shaw continued to adhere to the arguments of the late 1880s – an odd thing for the 'most advanced man of the day' to do, yet it is perhaps understandable; and, as will be seen, scepticism remained widespread, not least in Parliament which repealed aspects of the 1867 and 1871 Acts in 1898.

The particular circumstances that impelled Shaw to turn to the press and bombard it with letters on smallpox and vaccination from September 1901 to November 1902 are that London was threatened with an outbreak of the disease in the autumn of 1901; the authorities urged vaccination or revaccination; smallpox cases were isolated in ships on the Thames, whence the disease spread to Essex. In the event, there was no widespread epidemic in 1902, but no one was to know this, and with the 1871 and 1881 epidemics vivid memories a fierce controversy raged, with pro-vaccination opinion consolidating itself as the Imperial Vaccination League and anti-vaccination opinion consolidating itself as the Anti-Vaccination League. Professional medical opinion, as reflected in the pages of the *British Medical Journal*, was solidly behind the Imperial League; Shaw, though not a member, was seen as a supporter of the anti-vaccinist lobby. All the argy-bargying that ensued is now remote, a footnote of medical history, but it was real enough at the time. This explains the energy Shaw put into his 16 letters – ten to *The Times*, two to the *Saturday Review*, and four to the *British Medical Journal* – but it was the energy of a concerned (and thoroughly frustrated) public servant, not that of a man with a personal grievance to redress.

There is nothing in his private correspondence to suggest the reverse. Writing to his friend McNulty in 1894, he spoke feelingly about vaccination being 'a peculiarly filthy piece of witchcraft, which will probably be exploded even in parliament soon ...',[3] but this seems to have been an isolated outburst, and it was not until 1901, when he was a member of the Health Committee of the Borough of St Pancras, that he eventually spoke out, impelled quite plainly by civic rather than personal considerations.

His campaign began on September 1901 with an urgent letter to Ensor Walters, his ally on the St Pancras Borough Council and

Chairman of the Health Committee, in which he said that he had noted an increase of the number of smallpox cases. 'This means that we must act ... everything points to a devastating epidemic next spring if things are left as they are. It is better to frighten London now than to bury it next year ... But we must do something striking and vigorous at all hazards.'[4]

His first letter to *The Times* a week later, on 21 September, was everything Shaw had proposed to Walters – 'striking' and 'vigorous' in the rhetoric with which he tried to galvanize the public into facing the issue, and 'hazardous' in the way he confronted received opinion, knowing that pretty well everything he said would be taken up as, at best, contentious and, at worst, dangerously eccentric. His 'reckless bias' (and flair for the dramatic) is evident in the first sentence, which echoes the letter to Walters:

> Since it is better to frighten London in September than to bury it in April, it is as well to inform ... all ... whom it may concern (to the number of four or five millions of people) that St Pancras, and with St Pancras all London, is heading straight for an epidemic of smallpox next year.

This is a riveting opening, and the odds are that even the educated, secure reader of *The Times* would be sufficiently alarmed (the sentence is nothing if not alarmist) to allow himself to be swept on to confront the main points at issue, which are that poverty, overcrowding and squalor are breeding the disease, while 'the remedy urged on all sides is vaccination'. (The conclusion is nothing if not sarcastic.)

Thereafter Shaw launches into a wide-ranging attack on the inefficiency of the authorities and their failure to prevent the outbreak. He remembers the 1871 and 1881 epidemics: 'I myself, with satisfactory marks on my arm to certify me a vaccinated person, was one of the sufferers.' Plainly vaccination had not eradicated the disease and yet all the Local Government Board would do in its ignorance was cravenly to endorse the prevailing superstition while neglecting the central issue.

Summing up, Shaw reverts to the key issue of illegal overcrowding and the problem this poses. The law governing the number of inhabitants to a dwelling had to be enforced, 'whether our overcrowded constituents like it or not'. There were ways of making the Local Government Board do this: one way was to make him, Shaw, editor of *The Times* for three weeks; the other way was to wake up the President of the Local Government Board 'to an astonished consciousness that there is something else to be done to avert smallpox than to urge revaccination at a moment when the power of compelling even vaccination has been given up by the Government'.

This letter was to have successors in *The Times*. They depict Shaw pursuing his campaign into the byways of the controversy, but as the issues he raised are not issues any longer they may be left undisturbed. The letter cited above is a different matter. It was the best Shaw wrote on the subject, custom-built for arousing controversy, which was precisely what Shaw wanted to arouse. He may well have got more than he bargained for: as he was to remark, the reaction against him from his more excitable opponents included such choice descriptive phrases as 'ruffian and scoundrel' and 'rogue and blackguard'.[5]

Feelings ran high, not least in the principal organ of the medical profession, the *British Medical Journal*, which felt duty-bound to put Shaw down. He refused to accommodate them, so there ensued a duel that began in October 1901, lapsed for some months, and was resumed a year later.

The letter of 21 September 1901 to *The Times* cited above and a speech at a Borough Council meeting triggered the first reaction, a lengthy editorial article on 5 October 1901. The subject of the article is referred to as 'Mr G. Bernard Shaw, socialist, journalist, and playwright', whose 'case … displays a curious and interesting disturbance of mental equilibrium'. What this disturbance of mental equilibrium boils down to is that Shaw wanted the Local Government Board to close and demolish insanitary houses while all the time the Board 'actually proposes and even urges a means of small-pox prevention that does not involve any evictions. It wants people to get vaccinated and revaccinated'. The writer makes some heavy fun of Shaw's apparent desire not to risk his seat on the Borough Council (an unjust thrust), and then puts it that Shaw, having failed in the past to effect by fair means a revolution in house accommodation, 'now condescends to means which are not fair'. To the writer, 'it is a serious abuse of the present outbreak either to decry vaccination in the hope of hastening a reform in housing, or to promise that St Pancras if rehoused will be free from small-pox.'

Shaw responded three weeks later on 26 October 1901. Beyond

declaring that he stood by every word of his letter to *The Times*, he ignored the housing issue and concentrated on the lack of reliable statistical evidence regarding the efficacy of vaccination and the failure of the medical profession to avail itself of the science of statistics. This was not all:

> ... so far, the use of vaccination to prevent small-pox is, scientifically considered, as purely a piece of witchcraft as the use of a divining rod to discover water. By this I do not mean that it is ineffective; but that, as it is only a countryside tradition adopted by the medical profession, and as all efforts to discover the specific agent in vaccine lymph have failed, it can only be tested by statistics ...
>
> Personally, I profess neither vaccinism or antivaccinism. I am merely a much-perplexed public man trying to find out how much, if anything, can be saved from the admitted wreck of the largest hopes held out to the human race by Jenner and his disciples.

This, in the wake of over thirty thousand dead from smallpox in England and Wales since 1871, has a good deal to commend it; also, for all the pose of the 'much-perplexed public man', it is once again extremely 'partial' and irritating. It is meant to be. It is also very carefully written, with every word and phrase – no matter how highly charged – pointing to Shaw's intellectual detachment from the issue and his conviction that not enough was known about the subject to allow anyone to make any grand claims for the efficacy of vaccination. Not surprisingly, however, the *BMJ* chose not to see the letter for its virtues and wrote Shaw off, as it always did, as a public enemy.

That ended the first spat. The *BMJ* kept a close watch on him and was ready to pounce when a year later, on 19 August and 16 September 1902, he wrote to *The Times* about the difficulty of differentiating between general vaccinia and smallpox and between general vaccinia and syphilis, and, in the second letter, the statistics relating to the incidence of smallpox and smallpox prevention and the cost of revaccinating the entire population every ten years. All this was like a goad and the *BMJ* moved in hoping, no doubt, for a quick kill. The usual civilities are thrown overboard as the writer, unaware of Shaw's belief that effectiveness of assertion was the alpha and omega of style, declares Shaw's powers of assertion to be 'unsurpassed (we would not say unequalled)', agrees, with a show of suffering patience, to 'answer a fool according to his folly', touches on the pitfalls into which Shaw's 'exuberant fancies' lead him, and – the intended *coup de grâce* – says his letters to *The Times* are written out of 'the depths of an imagination utterly untrammelled by consideration either of probability or of possibility'. Shaw, the article concludes, 'is indeed a worthy ally of the National Antivaccination League, and that League is a very worthy ally of Mr Shaw.' As the Anti-Vaccination League was at this time being described in the *BMJ* as controlled by men who were 'either liars … ignoramuses … [and] cranks' (20 September 1902), Shaw could scarcely be said to have got off lightly.

He made some good points in his reply of 18 October, among these the reminder that many people were 'far more unsettled than [the *BMJ*] imagined'. After answering sundry charges, he comments: 'People who do not know whether they were vaccinated or not have not only high attack and death-rates, but low incomes, shabby clothes, unwashed shirts, and a number of other symptoms from which vaccinated people [that is, the well-off] are relatively free.' Shaw's flair for the concrete detail embedded in the tautly balanced phrasing contributes an angry vividness to the fact that the breeding grounds of the disease continued to fester in poverty-stricken slums.

The *BMJ*, impervious to this kind of literary 'punch' (though willing to concede Shaw's 'ready pen'), counter-attacked in the same issue:

> … no man is justified in writing as Mr Bernard Shaw does. A ready pen may be a dangerous weapon against the common welfare … and the harm which such writings as Mr Shaw's may do to the health and happiness of the English nation is so great as to make it a duty to freely expose his blunders and unhesitatingly animadvert on his methods.

Shaw was back on 8 November 1902. He complained that the correspondence was making heavy demands on his time. (The *BMJ* complained that his long letters were making heavy demands on its space.) He commends the journal for having made much progress in its attack on his personal character and suggests that he surrender the point.

Let it be granted that Mr Herbert Spencer, Dr Russell Wallace, Sir

William Collins, and the late Mr Gladstone may be dismissed, with myself and all other critics of vaccination, as hopeless cases of moral perversity which has for its object the disfigurement and destruction of the human race by small-pox, and for its weapon an unscrupulous misrepresentation of facts and documents.

This conceded, he goes on to 'demolish' all the contentions advanced by the *BMJ* as to the diagnosis of smallpox, vaccinia and syphilis, and to the cost of compulsory vaccination, adding several illuminating incidental remarks on the way:

> I am, as you rightly remind your readers, ignorant on these subjects. I am even dangerously ignorant, since I take part in the administration of the Public Health Acts. So are you: and if you are not anxiously aware of the fact you are not yet at the beginning of a suspicion of what public responsibility means ...
>
> And incidentally you waste my time; for I cannot claim that a dialectical victory over you is of any value. Any man with sufficient public practice to debate impersonally and to keep his temper (especially if he has a slight sense of humour to help him out) can ... tie you up in your own admissions.

The *BMJ's* response was to declare that Shaw, being angry at the exposure of misstatements 'now tears a passion to tatters all over the anti-vaccination stage across which he so gaily pirouetted in the *Times* before we called attention to the character of his gambols'. It gamely allowed him the opportunity to reply if he could say something 'short and to the point', which Shaw did a week later, on 15 November 1902:

> [I]t is not my custom to hit my opponents when they are down, or to deny them the Englishman's privilege of not knowing when they are beaten. Nothing that I can say can add to the completeness of your defeat on the scientific points raised by your attack on me. The personal points I have already conceded fully.

The editor had the last word, as he was bound to: '[Shaw's] method has been thoroughly exposed, and having failed to tempt us to aid him in obscuring the issue by following him through the curious pathological effusion which we printed for him last week, he has no choice but to brazen it out.'

So the argument ended, with both sides claiming victory. Rhetorically and dialectically, Shaw won hands down. As he rather unkindly indicated, the *BMJ* was no match for him in these respects. But rhetorical brilliance is not at issue here. The issues are those hypothetically evicted residents of St Pancras, about whom the *BMJ* challenged Shaw, and whether Shaw was or was not an anti-vaccinist, of which the *BMJ* had no doubt.

Those overcrowded tenements first. Did Shaw seriously advocate eviction? That first letter to *The Times* seems to say as much. That Shaw was an incipient authoritarian in public matters – that Socialism includes authoritarianism among its less engaging features – cannot be denied. Nevertheless, the answer here is no. He was playing the game according to his rules and (to recall the *BMJ's* plaintive remark) the 'unfairness' of these rules meant not a jot to him; he was pointing to the extreme contingency to gain the desired mean – sanitary housing. More effective civic hygiene, not brutal eviction, is what was needed, and the more 'recklessly' he expressed himself the more likely it was that someone would rise to the bait. This is precisely what happened. The fish rose to the lure – a splendid fish, the *British Medical Journal*, which proceeded to give him as much publicity as he could have wanted. As for his argument that improved housing and sanitation would eliminate the risk of smallpox, he was of course right and the *BMJ*, if it paid lip service to the 'problem' of the slums, skirted rather conspicuously round the reality of this issue. Even so, the *BMJ* was right to point to the fallacy of an argument that seemed to maintain that sanitation alone would be a cure-all; neither would vaccination alone, as the *BMJ* insisted. The proper application of both, a golden mean between the two extremes, was the solution. This was what Shaw was after – plus the added assurance of reliable statistical evidence.

Neither did he abandon his hypothetically unhoused tenants. He came up with an answer three years later, in *Major Barbara*, where the crime of poverty is eradicated by interested capitalism and the question of housing the homeless is answered in Perivale St Andrews. In the long run, this kind of 'sanitation' was, he argued, a far cheaper and more effective means of controlling disease – not only smallpox – than compulsory revaccination every ten years.

Was he opposed to vaccination?

What Shaw objects to in every one of the statements he issued is not vaccination as such, but the mentality that saw vaccination as the solution to the periodically recurring problem of smallpox. It had not proved a solution in 1871 and 1881; it was a frantic scrabbling to minister to the effect while neglecting the cause. Moreover, the medical profession, with it the *BMJ*, was '... defending a vested interest of enormous pecuniary value ...' This alone was enough to arouse his deepest Socialist suspicions and this was why he repeatedly called for a scientifically conducted statistical survey which would prove (or not prove) what was maintained more by hopeful hypothesis than scientifically verifiable fact. Hence his free use of such animadversions as 'superstition' and 'witchcraft' when describing vaccination.

All this admitted, Shaw often came close to defeating his own purposes and sounding exactly like a self-elected champion of the Anti-Vaccination League. He is not always as knowledgeable as his flow of medical terms may persuade one to imagine and he was inclined to go on at self-defeating length, trying to score points on relatively minor matters and thus blunting the main thrust of his argument. The impression sometimes gained is that, no matter how often he declared himself no anti-vaccinist, he was precisely this. On his own admission, he found himself impelled to argue against vaccination in council because vaccination did not cure diphtheria or scarlet fever.[6] The motives are impeccable, but one may wonder whether the 'reckless bias' of his argument was not too subtle for his audiences. Similarly, his notorious remark to Charles Gane, the Secretary of the Anti-Vaccination League, that 'vaccination is really nothing short of attempted murder',[7] is taken out of the context of the letter in which it appears and today made to represent Shaw's anti-vaccinist stance. The letter as a whole makes clear that Shaw's 'pathological' attitude to vaccination was grounded in exactly the same aversion as his 'pathological' attitude to insanitary living. As he said in the same letter: 'A skilled bacteriologist would as soon think of cutting a child's arm and rubbing the contents of the dustpan into the wound as vaccinating it in the official way,'[8] the official way then being blatantly negligent of proper sterile precautions.

Two major points emerge from the controversy. The first is contained in Shaw's words in a letter to Henderson: '[M]y part in the humanitarian campaign against vivisection, modern science generally, vaccination, "education," flogging &c &c are all part of my attitude as a "mystic."'[9] A 'mystic' can be as wrong about things as a mechanist, but Shavian mysticism was decidedly for, not against life. This is so obvious that one wonders at the *BMJ's* readiness to see him in the opposite role. The second point is that this set-to with the *BMJ* served excellently to hone the dialectical weapons Shaw would use in his medical satire four years later: after all that went before, *The Doctor's Dilemma* was inevitable.

# 3

# 1903–1904: Fabian Shaw

I

On 2 February 1903 the *Daily News* carried a letter to the Editor by Shaw. There was nothing unusual in this; it was a run-of-the-mill letter of a kind that Shaw was dashing off at the time to this, that or the other national daily, yet we may pause on it for what it reveals of Fabian Shaw at this stage of his career. It is a convenient peg on which to hang a discussion of Shaw and the Society with which he identified himself.

The letter was prompted by an argument arising from a lecture on eugenics Shaw had given a week before. This had been briefly and inaccurately reported and people wrote in to quarrel with him about it.

> ... [T]he lecture which has provoked this correspondence was founded on my conviction that no tolerable social life – that is to say, no improvement on the present abominable condition of civilized mankind – is possible without Socialism. And by Socialism I mean not only municipal gas and water, but the complete acceptance of Equality as the condition of human association, and Communism as the condition of human industry. This conviction ... has grown with my growth, and become strong enough to keep me rigidly to its point whilst the general Socialist movement has been swaying and wavering and wobbling and splitting in all directions before transient gusts of pro-Boerism, anti-Anglican School Boardism, and the rest of the accidents of party politics.

The letter goes on to state the general proposition of Shaw's lecture, which was that the human species had not evolved perceptibly within historic time and 'we have just reached that point in civilization at which Empires have always broken down'. They have broken down, and the British Empire was already showing signs of breaking down, because the management of such Empires over-taxed the political capacity of its human units. Shaw then turns to two correspondents, both of them well-known radical reformers, who had written to rebut him and asks whether their lifelong endeavours to improve the human condition have had any visible beneficial effect, whether his own endeavours have had any visible beneficial effect. He does not condescend to provide the obvious answer: none, and neither will there be any real advance by means of mere governmental reform which, governed by human incapacity, would be meagre. The remedy is obvious: a new sort of man.

> We have produced new sorts of horses, new sorts of apples, new sorts of flowers. We have always been trying to produce a new sort of man by the imposture which we call education ... Who, pray, is to educate the educators? We must breed our new sort of man.

Much of what Shaw says here has been heard before or will be heard again in considerably more weighty terms: the imminent breakdown of Empire was a theme of 'Civilization and the Soldier', the imperative to breed a new kind of man had by then, February 1903, received full dramatic treatment in the final draft of *Man and Superman*, which Shaw was then reading to friends. More than this, the letter reveals that Shaw's adherence to Fabian Socialism was an implicit endorsement of Fabian policy to stand aloof from the vacillation of party politics while steadily pursuing its goals through 'permeation' of existing political policies. The rhetorical 'Who, pray, will educate the educators?' invites an obvious response in context; but failing the advent of a new sort of man in the immediate future, the other answer would be, 'The Fabians, of course, who else?' After all, it was laid down in its Basis of 1887 that Fabians would promote their policy 'by the general dissemination of knowledge as to the relation between the individual and Society in its economic, ethical, and political aspects'.[1] As chief trumpeter of the Society, Shaw would speak and write on its behalf, disseminating knowledge, so to say, when and wherever the opportunity presented itself, as is implicitly done here. At the same time, because the Society allowed and encouraged the development of individualism within the bounds laid down by its Basis, Shaw could be his own Fabian self when and wherever he wanted to be, which meant that he could and would transcend gas, water and other mundane Fabian concerns by preaching the gospel of Shavian-Fabian vitalism whenever it suited his brief.

The particular issue here, that of breeding to produce a 'higher' kind of human animal, was a Fabian issue, not ever loudly enunciated because it was a delicate matter but certainly thought about and touched on in private discussion. Beatrice Webb confided to her diary that *Man and Superman* had delighted her as to choice of subject. 'We [the Fabian Society] cannot touch the subject of human breeding – it is not ripe for the mere industry of induction, and yet I realize that it is the most important of all questions, this breeding of the right sort of man.'[2] This was a generally topical issue as well, made so by Francis Galton whose studies into and publications on eugenics in the late nineteenth century indicated that the human race was in decline because of the indiscriminate breeding of the genetically defective and inferior. It is known today that Galton was wrong, but at the time and for many years thereafter his doom-laden message was taken seriously. Samuel Butler was troubled by the prospect; so were Shaw and Wells; so were Yeats, Lawrence and other 'advanced intellectuals' until well into the 1930s. Not only the 'intellectuals' of the radical left or the otherwise disaffected: politicians of liberal persuasion were similarly alarmed. Winston Churchill was very alarmed in 1906:

> The unnatural and increasingly rapid growth of the feeble-minded and insane classes, coupled as it is with steady restriction among all the thrifty, energetic and superior stocks, constitutes a national and race danger which it is impossible to exaggerate. I feel that the source from which the stream of madness is fed should be cut off and sealed off before another year has passed.[3]

Political correctness in Edward's day was not quite what it is today.

The Fabian element, rather the conjunction of the Fabian with the Shavian, may be detected in another matter. Shaw's letter is headed 'Lost Faiths'. Whose faiths had been lost? Not Shaw's. He had found his faith, been new-born into it. The sentence from the Fabian Basis quoted above includes the propagation of 'ethical aspects' of Socialism as a function of the Society. In 1884, shortly after joining the Society and before it had adopted a systematized form of Socialism as its basis, Shaw penned the Fabian Manifesto – Tract No. 2 – the rhetoric of which enhances the ethical consideration to that of guiding principle. Still earlier, in 1883, at the second tentative meeting in Edward Pease's rooms, before those who attended knew themselves as the Fabian Society or strictly what they would become, the urge was to reconstruct society not on economic or political lines, but 'in accordance with the highest moral possibilities', as the resolution at this meeting worded it. Socialism came later, when members saw that it endorsed their kind of morality.

Those years, the 1880s and on into the 1890s, were a great time for 'progress' – 'the mantra of the time', as Patricia Pugh puts it,[4] by which those whose faith was strong enough would refashion a new society for the new century. It was a reaction against the *fin de siècle*, a stock-taking and a refurbishing that the young feel is due when the century begins to turn. There was nothing new in this, but what vitalized the late nineteenth century with a spirit of particular and unique urgency was the void left by the collapse of revealed religion; also to many the collapse of *laissez faire* Capitalism. While the middle-aged and elderly and not a few among the young (those whose future interests were vested in their elders) continued to hold on to this, like passengers clinging to flotsam from a foundering ship, many of the young and hopeful struck out for an alien shore, determined to find something there that would sustain their need for spiritual sureties. The Fabians were no different; Shaw was no different, with the additional benefit that he could express himself on the matter far more lucidly and comprehensively than anyone else. As he does in this letter, which breathes proselytizing fervour, or, as he would have preferred to put it, 'moral passion', throughout. Whatever the form and whether the issue was 'gas and water' (the source of a good deal of satirical badinage from rival salvationists on the political left) or whether it was a more exalted entity, it was a salvationist message demystified and secularized.

There is a corollary to this: a sense of absolute rightness impelling the mission, inevitably a touch of intellectual arrogance. Shaw's arrogance shows in this letter. Fabian arrogance shows in the way members, self-educated by and large, middle class and 'intellectual', enclosed themselves in a somewhat exclusive and elitist clique; arrogance followed. One has only to open Beatrice Webb's diary – any page will do – to see this particular trait. There was a redeeming feature: as an early initiate, Edith Bland, enthused, the Fabians were 'quite the nicest set of people [she] ever knew'.[5]

Niceness can go a long way to cancelling less winning traits and Shaw employed his natural niceness to excellent effect, again as in this letter, where his belief that contemporary man – his very reader – was but a poor product of the evolutionary appetite is spelt out in a way that is more likely to amuse than offend. As a contemporary put it, '[O]ne of his principal weapons was a good-humoured insolence in controversy which assumed a truculence not seriously intended, and certainly not corresponding with any loud conceit.'[6] Not that offence was never taken: the world is full of irascible souls waiting to take umbrage at real or imagined slights. But when this happened Shaw never allowed his air of engaging engagement to be put at risk; and there were many occasions when fulminations against him would have warranted a wrathful rejoinder, whereas all he would do by way of retaliation was to adopt an air of impenitent meekness, no doubt on the excellent grounds that if his demeanour did not qualify him to inherit the earth it would certainly drive his adversaries to a frenzy. The Fabians were lucky to have such an infuriatingly nice person as their PRO.

But this niceness that Edith Bland observed was essentially an insider's, a middle-class, view. What, one should ask, about the working classes, in whose cause the Fabians strove to redress the evils of society? How effectively did the Fabians – and Shaw – come across to working men and women? The story of W. L. Philips is instructive in this regard. He was one of the first Fabians, a house painter, the only 'genuine working man' in the group, in his way a remarkable man, says a condescending Pease.[7] Philips was the author of Fabian Tract No. 1, *Why are the Many Poor?*, and a member of the Executive in 1887–8, then he gradually dropped out of the Society. Pease does not offer a reason for this and speculation might be ill-advised, were it not that the Fabians failed signally to include other working-class people in their inner ranks. Philips may well have defected because he gradually found himself an outsider among all those nice middle-class people. The bourgeois arrogance of its members created an ambience that was quite as exclusive in its way as class divisions.

Shaw's letter in the *Daily News*, so palpably addressed to an educated, 'intelligent' audience – an audience aspiring to education and 'intellectuality' should not be ruled out – points to an anomaly of his, and by extension the Fabian, cause. Dedicated to uplifting the weary, the huddled and unenlightened masses, his campaigns, in so far as they originated in the ink-horn, were conspicuous by their avoidance of contact with the masses. The same applies to the Fabian Society as a whole. Its tracts, pamphlets and books, to say nothing of Beatrice and Sidney Webb's cultivation of the politically powerful, were aimed at re-educating the already educated. Their rationale for this was sensibly pragmatic: convert those in power, persuade them to see the error of their ways, convince them that the situation was critical, and then reform, promulgated by the 'powerful' above, would drop upon the masses like the gentle dew from heaven. But was this Socialism in the all-embracing sense of the word?

One does not ignore what Shaw, the Webbs and other Fabians did among and with the working classes. It was an enormous amount. It is not as though aloofness from the object of their good works was a Fabian principle; but the question must be repeated whether, like many other intellectuals then and now, the 'masses' were preferably kept at a decent anonymous distance while those who 'knew better' fought their battles for them. This seems to have been the case. Fabianism fostered autocratic paternalism – of the nicest kind possible, of course.

The Fabians could not help being what they were. Shaw could not help being what he was, a downstart bourgeois Irishman, fated by this to see the world from a middle-class point of view, hence to see the working classes from the outside looking in. His depiction of the working classes in his plays bears this out. For all their vividness, vitality and immediacy, his Burgesses, Snobby Prices, Bill Walkers and Rummy Mitchens are created from the outside. They were created *for* the outside, for the mainly middle-class audiences for whom he wrote his plays and with whom he shared, or hoped to share, his point of view and set of values.

It should also be said that he depicted his working-class men and women with sustained belief in their individuality and right to equality of opportunity. He was utterly lacking in class-consciousness, except to sweep it aside as an irrelevancy. During 1904 he involved himself in precisely such a controversy carried on in the pages of the *Clarion*, in which he argued against the notion of a 'class war' in Socialism's struggle to bring Capitalist hegemony to an end: all classes, he said, had a vested interest in, were tainted by, the Capitalist system, from the most senior duke in the kingdom to the humblest bootblack in his employ; Marxian dogma had no bearing on the truth of the situation; class as such did not enter into the issue.

We return to the letter to the *Daily News* to pick up one strand left in abeyance – Shaw's passing, scathing dismissal of the educational system, 'the imposture which we call education'. As a product of this imposture in a variety of Dublin schools which had taught him nothing, he had personal cause for his strongly felt rejection of elementary education, the general import of which was that education, notwithstanding the improvements brought in with the passing of the 1870–81 Education Acts, continued to be a national disgrace.

He argued frequently and loudly (most lengthily and loudly in his 1910 'Parents and Children', the preface to *Misalliance*) for the redress of fundamental errors in the educational system. As it existed, it denied a child his humanity; it was a 'gigantic hypocrisy' in that its object was not to educate the child in the real sense of the word, but 'to relieve parents from the insufferable company and anxious care of their children'.[8] His pet aversion was that cornerstone of nineteenth-century liberal education, Latin, a dead subject retained in the curriculum because its proponents had a 'vested interest in torture'.[9] But other similarly unusable subjects, virtually the entire standard school curriculum, earned his scorn:

> [W]e get a whole body of teaching subjects masquerading as real subjects, and not only useless for culture, but actively and disastrously mischievous because of the unexplained but patent fact that when uninteresting studies are forced on the human brain they produce imbecility. That is why our educated classes are morally and intellectually imbecile … Civilization is dying of what it calls education …[10]

Shaw is easy to identify as an educational iconoclast, less easy as a builder of new icons, where he became woolly. He insisted on recognition of a child's humanity: he was a 'Fresh attempt to produce the just man made perfect,' as he said in 'Parents and Children'. One had a bounden duty to allow this humanity to develop as freely as possible, outside the prison house of contemporary schooling. Outside the prison house of the Edwardian family, as well. Freedom was a child's birthright, as much as it was that of his parents: 'If children were really free as adults were free, it would be found that intellectual capacity creates intellectual appetite, and that children grab eagerly at all the learning they can use. And that is all they can take in without injuring themselves.'[11] Shaw is speaking here in support of what he did as a schoolchild and failing to see that not all children are budding Bernard Shaws.

He qualified this call for freedom by invoking certain basic disciplines. Arithmetical and verbal literacy was necessary, and he insisted that 'children would learn reading and simple arithmetic for their own use if they led promptly to more freedom and more pence ...'[12] And he insisted on religious studies, not as a dogma but as a yardstick of moral behaviour, and on civics, so that children could grow up knowing something of the institutions that governed their lives. Once such knowledge and skills had been acquired, he advocated a Rousseauesque return to nature:

> [Children] should be taught how to use and enjoy the country without destroying trees or crops, and how to be as sanitary in their rambles as a cat. Instead of being forbidden to do as they like, they should be compelled to dispense with adult guidance, and depend on themselves to the full limit of their resourcefulness; so as to accustom them to that tyranny of Nature and circumstance from which they are only too willing to be shielded.

He did not dispense with adult guidance altogether, which would have to be unobtrusive and grudging of advice. 'Under such conditions,' he cheerfully concludes, 'real live learning would flourish on the boundless basis of human curiosity and ambition.'[13]

All those untended children free to 'ramble' through the countryside: it is more likely that real live savagery would flourish under such conditions. Even if it is agreed that Shaw's solution to the educational problem, evidence as it is of his boundless faith in human nature (at least in the Edwardian years), is impossible to the point of dottiness, it should also be admitted that his broad objective is beyond reproach: the inculcation of self-awareness, self-sufficiency and initiative in the young as far removed as possible from the claustrophobic tyrannies of the Edwardian home and school. It was Shavian vitalism striking at the very heart of Edwardian oppression.

This educational programme reveals Shaw as Shaw rather than as a member of the Fabian Society. In that less fancy-free organization he did not ignore social and political realities when it came to education. He actively supported Sidney Webb, the moving force in the Society for a reformed educational system, whose Fabian Tract No. 106, *The Educational Muddle and the Way Out*, was hugely influential in bringing about two Education Acts (the 1902 Act for the country at large, the 1903 Act for London), which Shaw applauded in more than one letter in the 'enemy' Liberal and Socialist press, hailing the measures as 'a magnificent piece of educational socialism',[14] the more 'magnificent' for having been almost entirely the product of Fabian 'permeation' of a Conservative government. Henceforth all schools would fall under the authority of local or county councils and, regardless of their religious affiliations, would receive financial support from the state. All schools could therefore, in theory at least, be subject to what-ever improvements of the system the state prescribed. It was a major step forward: the state cried a firm and for a while highly unpopular halt to sectarian in-fighting in education and put an end to the muddle that Webb had decried. The measure of the impor-tance of these two Acts is that they remained the cornerstones of British education policy for half a century and longer.

## II

Shaw went to Glasgow in early October 1903 to deliver two lectures, and writing to Trebitsch on his return to London he confessed that his successes as a 'mob orator' induced self-loathing. 'I am an incor-rigible mountebank; but I always suffer torments of remorse when the degrading exhibition is over.' He continued:

> And now the worst of it is that I shall have to set to work to write a Fabian Manifesto on the subject instead of setting to at a new play – or rather at the abominable book on Municipal Trading that I have to finish first. That is the secret of the greatness of my dramatic masterpieces: I have to work like a dog at the most sordid things between every hundred lines.[15]

Something of the self-loathing seems to have rubbed off on to this letter, which indicates quite a conflict between Fabian Shaw and playwriting Shaw, resolved here by an act of will which dictates the paradox that the 'sordid things' both impede and inspire the composition of 'dramatic masterpieces' – in this instance the booklet *The Common Sense of Municipal Trading* published in February 1904 and the tract *Fabianism and the Fiscal Question* published in March 1904.

*The Common Sense of Municipal Trading* was not strictly a Fabian project. Shaw undertook to contribute it to a Pro and Con series that a publisher, J. Eveleigh Nash, was contemplating and he went so far as to advertise it at the back of *Man and Superman* (as *Municipal Trading*) when that work was published in August 1903. In the event, Shaw decided to publish the book himself through Constable, probably because he wanted to promote it during his election campaign for the London County Council in March 1904.

Yet *The Common Sense of Municipal Trading* was Fabian through and through. The municipalization of services had been part of the Society's thinking for over ten years. It had published a number of tracts on the subject through the 1890s and into the Edwardian years and, when in 1908 it took up Shaw's booklet as Volume V of the Fabian Socialist Series, it was as though *The Common Sense of Municipal Trading* had found its proper roosting place in the end.

Pease makes the point that Fabian Socialism was an interpretation of the spirit of the time; the Fabians were not innovators so much as analysts of existing conditions and trends; in Shaw's words they pursued 'a peculiar opportunist policy'.[16] Thus with the municipalization of monopolies, which had been taking place in many of the great provincial cities in England for some time past. Birmingham was a prime example. If such cities could municipalize basic services, why not elsewhere, particularly London, the wealthiest city in the world and yet singularly backward in municipal management, where such services as its gas, water, docks and tramways were in the hands of private exploiters?[17] This is the question Shaw puts and answers in *The Common Sense of Municipal Trading*. It seems that he came to think well of the book, notwithstanding the 'abominable' with which he had typified it to Trebitsch; and he told Archibald Henderson in the first of his many letters to him – the letter in which he was to declare that in his plays his economic studies had played as important a part as a knowledge of anatomy does in the works of Michelangelo – that *The Common Sense of Municipal Trading* was in its way one of the best and most important of the books he had written.[18] No one seems ever to have agreed with him, not his contemporaries, no biographer and no historian of the Fabian Society. It is as though there is tacit agreement that it is a negligible piece, best relegated to the dustbin of better-forgotten Shaviana.

It does not show Shaw in top form: it is logically constructed and carefully argued; tables of figures, in fact all figures, are avoided; the abstract discussion is grounded in concrete examples, the more effectively to involve the reader in the realities of municipal government; the argument favours municipalization, yet it is balanced and moderate in the terms with which the pros and cons of the matter are assessed. It is a model discourse. Yet it misses the mark. This is not only because today the issue has lost it urgency; with the municipalization of services applied to a greater or lesser degree throughout the First World, one may discern a victory of sorts for modified Socialism, even in such rabidly free-market societies as the United States, even where the word 'socialism' is taboo. It misses the mark because Shaw fails to define his reader and presents his case in a no-person's land where neither the uninformed housewife nor the sceptical businessman will feel at ease or edified. It is surprising that the by then famous platform spellbinder, to whom the sizing-up of an audience was second nature, should have lapsed in this way; perhaps for once, as he half-indicated to Trebitsch, he did begrudge his time; and of course, because the book discusses the issue pro and con, it lacks the partiality with which Shaw invariably enlivened his discussions. But he never wasted anything, and over a quarter of a century later, when he returned to the same kind of discourse in the larger and much more complex *Intelligent Woman's Guide*, he showed that he had learnt from his lapse and, speaking as a Fabian Socialist to the intelligent women (and men) of the world through his intelligent sister-in-law, produced a masterwork of its kind.

In her history of the Fabian Society Margaret Cole cites three Fabian 'aberrances', that is to say three occasions when the Society adopted a line widely divergent from the consensus of radical and Socialist thinking.[19] The first of these aberrances was induced by the Boer War when, after furious internal squabbling, Shaw drafted *Fabianism and the Empire*, which supported the Tory government in its war against the two Boer republics in southern Africa. The second were the two education bills, touched on above, which the Tories adopted virtually holus-bolus from Sidney Webb, to the considerable indignation of Socialist organisations and the Liberals. The third aberrance was sparked off by the Colonial Secretary, Joseph Chamberlain – the radical hero of Birmingham, the glittering political figure of Miss Beatrice Potter's ardent hopes, the underhand and unscrupulous manipulator (Mrs Beatrice Webb's revised opinion) of the war against the two South African republics – Chamberlain, who, suddenly on 15 May 1903, after visiting South Africa, declared himself in favour of tariff reform by which the Empire would enjoy preferential trade while foreign countries would be obliged to pay import duties. To a country so accustomed to free trade as to regard it as inviolable this was tantamount to heresy and had it been anyone other than Chamberlain who had declared himself like this the chances are the statement would have caused a ripple of annoyance and then been forgotten. But Chamberlain was quite the foremost political personality of the day and his speech was explosive in its repercussions. His nominal boss, Balfour, was initially too stupefied to do anything about his subordinate's apostasy. *Punch* cartoons of the time show him as a woefully undecided Hamlet, not knowing whether to make a stand for or against tariff reform (16 September 1903) and as a cruelly depleted dummy saying whatever 'Joe the Ventriloquist' wished him to say (30 September 1903). In the end Balfour's indecisiveness induced Chamberlain to resign his office and stump the country proclaiming his belief in tariff reform. The government itself was split between free traders and reformers, with Balfour desperately trying to straddle both horses at once.

We are confronted once again with a controversy that historical hindsight tends to reduce in significance, yet it was important then and now and for more than one reason. It became one of the major issues of the election campaign that was then beginning to get under way. The election took place early in 1906 and the Tories were routed. Balfour, who had surprised everyone by surviving as long as he had, gave way to Campbell-Bannerman and gradually receded from the political stage; Chamberlain, whose health had declined markedly during 1905, suffered a stroke in 1906 and withdrew from politics. What hindsight makes clear is that the new Liberal government, though divided and lacking any firm set of policies, soon found themselves under increasing pressure to enact a series of major reforms (though not tariff reform) which marked a decisive break with the past. Flushed with victory as they would have been, they probably saw little significance in another outcome of the election: 41 seats to the Labour Party. They would have needed a Cassandra in their ranks to see this as marking the beginning of their not-distant demise. Shaw was no prophet either. This Labour Party was not Socialist, even though it included four Fabians and over twenty members of the Independent Labour Party, and he told readers of the Socialist *Clarion* that these 41 seats represented nothing more 'than a nominally independent Trade Unionist and Radical group ... I apologise to the Universe for my connection with such a party.'[20]

This was all in the future and in 1903 Shaw and other Fabians could only react as the immediate occasion prompted, and Shaw was up and about contributing his point of view on Tariff Reform from the beginning. The *Daily Mail* published his 'The Fiscal Policy of the Empire' on 3 July, taking care to point out that the views expressed were not necessarily those of the paper. Beatrice Webb also took care to tell her diary that the views expressed in the article were not necessarily hers or Sidney's – G.B.S.'s 'indiscretions' was how she described them.[21] Sidney would have preferred the Fabian Society not to take sides, much as he would have preferred it not to have taken sides in the Boer War, yet here was Shaw employing the tactic he had used over that war, using the press both to educate the public and to force Sidney's and the collective Fabian hand to fall in behind him. He is quite blatant in the way he draws fellow Fabians into his argument when, after having disposed of Chamberlainite tariff reform and free trade as economically and morally indefensible, he proposes a third, a Fabian option, as though to suggest that what he is saying is representative of and is indeed sanctioned by Fabian thought on the matter and that he, Shaw, is no more than the Society's obedient scribe. Beatrice and Sidney Webb are drawn in; also S. G. Hobson, a member of the Fabian Executive from 1900 to 1909; also H. W. Macrosty, a member of the Executive from 1895 to 1907 – leading lights therefore, all of whom by their presence in the article, provide the grist of Fabian authority to the Shavian mill.

If independence, opportunism and pragmatism characterized the Fabian Society as a whole, then Shaw was the most independent, opportunistic and pragmatic of them all.

Fabian Tract No. 116, *Fabianism and the Fiscal Question: An Alternative Policy*, followed soon afterwards. Shaw submitted his draft to the Society for discussion and emendation; it was adopted and published on 31 March 1904.[22] To anyone who had read Shaw's *Daily Mail* article, 'The Fiscal Policy of the Empire', this new tract contained little that was new. He abandoned his original theory that Chamberlain and the Empire had entered into a 'conspiracy', but for the rest served up much of the same again with a few trimmings on the side. He had plainly put the Society in his pocket with his article and kept it there through to the eventual approval of the official tract. 'It was perhaps the least successful of the many pronouncements written by Bernard Shaw on behalf of the Society,' says Pease,[23] who perhaps did not like being in anyone's pocket. Least successful certainly in that it tacitly assumed a victory for the Tories, Chamberlain and tariff reform in the coming election. Rather more successful, however, than Pease was inclined to believe in the way Shaw cleverly transposed his argument from the 'is' of the situation to the 'oughts' of the future,[24] which was the best he could do, given the division in the Society over the issue and the, to him, unpalatable aspects of both free trade and Chamberlainite tariff reform. Finally, although one would hesitate to hold *Fabianism and the Fiscal Question* up as a gem of sustained Shavian prose – it is not nearly as arresting as its forerunner in the *Daily Mail* – its occasional sparkle does raise the question of public inutility *vis-à-vis* stylistic utility. It is not a question Pease would have paused to ponder, much as he admired Shaw, public utility being his yardstick of worth, but the occasional satirical and always impeccably phrased thrust at this personality or that institution is pure Shaw. One notes, for example, the theatrical metaphor with which Shaw pins Chamberlain down:

> The stock Liberal gibe at Mr Chamberlain is to compare him to the harlequin with his coat of many colors. But the harlequin is the man who sets everything right. The performer who sets everything wrong in transports of elderly emotion is the pantaloon. Ever since the Fabian Society was founded it has had to struggle with a plague of pantaloons in politics; and it will perhaps be excused for saying that Mr Chamberlain, with all his energy, is hardly young enough to be a Fabian pioneer.[25]

One hopes that the pantaloon in question read this and smiled. And here, in the course of arguing for a reformed technical education:

> Our most famous and ancient universities are too venerable for reform. An attempt to adapt Oxford or Cambridge to modern industrial needs would be an act of Vandalism comparable to the turning of Westminster Abbey into a railway station. They are the only institutions of their kind in the world; and though it is conceivable that in the future their undergraduates and their dons may be represented by wax figures, and admission regulated by a turnstile, no real change is likely to be tolerated.[26]

Then there is this comment, more forward-looking than Shaw himself would have known, on the party that would soon sweep into power and his tract into oblivion:

> [T]he Liberals have spent their reputation. There is no more
> gratitude for them to abuse, no more confidence to betray, no
> more hope to defer. Until quite lately it was said of them that
> they were not worth voting for because they could not get their
> measures through the House of Lords. To-day it is impossible not
> to rejoice in the fact that so comparatively progressive an institu-
> tion as the House of Lords retains a veto on their powers of
> reaction.[27]

Seven years later that 'comparatively progressive institution' tried
to apply the veto to reformist legislation the Liberal government
was urgently pushing through Parliament. The confrontation
between Commons and Lords created an epic constitutional crisis
from which the Lords emerged battered and in no fit state ever to
attempt the veto again.

### III

While working on *The Common Sense of Municipal Trading* and
*Fabianism and the Fiscal Question*, Shaw penned his valedictory to
local government, published in the *Daily Mail* on 2 November 1903.
It was not a fond farewell. He had devoted six years to serving St
Pancras: a vestryman from 1897 to 1900, then, when the vestries
were upgraded, a borough councillor from 1901 to the end of 1903,
and he had had enough. He had been an excellent public servant
and contributed more than his fair measure in sundry subcommit-
tees of the vestry or council, serving at different times on the
Subcommittee on Health (twice), the Officers' Subcommittee
(which performed a personnel management function) and the
Subcommittee for Electricity and Public Lighting. Yet he did not
accomplish much. As a nominal 'Progressive', he was in a minority
in council and forever banging his head against vested interests of
one kind and another. His solid tradesmen fellow-councillors liked
him and always enjoyed a hearty laugh when he spoke, but they
were not prepared to vote with him. Still, being Shaw, he tried to
win them to his side. He tried to get the municipality to build a
crematorium in St Pancras: his colleagues laughed and thought he
was being morbid and sacrilegious. He tried to persuade them to

acquire a municipal monopoly on building: they laughed and turned to other matters. He proposed the appointment of additional sanitary inspectors: they laughed and thought he was being hysterical. He campaigned for free public lavatories for women: they did not laugh, they thought he was being disgusting.[28] By the end of 1903 therefore it was time to tell all and, as he said, tear his hair out and retire in disgust to the wider world outside St Pancras. He made the London municipal elections of 2 November the occasion for his article.

The headline is 'THE FRIVOLITY OF THE MOST FOOLISH CITY' and Shaw wastes no time in telling his readers that the day would provide an exhibition of frivolity that would occur nowhere else than in London, 'the most foolish city in the universe'. The municipal elections, which would involve nearly as large a population as a general election in Canada, would be taking place. 'And it will be treated as if it were a mere matter of gossip among a few tradesmen.' Shaking his head in incredulity, he piles it on: 'The whole business is beyond caricature ... No parodist can imagine anything so grotesque.'

The claim that the House of Commons was the best club in London was urged only by men who had never sat on a vestry or borough council committee. A borough council committee far outstripped any club dinner for sociability and amiability.

> That is what makes it so difficult, so unamiable, so ungracious, to betray the fact that most of the boon companions at these orgies are about as fit to be entrusted with the management of the huge revenues of the London boroughs as a Thames lighterman is to be trusted with the command of a first-class battleship.

He inveighs against the inability of the average councillor, whose eye cannot roam beyond the immediate saving, to understand the basics of economics; he ridicules local superstitions that impede the building of tramways: 'It is no use talking to [my constituents] about them. I have tried them with eloquence, and I have tried them with insult. Both are alike vain.' London remained intensely parochial and insular. 'The present relations between Russia and Japan [at war at the time] are almost mawkishly fraternal in comparison with relations between St Pancras and Islington, Holborn and Westminster. Its inhabitants never cross the boundaries if they can help it.' He had told his constituents about the four-lane tramways in France, which to them was proof of the degradation of France; he had told them about Dublin and Glasgow, which confirmed them in their resolution not to become provincial.

Shaw says: 'I am not myself a good party man in local politics' – a remark that should be borne in mind when considering his campaign, soon to be launched, to be elected to the London County Council. The division in local government between Progressive and Moderate is a delusive one and he advises the wise voter – 'not that I have met one, but still there are degrees in folly' – to back the candidate rather than the official line the candidate may be espousing. Here again one may discern the thinking that informed his campaign.

It is an extravagantly phrased but telling denunciation of local government as Shaw experienced it, telling enough for the *Daily Mail* to endorse the article in a second leader: an unusual experience for Shaw, who was accustomed to seeing himself criticized. It also provides a good example of the kind of attacking stance Shaw would adopt when he thought the public needed a dressing down. Not long afterwards, writing to Sidney Webb about another article intended for the press, he commented on his method, which amounted to being a conscious projection of 'individual, irresponsible, uncontrollable Shaw'.[29]

He may well have imagined that this attack on borough councils would conclude his career as an officially appointed public figure; it has the ring of finality. But Charlotte thought otherwise. Her husband's talent for this kind of work should not be squandered, she decided, and he was getting nowhere with his plays. She spoke to Sidney Webb. Could Shaw not be nominated as a candidate in the forthcoming election for the London County Council? Webb obliged, and Shaw, evidently not at all averse to the idea of running, was duly nominated as one of the two Progressive candidates for South St Pancras. The London County Council was a much wider world than the borough of St Pancras and, in addition, a Progressive majority in the LCC was a foregone conclusion. That would be a pleasant change for a man grown accustomed to banging his head against Moderate, that is Tory, indifference.

But he had to win the election first, and there were one or two problems to be overcome. One was that in the borough elections of 2 November South St Pancras had not returned a single Progressive to the council and the likelihood of persuading the good people of this district to do an about-turn when casting their vote for the county council was remote. Progressive party organisers regarded South St Pancras as a lost cause. Shaw himself said as much after the election: 'a Progressive forlorn hope' was how he described himself to the *Daily News*.[30]

Another problem was the main issue of the election, the contentious London Education Bill, which proposed to extend state control, thus financial assistance, to all church schools. As noted, the Fabians supported this Bill, even though it came from the Tories. The trouble was the Progressive ratepayers of South St Pancras, being nonconformist and hotly opposed to dipping into their pockets for nominally independent church schools, were unlikely to support a candidate who, though campaigning as a Progressive, spouted pro-Moderate education policy at them. To complicate the already complicated issue, pro-Education Moderates tended to look askance at a candidate who favoured their cause and yet marched under a Progressive banner.

None of this seemed to deter Shaw. Quite the opposite. He seemed to regard these problems as adding needed salt and vinegar to the situation and he mounted his cart and tootled on his trumpet for all he was worth. He knew enough about the politics and politicking of local government, he must have reckoned, to play his cards with practised expertise, no matter that the cards were stacked against him. Applying his maxim to sell the man and not the label, he tried his utmost to persuade voters to support Bernard Shaw, not the Progressive candidate, persuade them, if need be, by playing the paradoxical man to the hilt. He recognized the comedy in it all and turned his campaign into a romp. Idiosyncratic campaign letters flowed from his pen, he canvassed, he addressed public meetings, he sold his candidacy with the same fervour with which he usually sold himself in the public press and persisted throughout in presenting himself in as perverse a light as possible. The press itself probably paid him more attention than all the other candidates combined; some supported, some openly scoffed at him. Webb, returned unopposed in his constituency of Deptford, came in to help; he sent in members of the Fabian Society; wrote to every clergymen in the constituency, urging them to show their support; took charge of two-thirds of the constituency; fussed over Shaw's article 'County Councilitis', moderating its tone and editing its more outrageous statements to such an extent that the final version, when published in the *Daily*

*Mail*, was more controlled Webb than uncontrollable Shaw. Before the election Beatrice Webb could not make up her mind whether to be apprehensive or glad at the prospect of Shaw's winning. 'What effect G.B.S.'s brilliant slashing to the right and the left among his own nominal supporters will have, remains to be seen,' she wrote in her diary.

> The Shaws have been good friends to us and we would not like them to have a humiliating defeat. What that erratic genius will do, if he gets on the L.C.C., heaven will know some day, but I am inclined to think that in the main he will back up Sidney ... In the Fabian Society they have certainly managed to supplement each other in a curiously effective way – let us hope it will be the same on the L.C.C. But he is not likely to get in![31]

It is a confused and confusing comment but in the main she seemed to want Shaw to defy augury and win.

The election took place on 5 March 1904 and on that very morning Shaw produced his last rallying cry in the pages of the *St James's Gazette*. 'Are you and Sir William Geary [Shaw's fellow Progressive in the campaign] going to win?' 'Yes, easily, if the intelligent people of the constituency can be induced to vote. But 3,000 of them sat at home last time – reading my books, I suppose – and did nothing. If that happens again the old vestry gang will dispose of me as easily as a donkey disposes of a thistle.'[32] The donkey disposed of the thistle; Shaw lost decisively, though not humiliatingly, obtaining 1460 votes (his partner Geary received 1412 votes) to two Moderates who polled 1927 and 1808 votes. Beatrice Webb wrote Shaw off with an 'I-told-you-so' and a priggish:

> His bad side is very prominent at an election – vanity and lack of reverence for knowledge or respect for other peoples' prejudices; even his good qualities – quixotic chivalry to his opponents and cold-drawn truth ruthlessly administered to possible supporters – are magnificent but not war ... He will never be selected again by any constituency that any wire-puller thinks can be won.[33]

Shaw himself, energetically communicative before the election, became positively garrulous afterwards. Wounded vanity probably contributed to the spate of letters and self-drafted interviews that appeared in the press soon after the election, but there was more to it than that: he genuinely believed that he had been misrepresented and misunderstood; he had to clear the air and, of course, have the last word.

He enjoyed himself during the campaign; he would have liked nothing better than to upset the borough apple cart and, if elected, he would have seen himself making a real Progressive contribution to local government in London. His public persona after the election is more difficult to assess. It is not clear whether he was disappointed or secretly relieved. A little of both, quite likely. One thing is clear: his mistakes and miscalculations during the campaign did not come back to haunt him one bit.

He did not seek public office again. This was not for want of being asked, notwithstanding Beatrice Webb's dismissal of his future chances. A seat in Parliament would not have been beyond him; there was talk of this at various times, notably in an editorial article, 'G.B.S. as M.P.', which appeared in A. R. Orage's Socialist *New Age* four years after the county council debacle. One has to take tributes whence they come and Orage – a Fabian, a friend of Shaw's and editor of a paper partly funded by Shaw – can scarcely be thought an objective source. Even so, his flight of fancy in 'G.B.S. as M.P.' is real enough in defining the qualities Shaw would have been able to bring to Parliament: 'Anybody who has heard him in debate ... knows certainly that Mr Shaw was made for Parliament as surely as Parliament has not yet been made for him.' Orage sees Shaw as an Edwardian Socrates, and it 'is this that plainly points to Parliament as his natural sphere, the House of Commons being at present the only place in the British Empire where discussion is taken seriously and carried on with the necessary glare of publicity.' His active participation in the business of the House of Commons would afford the Empire a delight 'comparable only to the delight that must have been felt by the young Athenian lions when they followed Plato's master ... That is where Mr Shaw must be if the Empire is to make the greatest use of her chiefest intellectual asset.'[34]

But if Shaw did occasionally dally with the idea Orage puts forward here, it never went beyond that, for reasons this vignette from 1907 makes abundantly clear: he and Mark Twain were observed watching the Commons in action from the men's gallery:

> And there in the front row they lolled, sentient, alert, sublime as gods. As the drone of inanities from the pit below wafted up to

them they ... began to fidget. First they nudged each other. Next they chuckled. Then their pallid faces flushed. Presently, like toy balloons, their cheeks puffed out with tight-lipped laughter. And then they exploded and sat there quaking with uncontrollable, silent merriment.[35]

Shaw's Fabian-Socialist activities were by no means ended by his defeat in the LCC election; nor was this the only highlight of his Fabian career in the Edwardian years. A possibly even more brilliant display of Shavian fireworks was put up when H. G. Wells led the abortive revolt against the Old Gang of the Fabian Society in 1907, but this crisis, although news of it reached the press, was an in-house rather than a public matter. For the rest, Shaw continued to campaign, in print, debate and lecture, for the better world that the adoption of Socialism would bring. There was, for example, 'The Bitter Cry of the Middle Classes' in the *Tribune* of 14 and 15 August 1906, in which he drew yet again on his childhood experiences to discourse vehemently on the indigence of the middle-class 'proletariat' and reminded his readers that the Fabian Society was as committed to improving the lot of this under-privileged group as that of the working class. There was 'A Socialist Programme: The Gentle Art of Unpleasantness' in the *Clarion* of 9, 16 and 23 August 1907 where he had a field day being pleasantly unpleasant: 'Everybody knows that the rich live by robbing the poor. That is why no gentleman ever mentions it. To call a man of independent means a thief is, argumentatively, to hit a man when he is down: it is like mentioning the facts concerning a lady's inside to prove that she is not an angel.' Then there was an article in the *Englishwoman* of March 1909, 'The Unmentionable Case for Women's Suffrage', which advances so thoroughly original and Shavian a reason for granting women political rights as surely to have aroused the deepest Suffragist suspicions:

English decency is a rather dirty thing. It is responsible for more indecency than anything else in the world ... There is only one absolutely certain and final preventive for ... indecency, and that is the presence of women. If there were no other argument for giving women the vote, I would support it myself on no other ground than that men will not behave themselves when women are not present.

Hindsight may suggest to some that Shaw's endeavours on behalf of the Fabian Society amounted to an enormous expenditure of time and energy on what the past century has proved a ruinously misdirected mission. This is wide of the mark. What Shaw and other Fabians campaigned for and tried to achieve has been proved right, not wrong, by the excesses of totalitarian Communism, just as their mission has been proved right, not wrong, by the excesses of totalitarian Capitalism. To go back to the 'Fabian Basis' and a comment by Pease: Fabianism was an interpretation, based on ethical considerations, of the spirit of the time. John Palmer's 1915 article in the *Fortnightly Review*, 'Mr Bernard Shaw: An Epitaph', is remarkable for being both one of the most percipient and one of the most mistaken among the many criticisms of Shaw written at the time. He is perceptive here:

> Mr Shaw's inspiration ... is not aesthetic, but moral. We have to reckon with a moral fury where he most individually rages. The daemon which seizes his pen at the critical moment, and uses for its own enthusiastic purposes, is the daemon which drove Milton to destroy Salmasius ... That he talked Socialism was an accident of the time.

An accident of the time: the progressive spirit of the Edwardian years decreed the redistribution of wealth and a better deal for the working man: the rousing of a moribund social conscience. History has confirmed, not denied, the rightness of the Socialist movements that instilled this morality in Britain and other countries of Western Europe during the present century. Those interminable letters and articles Fabian Shaw gave the press on this theme contributed more than any other agency to its gradual public acceptance, to a revised frame of moral reference; and lest it be forgotten, those letters and articles enlivened political debate and controversy in the Edwardian years immeasurably.

# 4
# 1903–1905: International Shaw

Shaw produced nothing of substance from January 1901 to mid-1903. No major publication appeared, no play was staged except for occasional productions by the Stage Society in London or occasional performances outside London. The loyal Archer put it that 'it remains a monstrous and almost incredible anomaly that a writer whom such a critic as Dr Georg Brandes [the noted Danish philosopher and critic] can call "the most original dramatist of the British Empire of to-day" should never have had a single play produced by an established management in the West-end of London.' It was a sentiment Shaw was inclined to support. '[O]ur London system does cut off masterpieces,' he told Archer in response. 'Given theatres of the German type in England and my difficulties would be over at once ...'[1] His way ahead seemed quite blocked.

Yet he continued to work furiously to tilt the scales of fortune in his favour. He completed *Man and Superman*. At the same time, a young Austrian, Siegfried Trebitsch, began to translate his plays into German, and an American actor-manager, Arnold Daly, was beginning to promote his plays in New York. Three isolated and almost random activities, yet each would singly and cumulatively contribute to Shaw's emergence from the shadow of an indifferent world. Each is a story in itself.

*Man and Superman* first, because Shaw's struggle to get the play published reveals the suspicion, not to say hostility, with which he was held by the British (and to a certain extent the American) establishment at the time and because the response of his friends and peers to the publication reveals how lightly they regarded his gifts as a playwright.

Shaw decided in 1902 to get rid of Grant Richards as his publisher. '[Y]ou do not push the books past the point at which they replace their cost to you. *I* dont get the wages of a head clerk out of them …' He mentions that he is thinking of publishing *Man and Superman* himself and doing his own advertising, 'especially if I can induce my wife to take charge of the details'.[2] Fortunately he did not pursue this option to the letter; perhaps Charlotte sensibly declined to take charge of the details.

He investigated more conventional options in the next few months by approaching several leading publishing houses and he briefly employed the well-known literary agent, J. B. Pinker, who mentioned Methuen but failed to make satisfactory headway. Shaw impatiently approached Methuen direct. His letter to the firm tells one a good deal about his sense of himself as a marketable commodity at the time. He believed that a sale of at least 5000 copies of his books would be achieved by 'ordinarily energetic handling'. He assumed that Methuen were willing to deal with work of the higher literary class of the kind that he produced. The terms were a royalty of 20 per cent. The question of remainders did not apply. 'My books do not die after the first demand drops: they dribble away slowly but steadily.' He expected the publisher to bear the cost of printing, but undertook to correct printer's errors and generally make the book as presentable as he knew how. As a good Socialist, he required the contract to contain a 'fair wages' clause to apply to the cost of printing. The licence to publish – he never assigned copyright or stage right – was limited to the United Kingdom and the colonies; simultaneous publication in America was imperative because the book had to be copyrighted there.[3] Methuen turned him down without even looking at the MS: they appreciated, they said, Shaw's brilliant reputation but always endeavoured to avoid any occasion for friction and controversy; they would never, as author and publisher, see with the same eyes. Like other prominent publishers, they would no doubt come to regret their decision when Shaw's star began to rise, but at the time their rejection was probably sound. Shaw's terms would have seemed excessive and uncompromising: a 20 per cent royalty and the refusal to assign copyright from an author whose books and plays had not enjoyed more than limited appeal would have struck the firm as confirmation of Shaw's forbidding public image.

This and the likelihood of other rejections caused Shaw to go back to his idea of producing and marketing the book himself, at least in modified form. He would see to the printing; disciple of William Morris that he was, he would have been, and often was, difficult and fastidious in this respect, and his decision to supervise the printing, using Clark of Edinburgh who knew his ways by then, was wise. At least one likely source of friction with a future publisher would be eliminated.

As for publication, he had hit on the idea of getting this done on commission and negotiated along these lines with Longman's, who had an American house. Nothing was settled by May when, writing to an acquaintance, F. H. Evans, he asked whether he knew of a publisher who might be prepared to publish him on commission. Evans suggested Archibald Constable & Co.[4] This firm was descended from the Archibald Constable of Edinburgh who had published Scott's novels and then crashed in 1826; the new London-based firm was established in 1890 and initially headed by the grandson. Its venerable antecedents notwithstanding, it was a young firm and, although it had achieved several publishing successes by the early 1900s, the most notable being that it secured George Meredith when the grand old man broke with Chatto, it was not in the same league as other more senior and prominent publishing houses. It may have been for this reason that Shaw did not act immediately on Evans's advice, but sent the script to John Murray instead for a personal opinion. The reply was an unambiguous no: 'The object of the book is to cast ridicule upon – or perhaps I should say to assail – marriage and other social & religious institutions.' Respectable houses would not be inclined to publish such a book.[5]

Rejected again and increasingly anxious by then – mid-year – to see the book out before Parliament rose for the summer recess, he finally turned to Constable. The firm's two partners, Otto Kyllman and William Maxse Meredith, the novelist's son, turned out to be the kind of people he had been looking for. They were young – Kyllman was in his early forties, Meredith in his thirties – and prepared to risk their reputation on the dangerous revolutionary that was Shaw. Anyway, the financial risk was negligible: the agreement was that they would be Shaw's commissioned distributors; Shaw would be responsible for the printing. This agreement, 'formalized' in a few lines scribbled by Shaw on a sheet of letter paper, was to serve to the benefit of both parties until Shaw's death in 1950[6] – 47 years that were not without periods of vexation and exasperation on the part of the firm. As one commentator has put it: 'The revived house of Constable had Bernard Shaw as its chief author and irritant during the first half of the century ... but he was a valuable property to them ...'[7]

*Man and Superman*, printed by R. & R. Clark of Edinburgh, and published by Archibald Constable & Co. of Westminster, finally appeared on 11 August 1903.

Meanwhile Shaw's search for a new publisher in America was encountering as many obstacles as in England. His publisher to date, Herbert Stone of Boston, had failed like Grant Richards to promote the sale of his books and had to be jettisoned. Dan H. Laurence comments on Shaw's search during 1903: '[H]e had resorted to the transatlantic cable, and proof sheets of the play bounced from Harper to Macmillan to Appleton ...'[8] Shaw's letter to Macmillan in New York reflects an awareness of limited appeal in the United States: roughly 1000 copies on the strength of reviews and paragraphs, 'which I generally draw from the press in greater profusion than is at all personally convenient to me.' He would prefer the royalty system in America, his terms being 12.5 per cent on the nominal price of the first thousand copies, thereafter 15 per cent. He stipulated that the book be published under licence, the duration of which would be five years.[9] This stipulation caused Macmillan, on the point of accepting him, to draw back. They 'almost never' published under such conditions. Shaw had to have the last word: '[A] demand that the author shall also bind himself to you for life for better or worse, takes away my breath.'[10]

Other publishers – Harper, Appleton (who also objected to the five-year licence), and McClure, Philip & Co. – either dilly-dallied or, like their British counterparts, found the subject matter unsuitable. Shaw, eloquent on the subject of American lack of 'hustle', fully aware that the publication date in England was approaching and with it the certainty of an immediate unauthorized edition in the States, finally printed the book himself at the University Press of Cambridge, Mass. The book was set up from the first British proof and two unrevised copies were deposited in the Library of Congress on 12 August 1903, one day after publication in England.

This accomplished, Shaw could relax about finding an American publisher. He waited until 1904, by which time the effect of the English publication was such as to enable him to obtain considerably better terms with the publisher of his choice, Brentano's of New York: a 25 per cent royalty, which remained in force until the firm went bankrupt in 1933. The first American edition of *Man and Superman* came out on 1 June 1904.

The sales history of *Man and Superman* in the early years will be touched on in a later chapter, 'Edwardian Shaw'. Here one may remark that its success as a publication in both Britain and America underscores the pusillanimity of the established publishing houses of those two countries. The Shavian seeds they had disdained would become Constable's harvest in the years ahead.

True to form, *The Times* did not notice the appearance of *Man and Superman*: to the newspaper of record this was a non-event, even though (perhaps because) its distinguished theatre critic, A. B. Walkley, featured prominently in the preface. (A year later the American paper of record, *The New York Times*, noticed American publication in a cheerfully favourable leading article in its book review section of Saturday 18 June 1904.) Some London critics reviewed it, among them G. K. Chesterton and Max Beerbohm, both of whom made occasional admiring noises but preferred on the whole to find fault. Chesterton's main complaint, conveyed in a fusillade of paradoxes, was that the play, though 'fascinating and delightful', betrayed and embodied Shaw's besetting weakness, which was not to see things as they were;[11] Beerbohm's that, although this was Shaw's 'masterpiece, so far', it was not a play, its characters were 'not human enough, not alive enough'.[12]

The private responses were generally more interesting, revealing as they do how Shaw's friends and literary peers viewed him at this stage of his career. Beatrice Webb was one of the favoured few who listened to Shaw reading the play before publication. 'To me it seems a great work, quite the biggest thing he has done ... Possibly the unexpectedness of the success had made me over-value it, a reaction from a current in my mind of depreciation of G.B.S.'[13]

Shaw wrote to tell Beerbohm how wrong he had been in his review. 'This wont do. Your article in the Saturday is most laborious, most conscientious: the spasms of compliments almost draw tears, but the whole thing is wrong ... Most astonishing of all, you have before you in Bashville the Gay & Superman the Serious two terrific displays of literary bravura ... and yet you make the usual gull's apology – you, Max, a gull on such a point! – for complimenting me on my art. You idiot, do you suppose I dont know my own powers?'[14]

Replying, Beerbohm apologized for not having praised Shaw's delineation of the subordinate characters, but he would not retract on the issue of 'waxen John' and 'whalebony Ann':

Where your vision seems to me to be blurred and false is in the deeper business of human character ... Man doesn't strip to the

Laocoon, nor Woman to the Venus of Milos. Certainly not. But
no more does man strip to wax, and woman to whalebone. Each
strips to antique flesh and blood ... My specific objection to your
John and Ann is that neither ... draws any ordinary human
breath.[15]

Beerbohm would retract this objection, and handsomely, when he saw
the first production of the play at the Court Theatre two years later.

Gilbert Murray told Shaw that he thought *Man and Superman* a
most remarkable piece of work; like most of his friends, he was
anxious to point out just what was wrong with it, 'though I confess,
I cannot at the moment quite see what it is.' It made on him the
impression of an extraordinarily good thing gone somehow wrong.
'I wonder when you will write the real thing that is in you – the
thing that will not go wrong!'[16]

Shaw sent a copy to Tolstoy, who wrote back more in sorrow
than in anger. It was not sufficiently serious, he said. He detected
in Shaw a desire to surprise and astonish, which distracted from the
essence of the work, he said; anyway, he thought *Man and
Superman* reflected Shaw's thoughts in an embryonic state.[17]

Pride of place in this line-up of not always disinterested opinion
must go to William Archer, whose opinion was disinterested,
passionate and wrong. His letter, dated 1 September 1903 and
scrawled with a very blunt pencil, is a nine-and-a-half page denunciation of Shaw's hopelessly misdirected career to date; here we
limit him to his response to *Man and Superman*:

Well, you ... produce your 'Revolutionists' Handbook and
Aphorisms' – a glittering jumble of untested, unweeded, unhar-
monised thought, devoid of perspective or proportion, the old
humanitarianism cropping out every here and there through the
new Nietzscheanism, a good deal that is really profound in it, a
great deal that is hasty and superficial, and not a little that is
merely personal, crotchety, Shaw-esque ... I don't mean to say
that I despair of you as a dramatist; but I am bound to confess
that 'Man and Superman' rather dashes my hopes.[18]

Shaw replied to this; he could not otherwise: 'I find you more
modest than ever on my account. I feel as Harmsworth or Pierpont
Morgan might feel if you wrote to exhort them to turn over a new
leaf and make a little money.'[19]

All in all, Shaw's friends and associates did not fall over themselves to praise him. But public interest was quickening and the
first production of *Man and Superman* was not far distant.

## II

Archer's perennial lament over Shaw's wrong-headed approach to
the craft of playwriting tends to present him as a dour Scotsman
pedantically adhering to the litany of 'pure drama' in the face of his
friend's irreverent rejection of such a litany. This is only a fraction
of the picture. There was mutual esteem, loyalty and friendship,
which endured never-wavering disagreement and enriched both
lives; and there was the fact that Archer had a hand in directing
Shaw's career on at least three occasions, effecting far-reaching, one
is inclined to say fateful, consequences on that career. The first
occasion was when he got Shaw jobs as an art critic and book
reviewer; then in 1885 he invited Shaw to write the dialogue of a
play he had worked out, thus pointing him in the direction of, if not
quite launching him on, his career as a playwright. And then,
perhaps most fatefully, he told the young Austrian Siegfried
Trebitsch about him. This was in the spring of 1901 when Trebitsch,
visiting England, made a point of meeting Archer, known to him as
the English translator of Ibsen. Many years later Trebitsch remembered their meeting. Archer spoke despairingly about such
contemporary English playwrights as Grundy, Jones and Pinero
and their unmerited domination of the English stage. There were
unperformed, outstanding dramatic works which hardly anyone
knew about.

> The most important writer among them, one with whom I am on
> terms of close friendship, is a dramatist to his finger-tips, but a
> West End theatre would never put on a play of his. He has to
> make do with experimental theatres.
> Then for the first time I heard the name of Bernard Shaw.[20]

We may wonder whether Archer forgot himself so much as to
describe Shaw as a dramatist to his fingertips, but he said enough
to prompt Trebitsch to embark on a course that would alter his life.
He directed Trebitsch to a bookshop that stocked Shaw's works –
prominent bookstores would not have him, he said – and there

Trebitsch purchased the three volumes then in print: *Plays Pleasant,
Plays Unpleasant* and *Three Plays for Puritans*. He read *Candida* on the
train journey back to Vienna and was bowled over. 'I enjoyed the
strange fairy-tale of this poetic work as one of the most exquisite
gifts of a new and individual dramatic poetry. And afterwards, in
the tranquillity of my study, my enthusiasm grew and did not let
me rest until I had read all the ten plays.'[21]

After this, nothing would satisfy him until these plays had been
translated into German. He scoured the literary scene in Vienna
and elsewhere for a person both competent and willing to under-
take the task and found no one. Why not then secure the job for
himself? It was with this in mind that he returned to London early
in 1902.

Archer readily gave him a letter of introduction to Shaw.
Accounts differ as to how he overcame Shaw's initial reluctance to
have anything to do with him, although Shaw's version in his
'Translator's Note' which prefaces *Jitta's Atonement* is probably true
in spirit if not in all details. According to Shaw, this young Austrian,
quite unknown to him, presented himself at his door with the
request that he should become his interpreter and apostle in
Central Europe. Shaw tried to evade him; Charlotte spoke to him
instead and something about Trebitsch impressed her. She diplo-
matically manipulated a still sceptical husband to sit down to lunch
with Trebitsch. At this lunch, which took place at Adelphi Terrace
on 17 March 1902, the deal was struck. As deals go, it was more a
declaration of fervent intent on Trebitsch's part than a firm
contract: Shaw agreed to grant him translation rights for one year,
in which time Trebitsch would translate three plays and have them
either published or performed. It was a tall order and quite possibly Shaw expected Trebitsch to fall down on it; if so, he reckoned
without Trebitsch's determination. Within the year, battling against
the ignorance and caution of theatrical managers and publishers,
he managed to get *The Devil's Disciple* staged at the Raimund
Theatre in Vienna, other productions of other plays promised elsewhere in Austria and Germany, and his translation of three plays
– *The Devil's Disciple, Arms and the Man* and *Candida* – published as
*Drei Dramen*.

The production of *The Devil's Disciple* in February 1903 was, at
best, no more than a qualified success and *Drei Dramen* was heavily
criticized for inaccuracies of translation. Shaw's advent in German-
speaking Europe was not auspicious, but it was a beginning, and

soon, within a year or two, his plays were being staged for short runs throughout Austria and Germany, and critics were taking note of him as quite the foremost playwright in English and arguably one of the most significant in Europe. From then on his position in Germany and Austria went from strength to strength. There was criticism of the plays and of the translations, some of it severe, and the Burgtheater in Vienna shelved production of *Arms and the Man* early in 1903 when authority indicated that it might be 'inopportune' to stage it, the situation in the Balkans being rather volatile at the time. Shaw tried to make as much capital out of this 'censoring' as he could, to Trebitsch's embarrassment, but there was no controversy worth speaking of. There was no denunciation anywhere in German-speaking Europe, no confrontation with putative watchdogs of established political or social or personal morality. None of the perennial hostility of the English critics. It was a new experience for Shaw.

Thus began the Shaw-Trebitsch association – it was a collaboration really – that would survive two world wars and end when Shaw died. He owed his success in German-speaking Europe to Trebitsch, and he knew it. As he said in his 'Translator's Note', Trebitsch's translation of his body of work, both literary and theatrical

> was begun at a time when my position in the English theatre was one not of good repute, but of infamy ... I presently found myself a successful and respected playwright in the German language whilst the English critics were still explaining laboriously that my plays were not plays ... [M]y personal debt to him is incalculable.[22]

This tribute is the more generous because it does not breathe a word about the arduous apprenticeship in theatrical business and translation that Shaw was compelled to put Trebitsch through once his neophyte got going. Trebitsch was an innocent in many respects: innocent of the ways of the theatre, innocent of the vagaries of English idiom, to say nothing of his blank ignorance of the complexities of English social and political life; innocent, despite his admiration, of the subtleties of Shaw's texts. To complicate matters further, he was temperamentally poles apart from Shaw – Malvolio to Shaw's Feste, a hypochondriacal Malvolio at that; a difference revealed in Trebitsch's lugubriously melodramatic

*Frau Gitta's Sühne* and the ironic comedy Shaw made of it in his 'translation'. Shaw would have realized all this soon enough, but he had committed himself, and any kind of activity was preferable to the stalemate in England; so he set about instructing Trebitsch, lecturing him, moulding him in his likeness and being. His letters from 1902 onwards reflect this desire to set Trebitsch in the right direction, usually by dint of patient exposition and vehement exhortation sweetened with a compliment or two.

> Now you must make up your mind to undergo a most tedious and miserable apprenticeship to the stage over my plays. You are a sensitive & fastidious young poet: I am a sordid and disillusioned old charlatan. But I have built up these plays out of atoms of dust bit by bit, and planned them for the stage and corrected them for the press and rehearsed them for performance; and the result is that I can see at a glance these oversights that seem trifles to you. Siegfried Trebitsch: I tell you it is the trifles that matter when you are a man of genius.[23]

The same letter speaks of '48 appalling errors & ruinous oversights in the D's D alone'. (Two weeks later *Arms and the Man* was 'full of hideous and devastating errors' and *Candida* was worse.)[24] Shaw's German was elementary and he had to rely on a dictionary, but he was thorough and painstaking to the extent, as he told Trebitsch in the letter quoted above, 'Even I, who cannot speak German, have read your version aloud to a German ...' – the German being H. A. Hertz, the founder of the German Theatre in London and a member of the Stage Society executive. Trebitsch's English was better than Shaw's German – Shaw told him he wrote English better than most Englishmen, which is not saying much – but he needed correction; plainly he relied on Shaw's guidance, which is not to say he docilely accepted all Shaw's emendations. On one occasion early in 1903, trying to stick to his guns about certain details of translation, he told his mentor that 'in some things you are wrong', which prompted the inevitable rejoinder, 'My dear Trebitsch, *I am never wrong* ... I am omniscient and infallible,' which was followed by a cogent statement on the art of writing stage dialogue.[25]

As with the texts, so with theatre business. 'I know that the transfer of any work to the professional stage means desecration, prostitution, sacrilege and damnation. It means this *at best*.'[26] This is the cheerful prelude in the first letter on this topic (in anticipation of the production of *The Devil's Disciple*), after which Shaw proceeded in letter after letter to instruct Trebitsch on how he, as author, therefore the person best qualified to interpret the work in hand, should overcome the desecration, prostitution, sacrilege and damnation in which actors, theatre managers and others involved in the production of a play, not forgetting the critics, revelled. Shaw's philosophy in this regard is token of his personality (and a revealing reversal of his public manner): avoid direct confrontation, he advised; stick to your guns but use diplomacy to overcome those who would resist or try to overbear you. In a word, charm your co-workers into happy compliance. All this amounted to another tall order, in effect requiring Trebitsch, who would rather have challenged his opponents to a duel, to become what Shaw became, a byword in the theatre for gentlemanliness. But here again the young man learnt fast.

If Shaw owed Trebitsch a great deal, it is no less true that Trebitsch owed Shaw as much.

Other European translators of Shaw's work emerged after Trebitsch and during and after the Vedrenne-Barker seasons at the Court Theatre. The work they did in establishing Shaw as a playwright of global repute – some of his plays were appearing in translation in distant Japan and not-so-distant Russia, to say nothing of Western and Central Europe well before the First World War – falls beyond the scope of the present study. Suffice it to mention that Shaw found himself under great pressure to find translators before 1908. Trebitsch was bound to him by hoops of steel, the unwilling and not very competent Augustin Hamon of France by rather less tensile material and Hugo Vallentin of Sweden by his reliability, but Shaw's position overall was not secure. As he explained to Henderson in 1906, his copyright would lapse on the Continent in 1908 unless he exercised his rights before then. Consequently he had to appoint deputy Bernard Shaws in every country in Europe.[27] He succeeded perhaps beyond his expectations and by January 1908 could tell Trebitsch that he had seven other translators in Europe with all of whom he was under 'solemn contract'.[28]

These contracts – in time there would be many more than seven – would protect Shaw's business interests. His artistic interests were another matter. He could exercise considerable control over Trebitsch and, to a lesser extent, Augustin Hamon of France, but beyond these two he had no control whatever, because he did not know the languages. He admitted this to Vallentin: 'Do not send me the translations. I do not know a single word of Swedish; so I could not read them.'[29] Similarly all those other 'deputy Bernard Shaws' in Europe had virtually free hands and were bound by little more than their integrity, although we may be sure they were guided by plenty of advice, sought and unsought. It was not all plain sailing. Writing to fellow-playwright Henry Arthur Jones in 1908, Shaw admitted to the bother and expense it had been to engage suitable people and to get printing and publication done. 'The trouble, including occasional lawsuits, is sometimes so devilish that I curse the day when international copyright was invented ...'[30]

This was all Shaw could do to protect and promote his work in Europe. The protection and promotion of his work in the opposite direction – in the United States – was a different matter, easier in many respects, because there was no language barrier; more difficult, because in the early years of the century he found himself dealing with a personality who preferred to go his own way. This was Arnold Daly, the ever-hopeful maverick of the American theatre in the early 1900s.

### III

Daly's early career – as theatre factotum and bit player in pieces that flopped – was not one to inspire confidence in others. He had considerable self-confidence, not to say cheek, however, and in 1903 he decided to become his own manager and stage director, setting himself up in partnership with a friend Winchell Smith on a bankroll of $1350.00.[31] He read *Plays Pleasant*; in terms that said more about his motives than he would have realized he told Henderson, 'I felt as a prospector does when he strikes a big vein of gold.'[32] He set his sights on *Candida* and, working through Shaw's American agent, Elizabeth Marbury, secured the rights, an extraordinary and mystifying stroke of luck considering Daly's erratic history. Shaw knew nothing about him, asking the critic James Huneker – and Daly himself – whether he was anything to the late, and renowned, Augustin,[33] the answer to which was no. But he agreed to Daly's producing the play with the strict proviso that there would be no contract or reservation of rights – only permission to give half a dozen performances. He would hedge his bets with this young hopeful.

*Candida* was first performed as a special matinee at the Princess Theatre, New York, on 8 December 1903. This was not the first performance of the play in America, that honour going to the Browning Society in Philadelphia on 18 May 1903, but it was the first time the major critics noticed it. Their reaction was positive and, as they were to show time and again (with one notable exception), they were disposed to be far more open-minded in their reception of Shavian drama than their British counterparts. *The New York Times* marvelled 'how the play had been neglected these nine years ... it was so full of witty lines and bits of action that roused up spontaneous outbursts of delight, so deeply human and dramatic'.[34] Other critics felt much the same.

Daly, seeing that vein of gold glittering ever more brightly, moved his production from theatre to theatre and finally settled at the Vaudeville, later the Berkeley Lyceum, where it became the hit of the season. Swelling with success, he added *The Man of Destiny* to the bill (against Shaw's specific advice), playing both Bonaparte and Marchbanks in one evening until his health broke down. Shaw then wrote his antidote to the Candidamania sweeping the city, *How He Lied to Her Husband*, which replaced *The Man of Destiny*. Late in April 1904, after 132 performances, Daly took these three plays on tour, repeating his New York success wherever he went. From Shaw's point of view, although he made disparaging noises about the snivelling vogue of *Candida*, Daly had done well for him. In those lean years the royalty of $2534.00 for the New York season must have seemed like manna.

*Plays Pleasant* contained more gold than *Candida* and early in 1905, on 9 January,[35] Daly was back in New York with *You Never Can Tell* at the Garrick Theatre. *The New York Times* was not impressed. It headlined its notice with 'Mr Shaw a Success in Spite of the Actors' and strongly criticized most of the cast (but not Daly himself) for failing to bring out the full meaning of the text.[36]

Performances would have improved during the five-month run of the play – Henderson, who saw the production, was impressed – and *You Never Can Tell* may be accounted another Daly success. Even so, there were signs that his hour of glory was beginning to fade. To give credit where it is due, he had been an effective Marchbanks and his cast for *Candida* had been well chosen, but *You Never Can Tell*, if *The New York Times* is anything to go by, showed that he lacked the requisite touch for the more complex staging that this play demands.

Shaw would have been aware of such reported shortcomings; at the same time, he could not ignore Daly's continuing success with his plays. He gave his permission for a New York production of *John Bull's Other Island*, which had been earning him golden opinions in London. To Daly this opened up a vein quite as rich as that provided by *Plays Pleasant*.

Shaw's correspondence with Daly about the productions of *Candida* and *You Never Can Tell* as represented in *Collected Letters, 1898–1910* is so thin as to amount to nothing. He would certainly have written to him about these plays; it was not his way to leave a production to the mercies of a comparative novice, and the likelihood is that Daly, being the kind of man he was, paid scant attention to the advice being offered and conveniently mislaid letters, preferring to go his own way. Hence the less than immaculate production of *You Never Can Tell* and, to come to the next play in Daly's campaign, the dismal presentation of *John Bull's Other Island*.

*Collected Letters, 1898–1910* has nothing on the production of this play either, yet there is evidence that Shaw took pains in advising Daly about the casting and general tone of the production. This, a typescript dated December 1904 and headed 'Instructions to the Producer',[37] is clearly intended for an American director preparing the play for American audiences – Daly in other words. Daly, then, could have had no excuse, except his vanity and predilection for rushing under-rehearsed pieces into performance, for foisting on New York audiences a production that the critics panned. The *New York Journal* described the audience as 'sitting in fuddled bewilderment during the presentation of a thick, glutinous and impenetrable four-act tract'; the *New York Sun* said it was doubtful whether any play ever presented to a New York audience had proved so 'insufferably dull'.[38] *The New York Times* was one dissenting voice. The critic of this paper seems to have taken the trouble to acquaint himself with the text beforehand and was accordingly prepared to recognize and acknowledge Shaw's purposes and satire. Most of his review is in praise of the play – a 'masterpiece of satire' – rather than of the performance; but this also receives its measure of approval.[39] But dullness, or rather Daly's inability to raise the play above that level, won the day and *John Bull's Other Island* was taken off after only two weeks.

The failure rankled with Shaw. He told Eleanor Robson that Daly had disregarded his instructions as to the cast and so made an 'utter failure' of *John Bull*.[40] This, coupled with the fiasco surrounding his production of *Mrs Warren's Profession*, which was about to burst upon New York with all the force of a real-life Sutro melodrama, virtually put paid to Daly as Shaw's apostle in the United States.

The allusion to Sutro is to his London success *The Walls of Jericho* – about a ruggedly honest man's attempt to bring down the walls of hypocrisy and humbug surrounding London society – which had opened in New York on 25 September. Daly would certainly have seen the play, either there or in London and, although one hesitates to force an analogy, it is not inconceivable that his subsequent attempts to storm and breach the walls of New York were undertaken in some kind of emulation of Sutro's protagonist. He seems to have been that kind of man.

He also had an eye for the main chance, the chief beneficiary of such chance being himself rather than the author whose cause he was ostensibly serving; and *Mrs Warren's Profession* caught his eye as a promising source of revenue, even before *Candida*. He appears to have written to Shaw late in 1903 about producing it. Shaw told him flatly that 'There is no money in Mrs Warren; and it ought not to be played for money. But there are other considerations which make it well worth playing.' One consideration was that the actress who had made a great success of the eponymous role in the Stage Society production in 1902, Fanny Brough, was in New York. He encouraged Daly to secure her for the role. If Daly could get *Candida* into the evening bill and then have a few matinees of *Mrs Warren*, he would not be forgotten in a hurry; and his next season would begin in a rush. He also told Daly that 'the scandal would be terrific' but that the play, though startling by its apparent daring, was 'perfectly safe'.[41]

This letter blends encouragement with business-like advice, the essence of which from Shaw's point of view was that Daly should secure Fanny Brough for the main role and introduce the play to New York as quietly as possible; the essence of the letter from Daly's point of view was that there was no money in the enterprise. So he shelved *Mrs Warren* for the next 20 months and, it would seem, took it down and hurriedly put it into rehearsal only when *John Bull's Other Island* failed.

He ignored the advice Shaw had given him about giving a production of the play a low public profile; ignored the clause later written into the contract that the play should be advertised as being suitable for representation before serious adult audiences only; and ignored, when it arrived, Shaw's cable withdrawing his permission for the performance. He simply went ahead, and found himself overnight the target of a storm of abuse which would have flattened a less conceited man.

Vanity and the lure of dollars drove him. But there was another cause: envy of Robert Loraine's success with *Man and Superman*, which had opened at the Hudson Theatre on 5 September 1905. Here, suddenly, was an interloper, a rival who threatened to lift from his honest brow the Shavian laurels he had won with *Candida* and *You Never Can Tell*. *John Bull's Other Island*, a month after *Man and Superman*, was calculated to confirm his role as *the* Shavian apostle in the United States, but when it failed and Loraine continued to draw capacity houses, Daly resorted to *Mrs Warren* with all the heedlessness and alacrity of a gambler risking his all on one throw of the dice. In the course of its review of the play, *The New York Times* wondered why Daly had taken the risk: was it a 'blind unreasoning desire to revolutionize the moral state-of-being, or else a wholly unnatural and somewhat disgraceful attempt to win much tainted notoriety'? The critic's own answer is kindly, but Daly's behaviour on this occasion and his history as a whole suggests the second alternative.

Act I of our Sutroesque melodrama began a few days before the first performance, when *The New York Times* published correspondence between Anthony Comstock and Daly.[42] Comstock was secretary and special agent of the Society for the Suppression of Vice. A dedicated man, he boasted that since 1873 he had brought 3670 criminals to justice and destroyed 160 tons of 'obscene' literature and pictures.[43] He is immortalized in Shaw's designation of 'Comstockery' as 'the world's standing joke at the expense of the United States'.[44] An anecdote that pre-dates the controversy over *Mrs Warren's Profession* tells that Comstock, when asked about Shaw, replied, 'Shaw? I never heard of him in my life; never saw one of his books; so he can't be much.'[45] On 20 October 1905, however, he had heard of Shaw, if not yet read him, when he wrote to Daly: 'I am informed that you intend to put upon the stage one of Bernard Shaw's filthy products, entitled "Mrs Warren's Profession."' He darkly warned Daly against pleading ignorance of the law. Daly replied cheekily: 'You call "Mrs Warren's Profession" a "filthy" play. I cannot believe that you have read it; but, if so, your use of the adjective is decorative, but not descriptive.' He invited Comstock to attend a rehearsal of the play the following week. One wonders who leaked these letters to the press: probably Daly.

The next day *The New York Times* dutifully recorded the burgeoning drama, Comstock's response to Daly's invitation. He would not attend a rehearsal of the play. 'Why should I? It is not my purpose to advertise Mr Daly or the works of Mr Shaw.' Had he read the play? 'I have not. I have received a number of letters ... from people who have read the book, and they tell me that it is quite impossible.' Were the people who wrote to him men of letters? 'Whether they were men of letters or not is not essential. They are men of morality and decency, which is to the point.' Would he be attending the first night? 'The society did its full duty when I wrote a letter of warning to Mr Daly. If the play is put on it is up to the police, and I have not the slightest doubt that Mr McAdoo [the Commissioner of Police] will take the proper steps.'

Daly breezily brushed Comstock aside. 'I do not feel that I need any Comstockian advertising. He is altogether impossible.'

Shaw made his entry on the third day with a special cable. In the usual form of a self-drafted interview, it assumed that Daly was under threat of imprisonment.

> Let [Comstock] imprison Daly, by all means. A few months' rest and quiet would do Daly a great deal of good, and the scandal of his imprisonment would completely defeat Comstock's attempt to hide the fact that Mrs Warren's 'profession' exists because libertines pay women well to be evil, and often show them affection and respect, whilst pious people pay them infamously and drudge their bodies and souls to death at honest labor.

He touched on Comstock's achievement in destroying 93 tons of indecent postcards and the right of every country to have the government it deserves. Then he admitted (although he did not say it in so many words) to having called a retreat. He could not fight Comstock with the American nation at his back and the New York police in his van. Neither could Daly. He had advised Daly to run no risks. 'When this news reached me I had already cabled both Daly and my agent, Miss Marbury, to countermand the performance, because I think New York has had enough of me for one season.'

But – confusingly – he left the field open for Daly:

> Now I am bound to leave Daly free to accept the challenge and throw himself on the good sense of people who want to have the

traffic in women stopped … He is young and bold; I am elderly and thoroughly intimidated by my knowledge of the appalling weight of stupidity and prejudice, of the unavowed money interest, direct or indirect, in the exploitation of womanhood, which lies behind his opponent. I cannot save Daly.

This ended Act I of the drama with the audience of thousands wondering breathlessly whether Daly, now alone, would favour them with a second act. They had their answer on Sunday morning, 29 October. Yes, *Mrs Warren's Profession* had opened on Friday evening in the New England town of New Haven. New Haven! *The New York Times* blinked; the mayor himself wondered why Daly had selected his 'hidebound' town. New Haven was in uproar. Protests came from all quarters. The mayor, John P. Studley, immediately directed Chief of Police Wrinn to revoke Daly's licence and to inform him that *Mrs Warren's Profession* was 'grossly indecent and not fit for public presentation'. Daly was 'beside himself' and spent most of Saturday, backed by his manager, his press agent and a posse of attorneys, trying to get the mayor to withdraw his ban. Pressure, part political, part monetary, was brought to bear when ex-Senator Reynolds of New York, 'who was interested in the play' (interested because he owned New York's Garrick Theatre, where the play was scheduled to open two days later), intervened with an offer to furnish bonds, but Studley stood firm. So late that Saturday afternoon Daly left New Haven 'in high dudgeon … saying before he went: "New York will stand for the play if New Haven will not."' There is a hint that Daly was pinning his hopes on political support through Tammany Hall. If the right kind of pressure came from that body, New York could well be persuaded to stand for the play. Tammany Hall was as quiet as a church-mouse during the furore that followed.

Act II, scene ii returned the action to New York with Daly issuing a statement to the press: he would leave the question of presenting 'Mrs Warren's Profession' to the dramatic critics of the New York newspapers. If they said on Tuesday morning that the play was unfit, he would not give another performance. If they said it was fit, he would continue and run the risk of being arrested. He then spent what was left of that night and the whole of Sunday 'editing' the text and rehearsing. Daly's partner, Winchell Smith, evidently a smooth gentleman, explained. It was true, said he, that Daly had cut and changed some of the lines, but nowhere had Shaw's meaning been clouded. 'The changes are purely changes of words, made necessary by the fact that some of the lines … are susceptible of impure construction which were not at all intended.' Daly was also quoted: 'The play will positively be presented tonight, and if it is condemned by the jury of critics it will be withdrawn.' So ended Act II – on a high note of suspense.

Act III opened at the Garrick Theatre that Monday evening (31 October). The scene outside and in the lobby of the theatre was like a cattle market. People struggled to get into the theatre from as early as 6.30; extra police were ordered out to handle the crowd; between 2000 and 3000 people were turned away. Theatregoers, arriving in carriages, found their way blocked. Ticket speculators were offering orchestra seats at $30.00 and the top gallery at $5.00. *The New York Times* included some telling details in its report:

> … Three policemen in the lobby took turns in declaring to the crowds:
>
> 'There ain't no tickets; there ain't no seats on sale; there ain't no admission nor no standin' room on'y.'
>
> When the policemen got tired, the man in the box office stopped counting money long enough to emphasize their remarks. He counted money with exasperating coolness, and wrapped up dozens of parcels of it with red strips of paper, on which were printed the inscription, '$100.'

Every seat was taken, standing room was packed, when the curtain went up.

At the end of the third act, in response to repeated calls, Daly came before the curtain and addressed the audience. He mentioned adult men and women who should be allowed to face the problems of life; children, whose cherished illusions should not be shattered; the need for at least one theatre in New York devoted to the Truth. If public opinion forced the theatre to be closed and *Mrs Warren's Profession* to be withdrawn it would be a 'sad commentary on twentieth century so-called civilization and our enlightened new country'.

Silent in his box, Police Commissioner William McAdoo sat through three acts. Afterwards, cornered by the press, he was figurative and non-committal. 'I don't think this is a good test of trying it on the dog. The dog in this instance is rather high bred and the ordinary run of dog may have different ideas.' He left, leaving everyone guessing. Daly's jury, the New York critics, soon followed him into the night.

The next day would provide the climax: the verdict of the critics and the law.

Act IV of our melodrama opened on 31 October with an outraged cry: universal condemnation from the press. The *Herald* said that Shaw had reached the 'limit of indecency' with a play that was 'morally rotten'. The *Tribune* said it was an 'affront to decency and a blot on the theatre'. The *World* said it was a frank, brutal and a wholly nasty justification of prostitution. It had polled the audience the evening before: the result revealed a rather more broad-minded reaction: 576 of the 963 people in the audience had responded; 304 voted 'Fit', 272 'Unfit'. The *American* said the play was 'illuminated gangrene', the 'suppuration of a plague spot', and not permissible on a stage. The *Press* said it was Shaw's best play and in the same breath declared that it glorified the 'Scarlet Woman'. *The New York Times* said *Mrs Warren's Profession* was not only vicious in its tendency but also depressingly stupid, and had to be excluded from the theatre as a moral derelict. The notice pays considerable attention to the acting of Mary Shaw as Mrs Warren. She played the part very broadly and 'reflected to an astonishingly offensive, natural degree the abandoned creatures after whom she has evidently modeled her study'. She was not the Mrs Warren of the text (and certainly not like Fanny Brough of Shaw's London production). If this was so, then it would appear that Daly's sin in 'editing' the lines was compounded by his directing the actress to ignore Shaw's subtly ambiguous delineation of the character.

These reports had scarcely hit the news stands when McAdoo struck. He told Mayor G. B. McClellan that the production was 'revolting, indecent, and nauseating where it was not boring'. He then wrote to Daly, to the owner of the theatre, ex-Senator Reynolds, and the theatre manager, Samuel Gumpertz, telling them that he would prevent a second performance and arrest those participating therein. Later Magistrate Charles Seymour Whitman issued warrants for the arrest of Reynolds, Gumpertz, Daly and the other members of the cast. Gumpertz, the only one immediately taken in custody, appeared in court, pleaded not guilty to the charge of disorderly conduct, asked for an adjournment and was allowed out on his own recognizance on condition he appeared the next day with the other persons named in the warrant.

Daly meanwhile had decided that his jury of critics had returned a favourable verdict: performances would continue. Sales at the Garrick box office continued briskly throughout the morning and by one o'clock more than $10 000 worth of tickets had been sold. At four o'clock the box office was abruptly closed. A notice from Daly was posted on the door of the theatre: 'Further performances of "Mrs Warren's Profession" will be abandoned, owing to the universal condemnation of the press. Theatre closed to-night. Will re-open tomorrow night with "Candida," original cast.' Five hours later Winchell Smith issued a statement which cited the verdict of the press. The sensation that, through no wish of the management, had surrounded the production had drawn the wrong kind of audience on the first night. The management would have cancelled the performance even then, had it not been too late. 'There is no financial or other consideration whatever that could have tempted Mr Daly to give a second performance of the play after last night's experience at the doors, and after seeing the attitude of the papers to-day,' said he, as smooth as ever. He would not say why tickets had been sold until late that afternoon.

Our Sutroesque melodrama as a study of civic humbug (a critic dubbed the whole affair 'Mc'Adoo About Nothing') ends with a nice display of dramatic unity where it began – with Anthony Comstock in his office, adding *Mrs Warren's Profession* to his awesome collection of suppressed smut. His verdict: 'I had full confidence that Mr McAdoo would do his duty.'

There is an epilogue featuring the hero of these scenes: Daly himself. His attorney issued a statement: Mr Daly proposed to fight to the last and was confident the courts would take a liberal view. Daly had been reluctant to appear in court. 'But my dear fellow,' he had told his attorney, '… I have an engagement for luncheon and want to go to the races. Tell the Judge that I would be charmed to come down almost any other day and look at his little jail, but tomorrow it is impossible.' Daly was no stranger to humbug himself.

Eight months later, on 6 July 1906, the Court of Special Sessions acquitted Daly and Gumpertz. The liberal view had prevailed, but by then the damage had been done and Daly himself had failed to regroup and advance on other fronts. *Candida*, rushed in to fill the void left by the banning of *Mrs Warren*, tottered through one week. He continued to present his small repertoire of Shaw's plays, adding *Arms and the Man* in April 1906, but he seemed to have lost momentum. He refused to touch *Mrs Warren's Profession* again, to Shaw's apparent amazement: 'I cannot imagine why you did not stick to poor old Mrs Warren. She is bound to win in the long run.'[46] In the event, it was the Garrick business manager, Samuel Gumpertz, who produced the play in New York once the courts had cleared it, opening at the Manhattan Theatre on 9 March 1907 for 25 performances, and then taking it on tour, not with any great success.

Shaw's role in this affair is ambiguous, a mixture of desire and caution: desire to have the play presented and as much as saying that Daly could carry on with it if he wished, at the same time dissociating himself from the production should Daly proceed. He did not throw Daly to the wolves, but he wanted his cake and he wanted, if possible, to give the appearance of not eating it. When it was over he was convinced that Daly had let him down. He did not drop him precipitately; the association continued for some years, but Shaw gradually loosened the tie. 'Take that excellent young man [Loraine] as your model in future, Arnold. He made my fortune with Man & Superman, and is profoundly grateful to me for it. You ruin me with John Bull and Mrs Warren; and you expect me to be grateful to you for it. Shame!'[47]

The rebuke is deserved. Even so, coming after Mansfield's successes with *Arms and the Man* and *The Devil's Disciple* in the 1890s and preceding Loraine, Daly's productions of *Candida* and *You Never Can Tell* filled the gap at a critical time in Shaw's career and contributed importantly to establishing him in America. Shaw does not appear to have thought so, but infallible and omniscient Shaw was not always right.

# 5

# 1901–1910: Transformation

The press – Shaw's compliant ally in his self-advertising campaign at the turn of the century – began to realize its potential in about the middle of the nineteenth century and by the late 1880s, when Shaw began to work his way into the national dailies and weeklies, it had grown prodigiously to become a communication medium of previously unimagined range and scope. Several factors contributed to this: political interests, the development of technology, the increase of literacy, which produced an increase in the demand for reading matter, particularly of the kind purveyed in the cheap newspaper (one may cite as an example Corno di Bassetto's half-penny *Star*, the readership of which, if we are to believe Shaw, consisted of cyclists and products of the polytechnics). All this contributed to the growth of a propaganda machine of enormous potential; this was the vehicle Shaw leaped on during the Edwardian years.

The 'New Journalism' with its emphasis on vividness and readability came into being alongside the popular press. Shaw found himself in his element. He was a natural, a dedicated 'New Journalist'. Many would have said he was a natural, a dedicated 'Yellow Journalist', that is a writer with a penchant for the luridly sensational and terminologically inexact. Not true. Though bold and assertive in all he said, Shaw was never other than utterly scrupulous.

He prided himself on being a journalist. In the Preface to 'The Sanity of Art' he repudiates kinship with those who aspired to write 'not for an age but for all time' and plumps himself down among the journalists and their 'vulgar obsession with the ephemeral'. 'I am also a journalist, proud of it, deliberately cutting out of my works all that is not journalism, convinced that nothing that is not journalism will live long as literature, or be of any use whilst it does live.'[1] He set himself apart from the 'intellectual' school, 'intellectual' though he was in his own self-made way; decisively made himself a topical man, a man of the popular – and not so popular – press. He would stand firm on this throughout his career, a lowbrow among highbrows, a highbrow among the low.

The most graphic representation of the way Shaw took over the London press in 1890–1910 is in the 'C' lists and Index of Dan H. Laurence's *Bibliography*. The 1890s are dominated by his music reviews for the *Star* and the *World* and drama reviews for the *Saturday Review*, but there is a slow but certain entry into other papers on topics other than music or drama. Initially it seemed a matter of being 'in' with the editor. Thus it is the *Star* that features him in letters and occasional unsigned leaders, almost as though he has free access to its pages, not so much because he had served the paper well as Corno di Bassetto; rather because his greatly admired friend, the Socialistic H. W. Massingham, took over the editorship from O'Connor in 1890. The *Daily Chronicle* catches the eye later in the decade and it is because Massingham became its editor in 1895 and Shaw went with him, so to speak. Knowing the editor helped and Shaw capitalized on this, but even this need fell away as Shaw became better known and entry into a wider range of dailies, weeklies and other periodicals became easier, provided, as Shaw knew well, he remained newsworthy and produced the kind of fare city editors would want to use.

The press had become a major platform for his 'education' programme by the early 1900s. Certain newspapers recur, the Socialist *Clarion*, for example, and the Left-inclined *Saturday Review*, for which Shaw was writing occasional leaders; but there are new ones, not necessarily those that shared his political views. The rigidly conservative *Daily Express* quoted him, though critically rather than appreciatively; so did the *Daily Telegraph*, and he even forced his way onto the pages of the *British Medical Journal* during the battle over vaccination described in Chapter 2. Gradually all the national dailies, irrespective of their political hue, afforded him more space, either by quoting his public addresses verbatim or publishing self-drafted interviews, letters or articles by him.

This included *The Times*, which provides specific illustration of the response of the serious press to his career. It is worth noting what the newspaper of record recorded.

The entries from 1898 to 1907 under 'Shaw' in the index of that paper read like a sensational fever. Having had a letter printed in 1898, Shaw may have thought he had broken into that stronghold at last. Not so. For *The Times* of the following two years, 1899 and 1900, neither the playwright nor the controversialist nor, horror of horrors, the Socialist, exists, and in the following year, 1901, marked by two entries, he remains plainly not the stuff of which history is made. But in 1902 the scene changes with eight entries. No matter that *The Times* was going through a troubled period in its affairs with its circulation falling below 40 000 and closure threatening, it still had a duty to perform and part of that duty was to record, however unwillingly, that G. B. Shaw did suddenly exist. 1903 is a thin year for Shaw in *The Times* as in other papers, but in 1904 he begins to elbow himself back into its columns: ten entries, apart from the notice now being taken of him as a playwright. In 1905 seven entries, 1906 14 entries, and 1907 13, again apart from his work in the theatre, although his rising eminence as a playwright undoubtedly contributed to his recognition in other spheres.

His range of interests and activities as reflected in *The Times* was the well-known Shavian one, which is to say it covered everything where it seemed to him common sense had succumbed to fad or fable. His strong views on vaccination secured him his first platform. Suddenly in 1903, in the midst of his criticism of the Imperial Vaccination League, he is off on another tack: children on the stage. Apropos of this it is worth noting that he did not once throughout his 66-year career as a playwright include a juvenile in his casts:

> I assert as a master of common knowledge that the presence of children on the stage is as unwelcome to the thoughtless playgoer, whom they bore, as to the thoughtful and public-spirited playgoer, whose conscience they disturb. I assert that the child 'professional' is not only a social horror and a national scandal, but an artistic nuisance.[2]

His public stature is more firmly established during 1903 and 1904, when *The Times* carries an occasional report of a meeting he has addressed: 'Some Confessions of a Municipal Councillor' is followed a few months later by 'Mr Bernard Shaw on Municipal Trading'. His letters are now a regular feature of the paper: one on electric lighting in St Pancras and Marylebone, another on smallpox hospitals, then another (as if to show that the borough councillor has not submerged the music critic) on the Royal Opera:

> When a gentleman explains that in announcing *Don Giovanni* without cuts he meant *Don Giovanni* with cuts, he makes his position clear; and there is nothing more to be said except to apologise for having misunderstood him.[3]

Flogging in the Royal Navy, an issue that had engaged his attention in the 1890s, comes next in several letters, providing occasion for a good deal of heightened prose by his adversaries. Then a report on an address, 'Socialism for the Upper Classes'. Then (we have moved to 1905) it is women's hats at the opera, the Queen's measure to effect relief among the poor, the controversy over his article, written for the *Deutsche Neue Presse*, on Henry Irving.

Then it is back to flogging in the navy. Shaw suggests that new members of Parliament introduce a Bill for flogging old members of Parliament. Then (now in 1906) an address at the Imperial Institute to members of the University Extension Guild on the function of drama, the gist of this being that the creative writer was doing the highest constructive work in the world; he was creating mind, thus fulfilling a duty of a most indescribable sacredness. The theatre, rightly regarded, was not the mouth of Hell, but a church, in which people should be given, not what they wanted, but what they ought to have.

By 1906 *The Times* could scarcely keep pace with him; Shaw was not merely 'news' but a leading personality of the time. The transformation from relative obscurity to eminence took about five years.

This rise aroused a good deal of comment and controversy. Responses ranged according to whether one thought him a genius or a charlatan, thus from the admiring to the vicious. According to Beatrice Webb, Prime Minister Balfour thought Shaw 'the finest man of letters of to-day',[4] while Vice-Admiral C. C. Penrose-Fitzgerald, an apoplectic voice during the controversy about flogging in the navy, took a somewhat contrary view: '... the pseudo-philanthropists and effeminate doctrinaires who compose all the ranting brotherhoods and shrieking sisterhoods which are responsible for humanitarian leagues, anti-vivisectionist leagues, anti-vaccinationist leagues, and numerous other anti-common-sense leagues, supported by feeble-minded cranks ...'[5]

Shaw went to Manchester in 1906 to deliver an address to the Ancoats Brotherhood, a working men's association, on 'The Ten Commandments'. Two men, one an obscure and indigent clerk, the other already a distinguished public figure, have left their impressions of the talk he gave and the personality he projected. The clerk was Neville Cardus, later to become a highly regarded music critic and cricket commentator for the *Manchester Guardian*. He heard Shaw speak:

[Shaw] was not then regarded as respectable. As he stood on the platform, arms akimbo, in tweeds and still the red flame of Socialism in his beard, he told us to burn down the Manchester Town Hall and the Cathedral, for some reasons I can't remember but they were strictly reformative; and having digressed a while from the theme of his discourse, said, 'But now, ladies and gentlemen, let us return to our old friend God.' I didn't know at the time that this was a cheap joke; we revelled in the outrageousness of it, we had been repressed so long in our public discussions of the Almighty ... I remember nothing else of Shaw's talk that day except that I was electrified by the tempo, charmed by the accent and twinkle, astounded that anybody could say so much without a manuscript, an hour of it and not a fumble, not the omission of a semi-colon of speech.[6]

The second person was Winston Churchill, in Manchester the day following Shaw's visit to speak at the opening of the United Temperance Police Court Mission Bazaar. He had a bit to say about the virtues of temperance; he had a lot to say about Shaw:

We had yesterday in Manchester Mr George Bernard Shaw, who has been favouring us with his views on methods of human and social regeneration. Mr Bernard Shaw is rather like a volcano. There is great deal of smoke; there are large clouds of highly inflammable gas. There are here and there brilliant electrical flashes; there are huge volumes of scalding water, and mud and ashes cast up in all directions. Among the mud and ashes of extravagance and nonsense there is from time to time a piece of pure gold cut up, ready smelted from the central fires of truth. I do not myself dislike this volcano. It is not a very large volcano, although it is in a continual state of eruption. What is his remedy for the evil conditions which we see before us? It is very simple and drastic – he proposes to cut off the Lord Mayor's head ...[7]

In distant Edinburgh, *Blackwood's Magazine*, keeping as always a close and reactionary eye on developments in the south, decided that the upstart London Irishman had to be taken down, no matter that once (in 1900) it had foolishly allowed G. S. Street to write encouragingly about him. It adopted mockery as its weapon. Beginning with the publication of *Man and Superman*, thereafter throughout the Edwardian years in periodic bouts of ill-humour, it typified him as: '[T]he vestryman of dramatists. His work savours horribly of St Pancras. He has the sad art of transmuting every one he touches, big or small, male or female, into Progressive County Councillors.'[8] In 1907, in an episode which will be touched on in a later chapter, 'Edwardian Shaw', it allowed a pseudonymous 'Z' to abuse Shaw in terms that could have led to legal action had Shaw been the kind of person to take umbrage at libel.

The new conservative *Daily Express* criticized the 'clergy and ministers' for taking the likes of Shaw to their too trusting bosoms, declaring its disapproval in a leading article which may be taken as a model of the New Journalism in its most vividly 'yellow' form:

> The Socialist Fabian Society, of which Mr Bernard Shaw is the most prominent leader, numbers clergymen and ministers among its members. But Mr Shaw's attitude to Christianity is blasphemously hostile.
>
> Mr Shaw says:
>
> 'Popular Christianity has for its emblem a gibbet, for its chief sensation a sanguinary execution after torture, for its central mystery an insane vengeance bought off by trumpery expiation.'
>
> Socialism is indeed saturated through and through with Atheism.[9]

Not all commentators adopted doom and damnation as their theme. Some were able to summon up wry smiles. *Punch* frequently caricatured him in cartoons and articles. One skit, under the heading 'Man and Bannerman', purports to be a verbatim account of a lecture on the Prime Minister. Wells and Walkley were in the chair, each occupying half of it. Shaw's address began as follows:

> Ladies and Gentlemen, I flatter you by coming here this evening (*laughter*) to tell you the truth (*laughter*), and not only the truth but the truth about a very difficult subject (*laughter*) – about your Prime Minister. (*Roars of laughter.*) You won't, of course, understand what I say (*laughter*), being totally unused to the truth (*laughter*), and having not the faintest idea what it is when you hear it. (*Great laughter.*) But if there is one man who can tell it, it is I. (*Laughter.*) My friend Wells thinks he can (*laughter*); but he can't. (*Shouts of laughter, in which* Mr Wells *joined.*) My friend Walkley, wittiest and wisest of dramatic critics, with one exception (*great laughter*), since that over-rated windbag Aristotle (*roars*

*of laughter*), thinks he can tell the truth (*laughter*); but he can't. (*Renewed laughter in which* Mr Walkley *joined.*) ...[10]

There was no telling where he would pop up next, and there should be no surprise that on one occasion his name featured prominently in a women's fashion magazine. Dress, like eating habits, was a subject on which he held strong views and it needed the benefit of his wisdom as much as the economy of the country needed it. Indeed in Shaw's eyes Edwardian clothes were an extension of the confining, constricting – and wicked – economic system in which they were produced. A few quotations from this 'interview' will suffice:

I couldn't wear a thing which, after having been made clean and sweet, is then filled with nasty white mud, ironed into a hard paste, and made altogether disgusting ... As soon as we can get through this villainous phase of commercial civilization ... we shall get back the joy and colour of life, and loose, graceful garments and noble colours will follow as a matter of course ... [Y]ou [women] will sacrifice anything sooner than let us see you as you are ... A human figure with a curtain hung round it from the shoulders to the ankles looks like a badly made postal pillar ... [I]f you [women] confess your legs, you have no further use for your corset.[11]

He was featured in dramatic sketches by James Barrie and J. B. Fagan. Pinero had an oblique shy at him in his 1909 play *Mid-Channel*, written after Shaw's *Getting Married*. 'My dear fellow,' one of the characters says,

it's tryin' to say somethin' fresh on the subject of marriage that's responsible for a large share of the domestic unhappiness and discontent existin' at the present day. There's too much of this tryin' to say something fresh on *every* subject in my opinion ... [M]en and women will continue to be men and women till the last contango. I'm referrin', of course, to real men and women. I don't include ... individuals wearin' beards and trousers who dine on a basin of farinaceous foods and a drink o' water out 'o the filter. They belong to a distinct species.[12]

This is leaden stuff, although it probably raised a few sniggers. A

few – one imagines they were young – lifted their voices in frank
and cheerful celebration. One such, belonging to a Carolyn Wells,
broke into verse:

> *With Trumpets and with Shawms*
> Do you know the ecstatical, statical Shaw?
> His morals embarrass,
> His sophistries harass,
> His cryptical poppycock fills us with awe,
> With smothered guffaw,
> He flicks on the raw,
> Sarcastical, drastical, spastical Shaw.[13]

There are several more stanzas in this vein. It will be noticed that
Carolyn Wells does not greet the Shavian advent with unalloyed
rapture.

The foregoing indicates only a fraction of public response to
Shaw during his rise in the early years of the century. He came to
impinge on the sensibility of the time; the Shavian epoch was
dawning. Beatrice Webb, observing all this from close by, confided
her not-quite detached view to her diary:

> The smart world is tumbling over one another in the worship of
> G.B.S., and even we have a sort of reflected glory as his intimate
> friends. It is interesting to note that the completeness of his self-
> conceit will save him from the worst kind of deterioration – he is
> proof against flattery. Where it will injure him is in isolating him
> from the serious intercourse with his intimate friends working in
> other departments of life ...
>
> What a transformation from those first years I knew him: the
> scathing bitter opponent of wealth and leisure, and now! the
> adored one of the smartest and most cynical set of English
> Society.[14]

Shaw's emergence as a playwright contributed enormously to his
rise, and the responses there by professional theatre critics, by
fellow-playwrights, by scribblers induced by the advent of the
Shavian phenomenon to put pen to paper, added many miles of
print to the subject. Their reaction to playwriting Shaw will be indicated in the pages that follow.

# 1904–1907
# The Court Theatre

# 6

# 1890–1904:
# Private Venture, Public
# Enterprise

I

Shaw's early career as a playwright is bound in with the emergence in London of private theatres, generally called 'societies', during the 1890s. Modest though they were, they gave him his *entrée* to the theatre, and without this it is likely that his impact as a playwright on Edwardian England, when opportunity presented itself at the Court Theatre, would have been considerably less emphatic than it was.

Our account of these societies begins in 1885 when Jacob Thomas Grein, a devotee of advanced European drama, arriving in London from Amsterdam to take up an appointment as the representative of a Dutch firm of tea merchants, discovered a theatrical scene of mind-numbing puerility. Melodrama held the stage at most of the leading theatres, from the Lyceum, where the presiding monolith of the theatrical establishment, Henry Irving, was playing in a verse drama, *Faust* by W. G. Wills, to the Haymarket, where the Bancrofts were reviving Reade's *Masks and Faces*, and on to Drury Lane where a melodramatic 'epic', *Human Nature* by a forgotten playwright was drawing the crowds. If it was not melodrama, it was farce, generally English versions of French farces, although Pinero's *The Magistrate* at the Royal Court was demonstrating an original English flair for this kind of entertainment. In sum, what Grein discovered in London in 1885 was the stagnation that compelled G.B.S., as critic for the *Saturday Review* a decade later, to flood the theatrical landscape with incessant buckets of fresh cold water.

Grein was not alone in his dismay. Archer, already embarked on his long and illustrious career as a drama critic, was appalled by the way the theatre had been allowed to deteriorate and was saying so repeatedly; and a certain H. Mandell, similarly thwarted, had founded the Playgoers' Club in 1884, the first private theatre association in London, where members, students rather than practitioners of drama, discovered and discussed examples of avant-garde contemporary drama. Grein joined this club but continued to be frustrated by the absence of live avant-garde theatre. His opportunity to introduce change came when the directors of the Royal Theatre in Amsterdam, to whom he had recommended suitable English plays for production, including works by Pinero and Jones, rewarded him with £50 and gave him an additional £30 for his translation of *Little Lord Fauntleroy*. An appreciative Pinero and Jones presented him with a grandfather clock which he kept his whole life; he immediately invested his £80 in forming the Independent Theatre of London.

'Is a British *Théâtre Libre* – a theatre free from the shackles of the censor, free from the fetters of convention, unhampered by financial considerations – is not such a theatre possible?'[1] This was the question Grein and his associate, C. W. Jarvis, put about. One notes the reference to the stage censorship and the point Grein makes about evading its clutches: private theatrical societies stood outside its purview. Many responses to Grein's broadsheet were discouraging, but several prominent literary figures – George Moore, Hardy, Meredith, Pinero and Jones, among others – gave Grein the moral support he needed and he bravely decided to make Ibsen's *Ghosts*, already banned by the censor, his first production. A tremor ran through society. Irving, who was not easily moved, felt bound to declare his position:

> If those of the new movement imagine they are going to create literature for the English stage, which shall be absolutely foreign to British codes of morals, manners and social usage, they are making, I am sure, an egregious error. Ibsen, it is said, is in the future to be our dramatic teacher, and I learn from one of his prophets that his plays have abolished God, duty, the devotion of a mother to her children, and the obligation of man to his fellow-men – though perhaps it may not be regarded as quite complete by the rest of the world. Is any English playwright going to expound this philosophy to the public?[2]

Grein was warned that if he produced *Ghosts* a question would be asked in the House of Commons. The question was not asked, the Foreign Office putting a stop to any public display of crassness, but it could not stop private displays. 'Who is this fellow Ibsen, anyway?' was reportedly heard in the lobbies of the House.

Advertising his project, Grein announced that the 'object of the Independent Theatre is to give special performances of plays which have a LITERARY and ARTISTIC, rather than a commercial value.' He promised a wide selection of plays by various 'uncommercial' English playwrights and translations of plays by European luminaries. Walkley, writing as 'Spectator' in the *Star*, commented prophetically: 'Yesterday I received an invitation, innocent enough on the face of it, yet possibly to be valuable one of these days as an epoch-making document in connection with the history of the English stage.'[3]

Walkley was right: the production of *Ghosts* was a cultural shock of seismic proportions. Shaw reported to Archer in high glee: 'The performance was simply a tremendous success; and I fully expect that today the gloves will be off & the fighting agog in earnest.'[4] The gloves were taken off: critical reaction bordered on the violent and in the drama critic Clement Scott's famous leader in the *Daily Telegraph* there was foaming at the mouth. Grein instantly became 'the best abused man in London' and the Independent Theatre as villainous a society as ever functioned on the outer edge of the law.

Grein ignored all this and led his 'Independents' into the 1890s with a programme that remained ambitious and adventurous. It was with the sixth production in 1892 that he planted the Shavian beacon, *Widowers' Houses*. Years later, when theatre critic for the *Sunday Times* and in the course of panning *Misalliance*, Grein referred to that production: 'I have been Shaw's dramatic godfather. At my entreaty he favoured me with his first play, and I, then the best-abused man in London, produced it at the pain of debts and opprobrium.'[5] The Independent Society did not produce any more of his plays, both *The Philanderer* and *Mrs Warren's Profession* rousing Grein to ungodfatherly repudiation.

Business commitments obliged Grein to relinquish his directorship of the Independent Society in 1895. With his driving force gone, the Society languished and slowly died. Money was the perennial problem. As Shaw remarked, 'The disparagers ask what it is independent of ... It is, of course, independent of commercial success.'[6] Yet it had served its purpose in introducing advanced drama to London and it confirmed that Shaw's literary future, if he was going to have a literary future, lay in the theatre.

The momentum created by the Independent Theatre was taken up by other private theatrical societies: the 'forlorn hopes', as Shaw described them, doomed to financial disaster but the real makers of theatrical history. 'For my part, I take off my hat to them.'[7] One such society, the New Century Theatre, sponsored by Elizabeth Robins, Archer, H. W. Massingham, Alfred Sutro and Gerald Duckworth, had as its sanguine aim the eventual founding of a National Theatre. It put on a few plays in its early years, thereafter popped up only sporadically, most notably in its production of Gilbert Murray's translation of Euripides' *Hippolytus* in 1904. Not long afterwards, on 19 July 1899, at a meeting at the Fabian Frederick Whelen's house at 17 Red Lion Square, it was decided to form the Stage Society for the production of plays 'such as would be included in the repertory of any of the chief repertory theatres of the continent, but which under prevailing conditions of the English stage had no opportunity of production in England'.[8] Shaw and Charlotte were involved from the beginning, and Charlotte was elected to the first reading and advisory committee.

The meeting agreed that the Society would stage at least six performances a year on Sunday evenings, so that professional actors and actresses could provide their services. The arrangement worked well, although theatre lessees were initially nervous and the police suspicious. At the first 'meeting', on 26 November 1899 at the Royalty Theatre, with Shaw's *You Never Can Tell* on the bill, two police officers arrived to challenge the legality of the proceedings. Whelen, the chairman, argued the issue with them until the performance was safely under way. The Society did not hear from the police again.[9] The same production of *You Never Can Tell* was taken to the Strand Theatre a few months later for a run of six matinees. It was this public airing that impelled G. S. Street to place his appreciative article, mentioned in the Introduction, in *Blackwood's*.

A young actor, Harley Granville Barker, made his first Stage Society appearance in Ibsen's *The League of Youth* at about this time. Shaw did not see the performance. He saw Barker in a subsequent production, and in his words:

> [I]n looking about for an actor suitable for the part of the poet in *Candida* at a Stage Society performance, I had found my man in a very remarkable person named Harley Granville Barker ... I saw him play in Hauptmann's *Friedensfest* and immediately jumped

at him for the poet in *Candida*. His performance of the part – a very difficult one to cast – was, humanly speaking, perfect.[10]

This was the beginning of an association which was to become the most vital and dynamic in the history of twentieth-century theatre.

*Candida*, the sixth 'meeting' of the Stage Society, concluded the first season. Thanks mainly to Shaw, the Society was already well established. Membership was increased from 300 to 500 and the press was henceforth invited to special weekday matinees. There was cause for congratulation, but one may wonder whether Shaw was entirely satisfied. His plays were being performed and appreciated by fellow-members of the Stage Society; they would in due course be noticed by critics (though not by all), but he remained virtually unknown outside the confines of the coterie of members. As Beerbohm remarked of Shaw's standing at this time, '[His plays] were witnessed, and loudly applauded, by such ladies and gentlemen as were in or around the Fabian Society. Not that these people took their socialist seriously as a playwright. They applauded his work in just the spirit in which, had he started a racing-stable, they would have backed his horses.'[11]

We may also wonder whether Barker was satisfied. Shaw, for one, sensed a spirit of restlessness in his young discovery: 'My only misgiving with regard to you is as to whether the Stage, in its present miserable condition, is good enough for you: you are sure to take to authorship or something of that kind.'[12]

Nothing more promising presenting itself, Shaw and Barker continued to support the Stage Society, figuring prominently in its activities in 1900–4. *Captain Brassbound's Conversion* concluded the second season. The premiere of *Mrs Warren's Profession* came next, on 5 January 1902. Shaw and the management of the Stage Society thought the occasion important enough to warrant publication of the play in a special edition, which came out a few months later with a new preface or, as Shaw called it, tipping a perfunctory forelock to the convention, 'Author's Apology'.[13] It is worth pausing on this 'Apology' to note how Shaw viewed a production which he described at the time as 'the most notable in his career' and is at pains to commemorate.

He focuses first, predictably enough, on critical reaction to the play. 'Mrs Warren's Profession has been performed at last ... and I have once more shared with Ibsen the triumphant amusement of startling all but the strongest-headed of the London theatre critics clean out of the practice of their profession.' Grein, he says, 'the hardy iconoclast who first launched my plays on the stage along-side Ghosts and The Wild Duck, exclaims that I have shattered his ideals. Actually his ideals!... And Mr William Archer himself disowns me because I "cannot touch pitch without wallowing in it".' (In a letter to Archer, who protested that Shaw took the phrase out of context, he explained that 'a dramatist *must* wallow'.)[14]

The censorship question comes next and this – the banning of the play and the public odium that gathered round it – is the underlying theme of the entire preface. He says that *Mrs Warren's Profession* is one play of his which he would submit to a censorship committee without doubt of the result. Not, however, the censorship of the 'minor theatre critic, or the innocent court official like the King's Reader of Plays, much less of people who consciously profit by Mrs Warren's Profession', but a joint committee of the Central Vigilance Society and the Salvation Army, 'and the sterner the moralists the members of the committee were, the better,' because, by strong implication, *Mrs Warren's Profession* was woven of the sternest moral fibre.

He develops this in asserting the propagandistic element of his plays. This was not the first, nor would it be the last time that Shaw fused 'art' and 'propaganda', representing as they do the crux of his dramatic practice; but here, in the course of defending a play generally regarded as depraved, the passage is more than usually insistent:

> I am convinced that fine art is the subtlest, the most seductive, the most effective means of moral propagandism in the world, excepting only the example of personal conduct; and I waive even this exception in favour of the art of the stage, because it works by exhibiting examples of personal conduct made intelligible and moving to crowds of unobservant, unreflecting people to whom real life means nothing. I have pointed out again and again that the influence of the theatre in England is growing so great that whilst private conduct, religion, law, science, politics, and morals are becoming more and more theatrical, the theatre itself remains impervious to common sense, religion, science, politics, and morals. That is why I fight the theatre, not with pamphlets and sermons and treatises, but with plays.

The foregoing represents the gist of what Shaw describes as his 'arduous work of educating the press'. He now has to chronicle the success of the production. Here the man of the theatre takes over from the preceptor; more than this, the generous and appreciative side of his nature emerges.

It is not often that an author, after a couple of hours of those rare alternations of excitement and intensely attentive silence which only occur in the theatre when actors and audience are reacting to one another to the utmost, is able to step on the stage and apply the strong word genius to the representation with the certainty of eliciting an instant and overwhelming assent from the audience. That was my good fortune ...'

He mentions the difficulties the Stage Society and the players had to contend with; he tends to gloss over these, because in fact the problems, ranging from the 'terror of the censor's powers' felt by theatre lessees to the difficulties the cast encountered in rehearsing during the Christmas season, seemed insurmountable. Yet the cast bore it all, as Shaw points out, 'for a Society without treasury or commercial prestige, for a play which was being denounced in advance as unmentionable, for an author without influence at the fashionable theatres!'

The preface as a whole, seen as Shaw's appreciation of what to him was a significant event in his career, retains a good deal of its urgency and vividness. It details, almost incidentally, the difficulties with which he had to contend when trying to get his plays on stage; his awareness of his less than certain standing in the theatrical establishment; his knowledge that he had the entire body of critical opinion ranged against the kind of plays he wrote; his dependence on the actors and actresses, and reliance on the Stage Society. *Mrs Warren's Profession*, dealing as it does with an 'unmentionable' subject, raised special problems at the time, the most intractable being that imposed by the censorship. Yet the play was produced against all odds, and it was a special triumph for Edwardian Shaw.

After this, *The Admirable Bashville*, Shaw's only incursion into blank verse for the stage, which concluded the Stage Society's fourth season on 7 June 1903, came as an anti-climax. It was a jolly occasion and prompted some comment and discussion, but did not amount to much in itself.

This all but ended Shaw's active association with the Society, although two years later, in May 1905, he gave the Society the first two performances of *Man and Superman* at the Court Theatre. He kept faith with it throughout its long and worthwhile life (it survived until the outbreak of the Second World War) and he and Charlotte became life members. 'I owe the Society almost as much as it owes me,' said he.[15]

Barker meanwhile had been more active than Shaw in the Society. He had acted in *Captain Brassbound's Conversion* and *Mrs Warren's Profession* and in several other plays, including Somerset Maugham's first play, *A Man of Honour*. He had directed, among others, *The Admirable Bashville* and his own play, *The Marrying of Ann Leete*. Then opportunity came his way at last with a production of *Candida*.

This production – six matinees in all – was mounted on 24 April 1904 at a theatre which would soon assume an importance almost absurdly out of proportion to its erratic tradition, modest dimensions and remote location. This was the Royal Court Theatre on Sloane Square, SW1.

## II

The Royal Court Theatre began as something quite other than a theatre. It began as a dissenting chapel, built in 1818 on the south side of Sloane Square. Fifty years later the dissenters seem to have left Chelsea and the chapel fell into disuse. It was converted into a theatre in 1870 – the New Chelsea; then the Belgravia; then on 25 January 1871, after drastic reconstruction, the Royal Court Theatre, under the management of the actress Marie Litton.

W. S. Gilbert's burlesque, *The Happy Land*, was the most notable production of the early years, if only because its political satire obliged the Lord Chamberlain to intervene. Following on this, Pinero's farces – *The Magistrate* (1885), *The Schoolmistress* (1886) and *Dandy Dick* (1887) – made the Court one of the most popular places of entertainment in London.

In 1887 the old theatre was pulled down to make way for residences and gardens and a new Royal Court Theatre, on the east side of the square next to Sloane Square station on the Metropolitan line, was opened on 24 September 1888. The architects were Walter Enden and W. R. Crew who, in a period of architectural ugliness, seem to have taken pains to create no beauty. As *The Builder* said:

> The decoration is not much better than theatre decoration usually is, and the large vases and fronton ... with nothing

behind it, which forms the central feature of the skyline of the facade, belong to the most commonplace order of architectural accessories. The worst point, architecturally, is the manner in which the drum of the octagonal dome over the central part of the auditorium hangs in the air in front of the gallery. Nothing could look more unarchitectural and inconstructive.[16]

For the next ten years, the Court, under the management of Mrs John Wood and Arthur Chudleigh, later under Chudleigh alone, was virtually Pinero's theatre, as it had been during the last years of the old Court. His more portentous work – *The Profligate, The Second Mrs Tanqueray, The Notorious Mrs Ebbsmith* and so on – went to the West End proper; his lighter and frequently better work, pre-eminently the enduringly charming *Trelawny of the 'Wells'*, went to the Court.

After Chudleigh and Pinero various managers and playwrights came and went. There were one or two successes, there were several failures: the theatre on the fringe of theatreland went into decline. Then in 1903, as Shaw recalled, 'a gentleman with a fancy for playing Shakespearean parts, and money enough to gratify it without much regard to public support, took the Court Theatre ...'[17] The gentleman was J. H. Leigh. He had the theatre redecorated and structurally altered in various ways; then he and his wife, the actress Thirza Norman, produced and acted in a series of plays by Shakespeare. *The Tempest* in October 1903 was followed by *Romeo and Juliet* early in 1904. Shortly afterwards Leigh engaged John E. Vedrenne as his associate business manager. Their next production, Leigh and his wife decided, would be *Two Gentlemen of Verona*, at which point Barker made his entrance into the annals of the Court.

Thirza Norman approached Archer: could he recommend a suitable director (and actor) for *Two Gentlemen of Verona*? Archer could: Barker. In fact, Barker had written to Archer the year before, on 21 April 1903, asking his opinion on taking the Court for 'six months or a year to run there a stock season of the uncommercial Drama: Hauptmann – Sudermann – Ibsen – Maeterlinck – Schnitzler – Shaw – Brieux, etc.'[18] Now, approached by Thirza Norman, he must have wondered whether this dream was about to come true. He agreed to play the part of Speed and to direct the play, on one condition: that Leigh would allow him to give six matinees of *Candida* at the Court.

Leigh consented; Vedrenne had no objection; Barker was

enthusiastic and Shaw, now into his thirteenth year of failure, was sceptical – and full of ideas about the casting. 'But before I consent to such a hideous folly as it all appears to be, I must know who the people are.'[19] Of course he gave his consent and of course the 'people', the players that is, were acceptable. *Candida* was produced on 26 April 1904 with some success. Charlotte, who had guaranteed £160, received her money back; Shaw received £31.3s. in royalties, which, in a year that had been earning him precious little in Britain, was sufficient indication that such 'hideous follies' could conceivably be reperpetrated.

This was the question that Barker in particular was asking; that he had asked Archer the year before: could the experiment not be repeated? Those six matinees of *Candida* had shown that there was some demand for avant-garde drama. Could this demand not be encouraged? Could matinees at the Court not become a regular feature of London's theatrical life? The Stage Society had shown how it could be done privately; could something similar on regular public lines not now be inaugurated? If matinees were held on afternoons that did not clash with performances at other London theatres, would actors and actresses be willing to take part at a nominal fee of one guinea a performance? The Stage Society, once again, had shown that players were more than prepared to do this for the sake of the play rather than for money. Would Leigh cooperate?

Leigh would. He gave his full support as lessee of the theatre, and thereafter disappeared from the records. Vedrenne was willing to cooperate and would assume responsibility as business manager. Barker would be artistic director. Actors and actresses would be engaged on an *ad hoc* basis. Friends would be asked to back the venture with small donations of money. Only one person refused to shoulder any contractual obligation: Shaw. But he knew better than anyone else who would be supplying most of the plays.

The Vedrenne-Barker management of the Court Theatre – one of the most illustrious partnerships in theatre history – was ready to be launched.

III

The business partner, John Vedrenne, was born on 13 July 1867. The son of a merchant, he followed in his father's footsteps for a few years, combining trade with the duties of a vice-consul. Having always wanted to be a theatre manager, he left commerce as soon as he could and became, first, a concert agent, then later a theatre manager. He was manager at various times for Frank Benson, Forbes-Robertson and, as has been related, J. H. Leigh.

He proved himself a punctiliously correct, scrupulous and straightforward person. 'I lay my cards on the table,' was his credo. He was implicitly trusted and Shaw, among others, did not ever think it necessary to enter into any written contract with him. Lewis Casson remembered that Vedrenne got on well with the actors and actresses (an exception being Lillah McCarthy), although they often found themselves at a disadvantage with him, especially when discussing fees, by not being able to see his eyes behind the tinted spectacles he wore.

He was the least vocal of the Court triumvirate. His address at the celebratory dinner at the Criterion Restaurant in July 1907 was a model of brevity and anonymity. Clearly he was happiest not merely backstage, but back of backstage, although when occasion demanded he did not hesitate to leap into the limelight. His letters to the *Morning Post* after the first production of *Major Barbara* exhibit someone with the prestige and integrity of the Court very much at heart.[20] He will only rarely emerge from his office in the account that follows. He may be pictured there, a pessimist by necessity, quibbling over the cost of Jennifer Dubedat's wardrobe, fretting over the small returns, yet loyally backing the enterprise even when (in its later years) it plunged more and more deeply into the red. If it was chance that made him Barker's partner and thus gave his name a significance it would not otherwise have earned, chance could not have been kinder to Barker.

The other partner, the artistic director as he would be called today, Harley Granville Barker, was born on 25 November 1877 and 26 years old when he launched the Court venture. His father was an unsuccessful estate agent and the family was largely dependent on Barker's mother, from whom, as Shaw never tired of reminding him, Barker had inherited his 'self-willed Italianate' nature. She was an elocutionist and reciter of popular poems and had, as Irene Vanbrugh recalled, a good following. His mother introduced him to the public stage as an adjunct to her performance when he was still young. Irene Vanbrugh saw him on the stage of St James's Hall when she was a schoolgirl and he in his teens:

My first glimpse of him, while I was still at school, was as a boy
of about fourteen, long-limbed with a round, very intelligent face
and a shock of red hair ... [O]ne evening while we waited expec-
tantly for [Mrs Barker] to come on to the rather bare platform
there appeared instead the boy, full of confidence with a gay
charm, who, in a clear resonant voice, told us that his mother was
not well enough to come. 'So,' he said, 'I have come in her place
and will recite to you.' He was quite a success with the audience,
and his attitude was typical of his courage with a touch of bounce
which remained with him.[21]

One has to rely on impressions such as this to gain a picture of
Barker in his early years, because he was reticent about them. He
could not have had much formal schooling. On the other hand, his
early apprenticeship to the stage, his mother's training in speech,
deportment and other elements of stagecraft, his ever-widening
knowledge of classical texts and, a playgoer from an early age, his
familiarity with the contemporary stage made him quite exceptionally precocious in the world of the theatre.

His professional adult career began in the provinces in Sarah
Thorne's stock company; minor roles in London followed; then
came more provincial tours with various companies – 'the most
horrible and useless vagabond life I know,' he told Archer.[22] His
playing of Richard in William Poel's production of *Richard II* was
well received and he seemed destined for a successful acting career.
But there was something about him which lifted him above the
ruck whose precarious living he shared and attracted the attention,
later the friendship, of such people as William Archer and Gilbert
Murray.

He began to write. He collaborated with a friend, Berte Thomas,
and they completed four plays, one of which, *The Weather-Hen*, was
given a matinee performance in 1899. The play was no landmark in
theatrical history, but several critics liked it.

The turning point came when he joined the Fabian Society,
which led to the Stage Society. Shaw discovered Barker, Barker
discovered Shaw. 'We clicked so well together,' Shaw was to
remember.[23] Cajoled, chided and occasionally bullied by Shaw,
who was never backward in trying to steer him in a Shavian direction, Barker began to realize himself.

He was never anything but independent, influenced though he
was by his artistic 'father', Shaw. They differed in their approach to

the production of a play and his vocation was more purely of the theatre than Shaw's. The 'new' play, a new technique of presentation, a new theatrical system which included the formation of a National Theatre – these were Barker's fields. In 1904, in collaboration with Archer, he worked out a sophisticated and detailed 'Scheme and Estimates for a National Theatre', the seasons at the Court being in a sense the practical application of the scheme, a private experiment to prove a national need.

A National Theatre became Barker's ultimate dream, which he strove for over a decade to turn into reality. He saw himself, quite rightly, as the first director of such a theatre, and when nothing but disappointment came his way – and when the war finally dashed his hopes – he was defeated.

But the disappointments, the disillusionments, the estrangements were all in the future. The reality of 1904 was another matter altogether. Then it was Barker filled with energy and enthusiasm, confident that a National Theatre was imminent, grasping at opportunity when it presented itself at the Court. 'By the way, that young man is a genius – a cold-hearted Italian devil, but a noble soul all the same,' Shaw told Ellen Terry.[24] In those early Edwardian years, there was no hint of future division, only companionship founded in shared ideals and the challenge of a pioneering enterprise.

IV

The partners decided that the long-run system as practised at other theatres was out of the question. For one thing, it led to the abuses Vedrenne and Barker wanted to eliminate; for another, they had no full resident company for such ventures. To them, the ideal was the true repertory system, that is two or more plays performed in rotation, but as this was impracticable from several points of view, they decided on a series of short 'runs' – broken runs, because performances took place initially only on those afternoons when their players were free. There would always be the possibility of revivals for successful productions.

They kept to this policy throughout their three-year tenancy of the Court. As it happened, one or other successful play – invariably one of Shaw's – would have improved their financial position considerably had it been allowed a long run, particularly when evening performances came onto the bill, but the most they would then do was stage it for three to six weeks, once or twice for longer than this. An advertised bill was withdrawn only twice, once when Robert Vernon Harcourt's *A Question of Age* failed beyond any hope of salvage and once when a revival of St John Hankin's *The Return of the Prodigal* proved a flop. For the rest, a short run of matinees was the rule, even when a play lost money from the beginning.

As things turned out, this proved an excellent arrangement, if not – to Vedrenne's perennial disquiet – for financial reasons, certainly for artistic ones. By June 1907, when they left the Court, Vedrenne and Barker had produced 32 'uncommercial' plays in 33 months and, together with Shaw, had laid the foundation, in the midst of conservative London, for the new twentieth-century drama.

# 7

# 1904–1907:
# The Twenty-Nine
# Percenters

I

The 'twenty-nine percenters' should be considered first – that is, the playwrights other than Shaw who contributed to the Vedrenne-Barker seasons at the Court.

The call for new English playwrights, first sounded by Grein and continued by the Stage Society, had a meagre response in the 1890s and early 1900s. Grein's biggest fish, the only one worth mentioning, was Shaw; the Stage Society hooked two more, Barker and St John Hankin, but Shaw, with a drawerful of plays on offer, was their local standby. It was because of this dearth in modern forward-looking drama that, when the Court seasons got under way, Shaw actively solicited new plays from established writers. He mentioned Conrad, Hewlett, Wells, Chesterton and Kipling; there may have been others.

Joseph Conrad decided to try his hand, although his first meeting with Shaw was less than propitious. As Wells recounts this, it ended with Conrad mightily affronted by Shaw's manner and Wells, reluctantly abandoning the idea of arranging a duel, having to explain to him that this was Shaw's 'humour'.[1] The dour Pole would not be mollified and thenceforth, whenever he mentioned Shaw in his letters, he did so sarcastically. Still, in 1905 he gave the Stage Society a one-act play, *One Day More*, adapted from his short story *To-morrow*, and he unbent fractionally to remark of the production that '[T]he celebrated "man of the hour" G. B. Shaw was exstatic [*sic*] and enthusiastic. "Dramatist!" says he. With three plays of his own running simultaneously at the height of the season, he's entitled to speak. Of course I don't think I'm a dramatist.' Shaw urged him to write more plays, 'practically guaranteeing acceptance somewhere', said Conrad, which suggests that Shaw had the Court in mind. But no more plays came from Conrad's pen.[2] Maurice Hewlett, the celebrated author of historical romances, succumbed to Shaw's blandishments and gave the Court two plays which were presented as a double bill. Wells, also encouraged by Shaw, tried to master the intricacies of stage business and dialogue, but with no success worth mentioning, while Chesterton, badgered, bullied, abused by Shaw to bring forth the plays that resided in his capacious bosom, eventually obliged with the successful *Magic*, but this was in 1913 when the Edwardian 'revolution' in drama had run its course. Shaw does not seem to have approached Henry James, but James remained drawn to the stage in spite of the humiliation he had suffered in the commercial theatre with *Guy Domville* and offered the Stage Society a play, *Saloon*, rather late in the day, in 1908. It was not thought suitable and Shaw had to tell him, which he did in a letter of surprising brashness.[3] James defended his play vigorously and felt confirmed in his dislike of Shaw's work. Kipling, who disliked intensely everything Shaw stood for, had no difficulty in refusing to write for the Court.

There was, then, no queue of neophytes lining up behind Vedrenne and Barker, clutching brand new play scripts and clamouring to be staged. Shaw was on hand, of course. The statistics testify to the way he came to dominate the enterprise. During the three seasons at the Court, the first starting on 18 October 1904, the third ending just short of two years and nine months later on 29 June 1907, Vedrenne and Barker staged 32 plays, 11 of which were by Shaw. There were 946 performances – nearly seven performances a week – with four double bills and one triple bill, making a total of 988 performances of separate plays, Shaw's contribution being 701 – 71 per cent, which would certainly have been more had the management not adhered to its policy of short runs.

Even so, once the Court seasons got under way those few aspirant playwrights that there were – the balance of 29 per cent – gradually came into the reckoning. One cannot consign them to oblivion, as though they were incidental, expendable supporting players. They were not incidental and, notwithstanding Shaw's success, they were as much part of the seasons and as little expendable as Shaw. Vedrenne and Barker were committed to launching, not Shaw, but the 'new drama', and those relatively lesser lights that found their names on the billboards – the unknown as much as the known, the failures as much as the successes – added significantly to the momentousness of the seasons and to the sense that (in Galsworthy's phrase) a 'renascent drama' was being launched at the Court.

This 29 per cent comprises 16 playwrights, many of whose names read like a roll-call of the 'new' and 'revolutionary' at the turn of the century: from the Continent, Ibsen, Hauptmann, Schnitzler, Maeterlinck; from England, among others, Galsworthy, Murray (in his translations of Euripides), Masefield, Hankin and Barker himself; from Ireland, Yeats. The playwrights from the Continent were already well established, individually and collectively a force to be reckoned with, but denied access to English theatres by, not infrequently, the censorship and, more frequently, the pusillanimity of theatre managers. The English playwrights, on the other hand, were generally young and untried, in itself an indication of the way Vedrenne and Barker took their courage into their hands when producing them. Yet if we allow ourselves a longer view their judgment was remarkably acute at times. Most of those young men – and Shaw – went on from the Court to illustrious careers. They helped to mould the first half of the twentieth century, gathering as they did so, together with their Continental counterparts, five Nobel Prizes (Maeterlinck, Hauptmann, Yeats, Shaw and Galsworthy), three Orders of Merit (Masefield, Galsworthy, and Murray), one OM refused (Shaw), one Poet Laureate (Masefield) and dozens of other accolades, not the least being Barker's legendary reputation as a director. These distinctions do not all derive from drama, still less from the Court Theatre. All the same, they indicate the quality of mind and talent packed into not only Shaw's 11 plays but most of the other 21. Any account of the Vedrenne-Barker management at the Court must therefore include more than passing reference to at least the more prominent of these lesser figures; should include as well some reference to the always disinterested watching brief Shaw kept over them during the Court seasons.

II

Vedrenne and Barker originally planned to present Gilbert Murray's translation of the *Hippolytus* as the second play at the Court after an inaugural play by Shaw, but for reasons outlined in the next chapter it became the first. Although circumstances dictated this, a retrospective survey of the seasons confirms the peculiar rightness of its premier position. It asserted a mood, established a tone; it informed the venture with the spirit of dramatic excellence, irrespective of the tastes of one or other coterie.

Murray (1866–1957) was no fledgling translator-playwright. This brilliant Australian-born scholar, a Professor of Greek at Glasgow University when 23 and Regius Professor of Greek at Oxford in his early thirties, began his playwriting career in 1899 with an original work, *Carlyon Sahib*, an 'anti-imperialist' play which gave rise to quite an 'imperialist' uproar. Archer was impressed, more so when he heard Murray read some of his translations of the *Hippolytus*. Encouragement soon came from another source. Shaw attended one of Murray's readings and in proposing the vote of thanks said that 'he had felt, while the reading was in progress, that the Professor was reading one of his own original compositions, and being so generous as to give Euripides the credit for it.'[4] Then, hearing that Murray had completed translations of the *Hippolytus*, the *Bacchae* and Aristophanes's *Frogs* but was holding them back, he told him to stop behaving like a university professor and to send Euripides to the printer by the next post. 'Mind, by the next post. I am *durchaus* serious.'[5] Murray pleaded timidity and admitted laziness[6] but did as he was bidden and the plays were published in November 1902.

It was Archer's turn again. The New Century Theatre mounted a production of the *Hippolytus* in May 1904 at the Lyric Theatre. Murray recalled the occasion during his ninetieth birthday broadcast on the BBC: '[T]he first day there were about fifty people in the house. The second day perhaps a hundred. On the third the house was full. On the fourth I found a crowd stretching down Shaftesbury Avenue and thought I must have come to the wrong theatre.'[7] A success like this could not be overlooked and the inclusion of the *Hippolytus* in the Court repertoire later that year made good sense.

Ninety years after the event, it is difficult to determine the effect on Edwardian audiences of Murray's versions of Euripides. The Swinburnian metres he adopted sound false and 'stagey' to us, false in the 1920s when T. S. Eliot lambasted them in his essay, 'Euripides and Mr Murray'. Yet Murray's avowed intention at the time, 'to turn the written signs in which old poetry or philosophy is now enshrined back into living thought and feeling',[8] led to texts that made a reputedly unplayable dramatist playable. As Barker wrote, and he would have known better than anyone, 'He has made the plays live again as plays, that is the capital achievement.'[9]

Barker did precisely this in his first production at the Court. Working with Murray, he tackled the problems posed by the play as a practical man of the theatre: 'No principles can be invoked. There must be compromise and on a practical basis.'[10] The Chorus was a thorny problem. The Court stage was small, which made it next to impossible to effect any elaborate form of stylized movement. Another difficulty was the music. The composer and leader of the Chorus was Florence Farr, who achieved a melancholy ululating effect that did nothing to encourage clarity of diction. Barker disliked it intensely and said as much to Murray in several letters. It was 'torture to a musical ear (so I'm told)' – no doubt by Shaw – and he wondered if it would be possible to drop a little sound musical advice on her head.[11] Shaw, rather more directly and brutally, told his former mistress that her rambling up and down staircases of minor thirds was 'deplorable' and created a 'modern, cheap & mechanical' effect.[12] But this was only after the failure of the Chorus in the *Hippolytus*.

The critics responded warmly. Archer, as befitted the man who had 'discovered' Murray, extolled the virtues of the text, making bold to aver (his phrase) that it was a classic of translation and mentioning that this production was the 'first of a very interesting series of matinee performances'.[13] Others were in a lofty mood, none more so than Grein in the *Sunday Times*: '... the magnificent stateliness of professor Gilbert Murray's monumental translation',[14] was how he summed it up. Grein liked scaling the heights. Shaw was critical of some aspects of the casting. Writing to Murray he remarked that Aphrodite had 'the qualifications of a horse for a quiet family – no vices' but added: 'those Greek plays of yours ... are to me so fine that every single stroke in their production ought to be an inspiration.'[15]

The queues that had so gratified Murray at the Lyric did not form as readily at the Court. Even so, it was apparent that Vedrenne and Barker had got off to a promising start and another Euripides–Murray offering in the near future would, they hoped, consolidate their standing as purveyors of serious drama.

They decided on *The Trojan Women*, not as sensible a choice as they could have made. By then, some five months later, the critics, and the public to a certain extent, had become used to the Court matinees; novelty in itself could not be counted on as a drawcard any longer. A run of Continental playwrights – Maeterlinck, Hauptmann and Schnitzler – had begun to confirm certain critical prejudices, one of which was a strongly voiced antipathy to anything 'gloomy' and 'morbid'. If this reflected more on the quality of the English critics and English audiences than on the quality of the plays, the fact was a seriously depleted budget. Vedrenne-Barker may well have gone under had it not been for the success of *John Bull's Other Island*, which could be relied on to provide a financial cushion for *The Trojan Women* should it also be castigated for doling out yet more distressingly heavy doses of 'gloom' and 'morbidity'.

Archer advised Murray not to let Barker produce the play, which he thought unsuitable for several excellent reasons.[16] But Barker, who could be very stubborn, went ahead, putting the play into rehearsal while Murray was on a Mediterranean cruise.

The production had a mixed reception. Shaw was not impressed with the acting, telling Gertrude Kingston, who played Helen, that *she* was 'magnificent' but that nothing else in the whole affair was really classical.[17] Barker himself seems to have had mixed feelings, writing to Lady Mary Murray, Murray's wife, that they had tried their present best but 'the truth is we're not big enough people for it ... Oh it is a big thing ... we'll have a classic drama in our time.'[18] He also hoped the play would pay its 'rather costly way,' but it does not seem that it did. *The Trojan Women* later came to be considered one of Murray's most powerful anti-war pieces, but in 1905 this very quality so soon after the Boer War may well have kept audiences away.

The critics were respectful on the whole, except Walkley, who complained at length. The play, he said, 'wallows in the sufferings of captive women ... we have one prolonged wail ... and to be plain, we do not like it.' He continued to complain about the inaudibility of the Chorus, which suggests that Shaw's advice to Farr had fallen on tone-deaf ears.[19] Walkley's name has cropped up occasionally in these pages; more will be said about him in due course. Here it is sufficient to remark that as the drama critic of *The Times* he wielded his cultured and witty pen in unremitting resistance to the 'new drama', to Shaw in particular and to anything on the stage that seemed to flout the Aristotelian canons of dramaturgy. Shaw would have noted his complaint; he would by this time have made a fair collection of critical antipathies and prejudices – all grist for his anti-the-critics mill. The time would come when he would fling this grist, the accumulation of some 15 years of prejudice, right back in the critics' faces.

The impact on Shaw of Murray's translations of Euripides may be touched on. *Major Barbara*, which followed later that year, on 28 November 1905, was the product of considerable discussion between him and Murray – so much toing and froing of opinion that one could argue a loose collaboration rather than Murray's scholarly mentorship in the writing of the play. It is not the more superficial 'borrowings' that are significant – Murray as the model for Cusins, his wife as Barbara at least in part, and Murray's fabled mother-in-law, Lady Carlisle, as Lady Britomart – not this so much as the degree to which the play has been immersed in the spirit of Euripides, particularly the spirit of the *Bacchae*. It does not stretch one's critical faculty to see *Major Barbara* as an updated version of Murray's *Bacchae*.

It was, then, no accident that when *Major Barbara* went into evening performance early in 1906 the afternoon companion piece for part of its run was Murray's third Euripidean contribution to the Court, the *Electra*, which opened on 16 January for six matinees. It did not have the same impact as the earlier works, even though Florence Farr had finally been relieved of her musicianly duties. The critics were respectful, however, as they felt themselves bound to be. The play was a classic after all, and this one, though tragic, did not wring critical withers quite as wrenchingly as its predecessor had done. Shaw's comment to Murray is interesting for the light it throws on his own aesthetic of drama, which apprehended the sublime in direct proportion to which it assumed the absoluteness of music: 'The play is immense! I feel we must do that sort of thing again and now. But there are parts of it that go beyond acting: acting is only possible half-way up the mountain: at the top they should efface themselves and utter the lines.'[20]

Euripides and Shaw: they were the high points of the Court seasons. If the most tragic of all the poets had to give way in point of popularity to the most comical of contemporary playwrights, he (aided by Murray) established his own respectful and appreciative following. Enough of a following to warrant promotion for the *Electra* and the *Hippolytus* to the evening bill, two weeks for each, in March 1906. This connection between Shaw and Murray-Euripides did not go by unnoticed. One critic, Norman Bentwich, noting the juxtaposition of these productions with *Captain Brassbound's Conversion*, drew a comparison between the two with Shaw's 'disintegrated' kind of play coming off decidedly second best *vis-à-vis* Euripides' 'elemental' drama.[21] He may have considered his comment more carefully had he realized the degree to which Shaw had absorbed Euripides through Murray by this time.

## III

St John Hankin (1869–1909), the first of the up-and-coming English playwrights to be presented at the Court, was one of the most interesting of the new crop, if only because his untimely death highlighted his unfulfilled promise: he committed suicide by drowning, believing himself to be suffering from an incurable hereditary disease. He was a journalist and occasional playwright during the 1890s and early 1900s and then, when ill-health forced him to retire to the country in 1905, he devoted himself chiefly to his plays, although he continued to write occasional pieces for journals. His articles on English drama, four of which were placed in the *Fortnightly Review* in 1906–8, are uniformly pessimistic. He had no illusions about the commercial potential of the kind of play he or such contemporaries as Galsworthy and Masefield were writing: an endowed theatre was their only hope. Reviewing Shaw's *Dramatic Opinions and Essays* in 1907, he offered a gloomy diagnosis and prognosis of English drama. Unlike politics, sociology, literature and the fine arts, all of which had moved considerably in England over the past 15 years, the English theatre had remained rooted in 1890.

> The plays, the actor-managers, the actors are unchanged ... At times, of course, some movement seems to be taking place. There is supposed to be one going on at Sloane Square just now. But that is a mere ripple on the surface of contemporary drama. The bulk of our playhouses are quite unaffected by it. It will soon die away, and the English theatre, which seemed to be stirring for a moment uneasily in its sleep, will turn over and doze off again.[22]

Hankin's two incursions onto the stage before 1905 were unremarkable. The first, in collaboration with Nora Vynne in 1893, was *Andrew Paterson*, which, though produced, was so signally unsuccessful as to keep him away from playwriting for ten years. The call for plays by the Stage Society encouraged him to try again and the result, *The Two Mr Wetherbys*, was produced by the Society in 1903. His next play, *The Return of the Prodigal*, was taken up by Vedrenne and Barker for the Court and it was immediately apparent that the new indigenous drama might not have only Shaw to draw on.

It was presented on the afternoon of 16 September 1905, when the Shaw boom was at its height, and almost with one voice the critics cried out 'Shaw!' One critic exclaimed 'Pshaw!' Grein enthused, 'Mr St John Hankin has established his claim to rank in intellectual force with George Bernard Shaw';[23] Walkley mildly suggested that Hankin's prodigal, Eustace Jackson, had read the works of Mr Bernard Shaw[24] and Beerbohm, who rather liked lecturing his fellow critics, told them:

> Mr Hankin has been much likened by the critics to Mr Bernard Shaw. It is quite true that Mr Hankin has come – what young playwright, nowadays, would fail to come – somewhat under Mr Shaw's influence. But the likeness of Mr Hankin's play to what Mr Shaw would have made of it is a merely technical and super-ficial likeness.[25]

Apart from the Shaw likenesses, the critics saw a good deal to commend. Archer, plainly more sanguine in his expectations about the new drama than the subject of his review, said he was 'delighted at the warm reception of the comedy by the critics in general. Ten, or even five, years ago such a piece would have been received with bewilderment, and probably with contumely. Clearly we are advancing in intelligence.'[26] Even the *Observer*, usually ill-humoured about the Court productions, conceded that the play had some merits.

*The Return of the Prodigal* inverts the traditional formula in that the prodigal son returning home causes no joy, causes instead a good deal of embarrassment to his family: social embarrassment, financial embarrassment, public-political embarrassment. It is made clear in a series of satirically pointed, well observed scenes that the family, father and brother in particular, would prefer its prodigal to return to its errant ways, charming though he may be, and as far from home as can be managed. The prodigal obligingly agrees to do this, having been promised the customary retainer. If there is anything Shavian about this, or what the critics would have seen as Shavian, it is probably in the inversion and the series of discussions that develop from this. The satire that emanates from the situation is Hankin's own, and it is conducted in delicately pointed, witty dialogue, quite unlike Shaw's vividness and vigour. Where Hankin falls short in this play is in precisely a lack of variety and vigour (as Shaw would point out), and in his cynical detachment from his characters. He was to do better, and be more engagingly himself, in his later play, *The Cassilis Engagement* (1907), but Vedrenne and Barker refused to use it at the Court, deciding instead to revive *The Return of the Prodigal* for an evening run, to Shaw's considerable and justified annoyance. He wrote to Vedrenne deploring the decision to bring it back when *The Cassilis Engagement* was available. His letter indicates how essentially un-Shavian Hankin was:

> I am greatly depressed by this Prodigal business, because it shows that you neither of you understand [*sic*] what has made the Court possible. I have given you a series of first-rate music hall entertainments, thinly disguised as plays, but really offering the public a unique string of turns by comics and serio-comics of every popular type ... Make no error, VD; that is the jam that has carried the propaganda-pill down ... Now consider the Prodigal from this point of view. It has an idea in it, no doubt. But it has only one part in it, and that not a very entertaining one. No heroine, a father who is only a butt, nobody except Matthews whom one remembers. Compare Cassilis. It also has an idea; but it has lots of turns to back the idea up ... Here is value for everyone's money, and the play Hankin's best so far.[27]

Shaw was right. *The Return of the Prodigal*, when brought back on 29 April 1907, was a complete failure. It limped through a little over a week of its allotted four weeks, losing money all the way, and was then taken off.

Six months before, on 23 October 1906, Hankin's next play, *The Charity that Began at Home*, was put on for the usual series of matinees. Critical response ran the gamut of opinion, ranging from very decidedly Hankin's best play to date (Archer), to rather a loose go-as-you-please effort but bearable (Walkley) and pretentious drivel (the *Observer*).[28] Like *The Return of the Prodigal*, this was a play round a single idea, the idea here being the nature of 'charity', in debating which Hankin mildly satirized the privileged classes for their comfortable and sentimental delusions. The play is diverting, but the central idea is too thin for four acts and the action is attenuated beyond the bounds of plausibility. The public thought so and withheld its support, and the production lost heavily.

Barker did not use Hankin again, although his later plays, *The Cassilis Engagement* and *The Last of the De Mullins*, both of which are greatly superior to the two produced at the Court, were available after the management had moved to the Savoy in 1907. It seems that Barker did not get on with Hankin, who was evidently a bad-mannered, difficult man – a conceited, colossal and avowed snob, Shaw said of him.[29] Yet Shaw appears to have liked him. There is evidence that they corresponded and he thought very highly of *Cassilis* and *De Mullins*. When Hankin died he felt moved to issue a statement to the press:

> Hankin's death is a public calamity. He was a most gifted writer of high comedy of the kind that is a stirring and important criticism of life ... He suffered a good deal, as we all have to suffer, from stupid and ignorant criticism; but even the critics who were not stupid quarrelled with his style, which was thought thin, because it was not their style. As a matter of fact, the thinness was a quality, not a defect. In his recent letters to me there was nothing that prepared me in the very least for the shock of his death ... I very deeply regret it, not only on personal grounds but on public ones.[30]

This is a generous tribute, too generous if the neglect that has befallen Hankin since his death is anything to go by. But Shaw was right: if Hankin lacked 'body' he was not 'thin', and his anti-establishment views and sardonic depiction of Victorian-Edwardian middle-class attitudes were conveyed in dialogue that was always elegant and poised. If he is ever revived, and he should be, it will be seen that his contribution to the Edwardian 'renascence' of drama was substantial.

## IV

The third of the more important of the twenty-nine percenters was Barker himself, whose playwriting career began with *The Weather-Hen* in 1899, in collaboration with Berte Thomas. This was followed in 1902 with *The Marrying of Ann Leete*, which had the critics pausing to take note, if generally rather negative note. Shaw thought it an 'exquisite play',[31] and perhaps it is in its impressionistic evocation of situation and conflict. Revived at the 1993 Shaw Festival at Niagara-on-the-Lake and sensitively directed, it proved its enduring worth. But at the time Walkley spoke for most of his fellow-critics when saying, 'It must be difficult to write a play in four acts ... and throughout them all to keep your audience blankly ignorant of the meaning of it.'[32] This is a justified criticism. *Ann Leete*, about an eighteenth-century 'new woman' who marries her gardener, shows naturalism driven to the extreme in cryptic fog-bound utterances. Critics were later to make a good deal of Barker's 'Shavian' qualities, but *Ann Leete*, which is prototypical Barker, is so un-Shavian as to be seen, technically if not in its 'modernity' of outlook, as an exercise in the opposite direction. Barker is Debussy to Shaw's Verdi. Shaw may well have suggested when Barker was working on *The Voysey Inheritance* that more direct communication with the audience – a touch of Verdian brass among the muted arpeggios – was a prerequisite of effective theatre. Twenty years later he did say as much when Barker sent him the text of *The Secret Life*. Barker's response points to what was innate in him as a playwright: 'What you say about clarity ... is of course the soundest sense ... I *may* yet arrive at clarity but I must work through my Ann Leete vein to do it, for that prevails in me.'[33]

Barker's next play, *The Voysey Inheritance*, was the fifth production of the second season at the Court, opening for the usual series of matinees on 7 November 1905. Archer withdrew his previous criticism of Barker's efforts and years later was able to look back on that Tuesday afternoon and claim that it represented a redletter day for him and a noteworthy date for modern drama, because it inaugurated the career of what, to him, was one of the most important playwrights of the age.[34] Beerbohm admitted that he had often maintained that no 'mime could ever possibly write a good play', but that *Voysey* obliged him to bow, corrected. 'May [Barker's] very bright intellect never grow dim. I may have to suggest anon that he is too purely intellectual to be perfect. For the present, though, let there be nothing but praise.'[35] Walkley grumbled. As he almost always grumbled after going to the Court one may be inclined to dismiss this grumble as one among many, but the basis of his complaint on this occasion is worth quoting; and anyway it is time to observe him in full buzzing flight:

Yes, decidedly the Court is our 'Shavian' theatre. Mr Shaw's own plays are shown there nightly, and in the afternoons they give new plays by the younger men, all different in essentials, but alike in the one particular that there clings to them a faint aroma – observe that we resist the temptations of saying the taint – of Mr Shaw ... Mr St John Hankin's *Return of the Prodigal* had been delicately scented with a Shaw *sachet*, and now *The Voysey Inheritance* of Mr Granville Barker gratifies your nostrils with *triple extrait de* Shaw. You recognise the subtle perfume whenever the personages fall to giving solemnly nonsensical or nonsensically solemn explanations of life, morality, and one another. Mr Barker has a story to tell, an interesting story in itself ... But at periodic intervals, overcome by the atmosphere of the Court Theatre, he feels compelled to offer a gloss, a Shavian gloss, on the facts. Then all is confusion, 'new' morality, Nietzschean 'transvaluation,' and goodness knows what.[36]

This invites the question: how 'Shavian' is *The Voysey Inheritance*? Barker would have asked at least three of his associates to comment on the play: Archer, Murray and Shaw. Archer, on his own admission, refused because he had come to despair of getting Barker away from the 'Shawesque' in his writing[37] – a mystifying attitude considering the highly personal style of *Ann Leete*. Murray's response was positive:

[T]he root situation ... is very good indeed ... the main characters and construction good ... I see what you mean about a lack of driving power ... But I think that came from uncertainty ... about the main problem. If you get that clear – to speak roughly, that the old man is wrong and a failure and Edward right – I think you will find that the driving power is mostly achieved.[38]

Shaw's letters to Barker about Barker's plays have not survived (it is inconceivable that he would not have written to him about them) and one is therefore obliged to offer informed guesses about the extent and kind of encouragement and advice he gave Barker. His letter to Vedrenne already cited (26 February 1907) about Hankin's *Return of the Prodigal* indicates what he liked in *Voysey*, its series of 'turns': the 'Booth turn, the Clarence turn, the wicked solicitor and the comic old deaf woman that consoled the house for the super drama.' He may have advised Barker about the importance of such 'turns' or Barker may have taken his cue from *John Bull's Other Island, Man and Superman, You Never Can Tell* and other 'series of music hall entertainments' already staged at the Court. In addition, Shaw would have satisfied himself that Barker had worked through his Ann Leete vein to achieve a sufficiency of explicitness, which went with the 'driving power' that Murray mentioned. But he would not have tried to get Barker to rewrite the play in any Shavian way. This was not how he worked. He once remarked that literature was one of those things in which no man could help another,[39] so, generous as he would be with his opinions and advice, he would not have tried to undermine the governing concepts of Barker's play.

To return to Walkley's opinion about the Shavian 'aroma' the play exuded, certain influences can be argued, most conspicuously that it is a 'discussion drama' and the issues are, as Beerbohm observed, intellectualized rather than lived through the emotions. As Beerbohm observed about Hankin, it would have been difficult, perhaps impossible, for any young playwright trying to break into the new drama to avoid a touch of Shaw. This admitted, one has to see *The Voysey Inheritance* as the work of an independent and original mind. Its resonances – autobiographical, Victorian-domestic, social and allegorical – the idealistic 'new age' confronting and repudiating the corrupt legacy of the 'old' – achieve Barker's ideal of a 'symphonic effect' most satisfyingly. Barker would come to prefer *The Madras House*, which is also richly orchestrated, but the past ninety years have tended not to support this view. As Archer said, *Voysey* is one of the most important plays of the time and Shaw would have been the first to agree.

If something of the 'aroma' of Shaw may be nosed in Barker, something of the 'aroma' of Barker can certainly be nosed in Shaw. The dining-room table that dominates the set of Acts II, III and V of *The Voysey Inheritance* impressed him as a fine stroke of naturalism. 'I defy you' – he wrote to Archer – 'to deny that the staging of The Voysey Inheritance produced much more illusion than the staging of The Second Mrs Tanqueray.' After this he was easily persuaded to bring a 'huge motor car' onto the set of Act II of *Man and Superman* when the play was brought back to the Court in 1907.[40] Not long afterwards he used a large table on the set of *Getting Married,* but it is moot whether this was cribbed from Barker: he needed it there as a necessary naturalistic constituent of his Bishop's kitchen. There is another, a later and more dynamic influence: we have Lillah

McCarthy's word for the way Shaw listened to Barker reading his *The Madras House*, grinning all the time, and then going off to write *Misalliance*.[41]

*The Voysey Inheritance* was a success at the Court and was brought into the evening bill for four weeks in February 1906, the first play by someone other than Shaw to be elevated in this way. It has been revived regularly since then and has become part of the cyclical repertoire of the uncommercial theatre.

V

John Galsworthy (1867–1933) was the next important member of the band of twenty-nine percenters. His friend Edward Garnett suggested to him that he write a play for Barker and Vedrenne, but Galsworthy, having just completed *The Man of Property*, the novel which was to make him famous, was not drawn to the idea. He saw himself as a novelist. There may have been other reasons: he had once written a play but had found it unsatisfactory; he had no reason to believe he would do any better the second time round. Another possible deterrent may have been the Court's image as 'Shaw's theatre' and he disliked Shaw's plays. He may well not have relished the idea of playing second fiddle in the Shavian concerto. He told Garnett, when *John Bull's Other Island* and *Man and Superman* had made Shaw the talk of the town, that he had received a letter from Conrad. 'Shaw seems to have endorsed [Conrad's] play; but that little play has more *drama* in it than any or all of Shaw's own – *he* is not a *dramatist*.'[42] The dislike was aesthetic rather than personal. He and his wife lunched with the Shaws. 'G.B.S. very garrulous and affable. As a man I greatly prefer him to the author of his works and speeches, he has a good face.'[43]

He overcame these doubts and prejudices to begin writing *The Cigarette Box*, later changed to *The Silver Box*, in January 1906. He completed it in six weeks and sent it to Barker who immediately accepted it for production. Vedrenne, for his part, would always remember with awe the young man who confessed to him that he had tried to write a play once before but, finding it unsatisfactory, had destroyed it.[44] In Vedrenne's world, playwrights did not find their plays unsatisfactory, still less destroy them.

Garnett commented on the presence of a thesis in the play. Galsworthy responded: 'As to the thesis – this I must keep, or start a fresh play which I'm not inclined to do. Aesthetically you're right, but I want to be played.'[45] He was not subordinating aesthetic principles in order to 'be played' at the Court and indeed was true to the principle throughout his life that 'the writer who steadily goes his own way, and never writes to fulfil the demands of public, publisher, or editor, is the writer who comes off best in the end.'[46] He developed this in an article in the *Fortnightly Review*, asserting: '"THE MORAL" is the keynote of all drama. That is to say, a drama must be shaped so as to have a spine of meaning.' The average modern play had no such moral; it had in fact a distorted moral that had 'infected its creators, actors, audience, critics; too often turned it from a picture into a caricature'.[47] There is more in similar vein and, all in all, he was more Shavian in his outlook and beliefs, and not only in his detestation of popular drama, than he would have cared to admit. As for *The Silver Box*, the 'thesis' (or 'moral') would certainly have appealed to Shaw and Barker, the 'spine of meaning' of the play being a criticism of class privilege.

Galsworthy involved himself in the production, writing to Barker about the staging, the casting and sundry 'keynote' aspects of characterization; he told Garnett:

> I've been at rehearsals all day ... On the whole, not quite so bad as I expected, but bad enough. None of one's personal conceptions quite realised – naturally. I met Shaw, who told me he'd read the play and thought it 'very fine.' Hm![48]

*The Silver Box* opened for a run of eight matinees on 25 September 1906 and was an immediate success. Galsworthy's reaction was modest. 'The play seems to have struck a good many people ... the odd thing is I can't tell in the least what it's like.'[49] The critics were impressed. They spoke at length about the 'stern realism' of the piece, although Purdom, who evidently saw the production, mentions that Barker gave the play a poetic quality quite unlike the realism of subsequent revivals.[50] Grein saw Galsworthy as a kinsman of Barker's; Archer, more sensibly, drew a comparison between *The Silver Box* and Hauptmann's *The Thieves' Comedy*; Walkley heaved a lengthy sigh of relief that Galsworthy was not another would-be Shaw and the *Observer* so far forgot itself as to admit that the play was 'Very interesting from every point of view.'[51] Generally there was readiness to acknowledge the arrival of a major new talent.

The play came into the evening bill for a three-week run a few months later in April 1907, and Shaw criticized Barker and Vedrenne at length for the quality of the production, which was 'disgraceful in the highest degree to the theatre'.[52] Not long afterwards he publicly complimented Galsworthy when replying to the toast 'The Authors of the Court Theatre' at the complimentary dinner to Vedrenne and Barker, saying that *The Silver Box* brought onto the stage penetrating social criticism and 'that charm of wonderfully fastidious and restrained art that makes me blush for the comparative blatancy of my own plays'.[53]

Galsworthy's next play, *Joy*, was presented at the Savoy under Vedrenne and Barker. It was a failure, as it deserved to be. This concluded his association with the Court management, but it did not end his association with Barker, who directed his next play, *Strife*, in 1909 and *Justice* in 1910. The latter play was presented in repertory with Shaw's *Misalliance* and Barker's *The Madras House*. Galsworthy stole the thunder, Barker had a mixed reception, Shaw got the boos and hisses. As far as Edwardian England was concerned, there was another star in the firmament of the renascent drama, and there were times when it shone more brightly than Shaw's.

## VI

John Masefield (1878–1967) found his way to the Court via *Captain Brassbound's Conversion*. The story comes from Stier, the musical director at the Court, that Barker wanted to introduce some sea shanties into the second act and Masefield, coming by chance to his office at the theatre, offered the information that he had been making a hobby of composing sea-songs.[54] In due course Masefield's shanties enlivened the production of *Captain Brassbound's Conversion*. His interest quickened by this entry into the theatrical world, he began writing a play, *The Campden Wonder*, which he completed and submitted to Barker within a few months. Barker and Shaw promptly accepted it.

It was presented in January 1907 for eight matinees in a double bill, its companion piece being Cyril Harcourt's *The Reformer*. It was a badly judged combination. Harcourt's play, billed as a 'very light comedy in three acts', was frivolous and forgettable, a reminder that not all of Vedrenne and Barker's selections were well made;

not only this, its light-heartedness accentuated what Shaw was to describe as the Grande Guignol element in Masefield's piece, placing it, as far as the critics were concerned, beyond the pale. They condemned it out of hand. 'Horror for horror's sake' was Beerbohm's judgment; he also wrote a cruel parody of Masefield's dialogue; 'gratuitous distress of mind and nerves' said Walkley in his usual magisterially dismissive way; 'Mr Masefield's very horrible little interlude,' said the *Evening Standard*.[55] The gloom and morbidity theme with which critics had assailed Murray's *Trojan Women* and several other plays was back with interest.

Shaw's role in the planning of the seasons was considerable, but he was not always able to voice a deciding opinion about the selection of plays. He does not seem to have had any say about this particular bill, which made him all the more critical when writing to Vedrenne about it. The trouble was the pairing of two incompatible pieces.

> The Camden [*sic*] Wonder is an ideal Guignol item, and will be safe if it is rightly placed. It should never have been put after The Reformer: that bill, believe me, was a mistake all through. The Reformer has no business at the Court at all ... and it killed the Wonder, which is a magnificent play ... and only needs a proper position in a Guignol program to bowl out the critics and be the talk of the town ... That play has magnificent artistic qualities and its lines haunt one symphonically.[56]

*The Campden Wonder* is not as good as Shaw believed it to be. Perhaps he and Barker allowed themselves to be unduly impressed by the 'otherness' of the piece – the density of the rustic speech and the stark paradox of the plot, which revolves round a false confession of murder and the consequent hanging of innocent people. All the same, the pounding the critics meted out was cruelly in excess of the shortcomings of the play, so excessive that it might well have put an end to Masefield's career as a playwright (and it became quite a respectable one) had it not been for the support he received from Shaw. This came out in the course of a trenchant attack on the critics at the complimentary dinner to Vedrenne and Barker, already mentioned. Shaw invited his audience to consider first-night notices of new productions:

> There you will find a chronicle of failure, a sulky protest against this new and troublesome sort of entertainment that calls for

knowledge and thought instead of for the usual *clichés*. Take for example the fate of Mr Masefield. Mr Masefield's *Campden Wonder* is the greatest work of its kind that has been produced in an English theatre within the recollection ... of any living critic. It has that great English literary magic of a ceaseless music of speech – of haunting repetitions that play upon the tragic themes and burn themselves into the imagination. Its subject is one of those perfect simplicities that only a master of drama thinks of. Greater hate hath no man than this, that he lay down his life to kill his enemy: that is the theme of the *Campden Wonder*; and a wonder it is – of literary and dramatic art. And what had the press to say?

Shaw then told his audience what the press had said and he did not mince his words.[57]

There was a sequel to this, a letter to Shaw from Masefield, in which he explained that he had left the dinner early and so missed Shaw's speech, but had read and heard about it:

I will not thank you, because the praise of a great writer is beyond thanks: but I should like to tell you how very deeply I have felt your sympathy. My play did not succeed, and I have felt its failure keenly, not on my account but because of Barker. It was bitter to me to think that my work should have brought him all that abuse as well as a heavy money loss. You will know how very greatly you helped me in the weeks of bitterness, by something you said to Yeats about me. Now that the bitterness is forgotten you give me encouragement to begin again. I am proud that the head of my art should have liked any of my work; but what I feel most deeply is that you, who now stand where the critics cannot hurt you, should yet think of a beginner's feelings, and go out of your way to give him confidence & a hearing.[58]

## VII

A case could be made for billing Laurence Housman (1865–1959) among the five discussed in the previous sections, except that his solitary contribution – *Prunella* – was done in collaboration with Barker and did not establish him as a playwright in his own right. The collaboration came about when Barker asked Housman (as

Housman relates) to write a 'grown-up fairy tale play for the Barker–Vedrenne management then about to start at the Court Theatre; and when he did so God gave me the grace to say that I could not do it alone; but only if he would do it with me'.[59]

Housman was obviously a considered choice. He had already made a name for himself as a poet and writer of fairy tales, and a 'grown-up fairy tale' of the kind Barker had in mind would have suited his talent. He had also written a religious play, *Bethlehem*, which, the Reader of Plays having refused to license it, he had produced privately. One may speculate about Barker's decision to work with Housman: he would have seen the need to assist Housman in writing for the stage; perhaps also he would have relished the opportunity to exercise the 'Ann Leete vein' in himself, specifically the poetic element, and looked forward to indulging it even while working, as he would have been at this time, on the hard-headed realism of *The Voysey Inheritance*.

Barker and Vedrenne had high hopes of *Prunella*. As part-writer, director and leading man (he played Pierrot), Barker had a special interest in the play, but the cost of production was going to be much higher than usual. Writing to Gilbert Murray to ask if he 'could find' £200 to support the venture, Barker remarked that 'The chances of the play doing well seem to me quite good as such things go.'[60]

*Prunella* opened on 23 December 1904 and failed, disastrously at first, 'so bad' – as Barker wrote to Murray – 'that we seriously discussed to-day whether or not to close on Saturday and cut all the loss we could.'[61] Nothing so drastic was done, fortunately. The play trickled through its advertised three weeks and retired on a heavy deficit. Yet there was some awakening of interest towards the end of the run, enough to warrant matinee revivals in April 1906 and May 1907. It ended as one of the most popular of the Court productions and became the most often played of all the dramatic works bearing Barker's name. When published it ran through 14 impressions in 20 years.[62]

Housman recalled that practically all the critics found fault with everything except the music (composed by Joseph Moorat). This is not so. Some critics were disconcerted to discover, not the usual Christmas entertainment, but, in Archer's words, 'a pathetic, almost tragic fantasy, not without a touch of bitterness', and reacted with customary grunts of disapproval. However, the more discerning counterbalanced the fault-finders with generous words of praise.

Beerbohm's appreciation when the play was revived a second time at the Court was definitive for its time and may still be valid: '*Prunella* does not wither. It is as delicately fresh a thing as ever. In despite of its fragility, it is one of the most "important" of modern English plays; for it is the most spontaneously poetic.'[63]

The only fault, and Vedrenne and Barker could scarcely be blamed for this, was that the production opened four days before Barrie's *Peter Pan*, and *Prunella*, for that matter all other seasonal entertainments, had no option but to take back seats while London and soon the entire English-speaking world went into unending rapture.

*Prunella* and the Court started Housman off as a playwright. As he wrote: '... after *Prunella* all the rest – now well over a hundred.'[64] He was prolific and distinguished rather than celebrated. His other reputation as the most censored British playwright ever reflects on the tradition of inanity maintained by the Lord Chamberlain's Reader of Plays, not on Housman.

The remaining English playwrights may be briefly mentioned. The first was Robert Vernon Harcourt whose comedy in three acts, *A Question of Age*, was presented on 6 February 1906. This was Harcourt's second play; his first, *An Angel Unawares* (1905), attracted sufficient attention to earn a fawning notice from the *Sketch* of 26 July 1905, which reminded its readers that Robert Vernon was a son of the famous statesman and the grandson of the historian, Motley. He was also, 'dramatically, Mr Bernard Shaw's godson. It is "G.B.S." who has incited and spurred him to write plays, and from the older dramatist the younger has received valuable hints and much good advice.' Impeccable credentials, to be sure, but they were not enough to save *A Question of Age*, which was taken off after two disastrous performances. Harcourt's greater service to drama would come in 1909 when, as an MP, he repeatedly asked the question in the House which led to the Parliamentary investigation into dramatic censorship. *A Question of Age* had a companion piece, the one-act *Convict on the Hearth* by Frederick Fenn, which Walkley thought should be immediately promoted into the evening bill. About a young convict's return home after a spell in gaol, it is an engaging but slight work and no tears were shed when it also disappeared.

Maurice Hewlett was one of the few established men of letters who responded to Shaw and Barker's plea for plays and his double bill, the two-act *Pan and the Young Shepherd* and one-act *The*

*Youngest of the Angels,* followed Harcourt and Fenn at the end of February 1906. The production appears to have been as meticulous as any at the Court but not even Barker's magic could hide the fact that Hewlett had no dramatic flair. The plays ran their allotted course and then sank from sight, taking Hewlett's ambitions as a playwright down with them.

One other 'unknown' should be mentioned, although this particular one, Elizabeth Robins, had made a name for herself as an actress, particularly in Ibsen, as a champion of the advanced theatre, the 'New Woman' and other modern issues. She was then making a fresh reputation for herself as a novelist. Her play, *Votes for Women!,* subtitled 'A Dramatic Tract in Three Acts', based on her novel *The Convert,* was taken up for production at the Court in 1907. Its highly topical suffragist theme aroused keen interest before and during its run. There was talk of a suffragist demonstration, 'an exciting rumpus', as the *Standard* excitedly put it, but disappointingly 'no raucous cries of Amazonian frenzy rent the theatrical air'. The play put many critics, male chauvinist to the core, in a waggish mood. The *Observer* commented: 'Where over the sufferings of the betrayed damsel we used to be asked to drop a tear we are now asked to drop a vote into the ballot box,' and Beerbohm said, 'Neither as a dramatist does Miss Robins thrill me, nor as an evangelist does she win me.' The play is rather unpersuasive and flat in the reading, particularly when the public world of women's rights is narrowed down to the private world of the suffragist heroine and her lover, which is presented with a fair amount of heavy breathing. It needed a woman critic, invited by the *Tribune* to record her response, to point out that the heroine's renunciation of personal happiness in favour of her cause was 'curiously symbolic of the intensity of purpose, the depths of self-sacrifice underlying the movement of "Votes for Women"'.

Everyone was won over by the theatricality of the second act, which depicted a suffragist meeting at Trafalgar Square. As the *Daily Telegraph* said, '... nothing more complete in detail, more "actual", more "alive", than this picture of the Trafalgar Square meeting has ever been witnessed.'[65] A photo in the *Sketch* of 15 May 1907 confirms the remarkable effectiveness of the scene and testifies to Barker's genius as director. It was a triumph of naturalism – so much so that one gentleman onlooker, foregrounded stage left, looks uncannily like Sidney Webb. It would have been like Barker (and Shaw) to advertise a Fabian presence in this way.

*Votes for Women!* was not formally revived either at the Court or the Savoy, but when Hankin's *Return of the Prodigal* had to be taken off the evening bill, *Votes for Women!*, which had just completed its run of matinees, was hurriedly pushed into the vacant slot and ran successfully for several weeks.

This concludes the line-up of English playwrights at the Court in 1904–7. There was also a contribution from Yeats – his one-act *Pot of Broth* – and contributions from a handful of leading Continental playwrights: Maeterlinck, Schnitzler, Hauptmann and Ibsen. Although Ibsen was afforded some grudging acceptance, reception of the others offers a dispiriting insight into critical and public prejudices at the time. New advanced English playwrights had at best only a slim chance of success, but established contemporary European playwrights had no chance at all.

These were the twenty-nine percenters. The seventy-one percenter, Shaw, could not have had better backing, not always financially, but almost always artistically.

# 8

# 1904–1905: Shavian Farragoes

## I

'Farrago' was Walkley's choice epithet, and the one in question was Shaw's first play at the Court, *John Bull's Other Island*, by which he hoped to bring London to its knees.

He wrote *John Bull* in 1904, in a rush, against time, but a play on the perennial 'Irish Question', or as he put it, 'on the contrast between Irish and English character',[1] had been in gestation since 1900 at least. It was at this time that he first sounded W. B. Yeats on the matter. Yeats seemed to like the idea, but nothing came of these early overtures. For one thing Shaw had yet to write his Irish play, for another Yeats had yet to establish his Irish Literary Theatre.

The situation had changed by late 1904. The Abbey Theatre, under the directorship of Yeats and Lady Gregory, opened in December 1904, but by then Shaw had another venue – the Court; and, as he reported, 'The play was at that time beyond the resources of the new Abbey Theatre … It was uncongenial to the whole spirit of the neo-Gaelic movement …'[2] Both observations are probably true. On the other hand, Yeats expressed no doctrinal or other objections when he responded to the text Shaw sent him. He was disappointed in the first Act and agreed with Shaw that the play was too long; for the rest he found only praise. 'I thought in reading the first act that you had forgotten Ireland, but I found in the other acts it is the only subject on which you are entirely serious.' A backhanded compliment, but there is no doubting Yeats's positive reaction and the intimation that it was suitable for his theatre: '… I mean that we can play it, and survive to play something else.'[3] After such an appreciation it is surprising to find him telling Lady Gregory a few weeks later: 'I have seen Shaw's play; it acts very much better than one could have foreseen, but it is immensely long … It is fundamentally ugly and shapeless, but certainly keeps everybody amused.'[4] At all events the Abbey Theatre did not produce *John Bull's Other Island* until 1916, leaving Louis Calvert (the original Broadbent) to take the Court production on tour through Ireland in 1907.

While Yeats dithered over the Irish rights, Vedrenne and Barker and Shaw were working full tilt to get it ready for the Court. It was neither Barker's nor Shaw's first choice. Both wanted Shaw for the first production, but Barker wanted *Man and Superman* while Shaw wanted *Captain Brassbound's Conversion*. Shaw, pursuing his old dream, wrote to Ellen Terry about playing Lady Cicely Waynflete, tempting her in a characteristically offhand way: 'Lady Cicely would get no salary, of course. £25 and "find her own gowns" is the sort of thing the Court runs to.'[5] Ellen Terry turned this down in her characteristically charming way. Shaw, for his part, turned down Barker's idea of doing *Man and Superman*. 'I think the Superman would need a cast of more weight and splendour than Rule Britannia'[6] – this being the working title of the Irish play.

So *John Bull's Other Island* became the first Shaw play, but not the first play under the management. Shaw refused flatly to rush it into production. He wrote to Vedrenne that the projected opening date of 18 October was too early: '[I]t would be throwing away money to produce it before parliament meets again.'[7] Now that opportunity was presenting itself, Shaw's flair for theatre business was emerging. His flair for publicity came out in a self-drafted interview in the *Daily Mail*. Like all his plays, he said, this new play was very good, 'of first-rate workmanship and material, and ... calculated to ... wound and bore and irritate the romantic playgoer beyond endurance.'[8]

He completed the first draft in August 1904 while he and Charlotte were on holiday in Scotland. He worked against time and in uncongenial conditions; and he had to interrupt composition to write a curtain-raiser, *How He Lied to Her Husband*, completed in four days, for Arnold Daly in America. Then he was to discover that revision and staging took him longer than the writing. He worked 'like ten galley slaves'[9] against the projected opening date of 18 October. He objected frequently and strongly to this, blaming Barker's Italian blood for 'arbitrary and totally premature dates'. The premiere was postponed a fortnight.

The working title, *Rule Britannia*, was discarded. He told Barker: '[I]t is too frankly a jest: and we shall have to play off the piece as a very advanced and earnest card in the noble game of elevating the

British theatre.' Though put flippantly, the observation is worth keeping in mind. Nor was it the only suggestion that Shaw was aiming high with his new play. His letters to Barker from Scotland illustrate his total involvement in all aspects of the production. Staging and casting were discussed in letter after letter. In all these Shaw's completeness as a man of the theatre emerges strongly, as does the impression, gathered from the urgency and vehemence of the correspondence, that he was concentrating all his resources on achieving a production which would inaugurate the new Shavian drama beyond critical denial. He exceeded himself in one respect: the play was too long, and he had to begin the hurtful task of cutting. 'All the tissue seems to me to be vital: I can't get the blue pencil in without cutting an artery.' The play remained very long – as every critic observed – but Shaw would cut no more arteries, not even when Barker asked him to make the play suitable for evening performance. Shaw refused on the grounds of artistic principle and time, adding that the play, having served its turn, could as well be dropped. It had certainly not served its turn, as matters turned out.

Shaw directed, as he would all of his plays at the Court. It was, then, as author-director that he wrote his 'Instructions to the Producer' in December 1904 apparently for Arnold Daly, who produced *John Bull's Other Island* in New York in October 1905.[10] A good deal of what he said was intended to pre-empt misrepresentation of Ireland and the Irish. Thus, the Round Tower did *not* look like a medieval castle, an Irish land agent's house was *not* a thatched hovel and all Irishmen did *not* wear 'very long frock coats with large holes in them stuffed with wisps of straw, knee breeches and battered hats with clay pipes stuck through them'. There are instructions about how the characters should be required to dress and speak, all pointing to Shaw's insistence that they had to be seen to be what they are, not what stage stereotyping would make them.

As for casting, Shaw reminds Daly that Broadbent is 'nearly the whole play ... a big man with an imposing personality ... thoroughly likeable and goodnatured through all his absurdities'. He would get endless laughs until he begins to play for them. 'In England the part was created with immense effect by an actor who played Falstaff successfully, and had never played in a coat and trousers in London before.' All the other male characters are similarly touched on but the female roles are dismissed with a summary 'The women may be left to themselves: if they cannot find their way for themselves, no instruction will save them.'

'Instructions to the Producer' was written after the successful opening of *John Bull's Other Island* at the Court, when Shaw's involvement in the production would have made him supremely aware of the play's theatrical requirements. Daly could not have asked for more exact instructions but, as we know, the play failed in New York. Interestingly, Shaw has nothing to say about the piece as a 'play of ideas'. These, like the female parts, had to find their own way and speak for themselves.

*John Bull's Other Island* had the critics out in force. Shaw was good copy and the play itself, even to the most reactionary critic, was obviously going to be topical and 'relevant'. That it might also possibly be a major theatrical event did not enter into critical reckoning. Notices were long, often confused, oddly contradictory.[11] The main complaint was that *John Bull* was not a play. Most critics were united on this point. Archer said it was not a play, the *Athenaeum* said it was not a play, the *Daily Telegraph* said it was not a play and the *Daily News's* E. A. Baughan (whose name, like Walkley's will recur in these pages) said it was not a play. Walkley wrapped it all up with:

[T]he play is a disappointment because of its wilful, perverse disregard of anything like construction. It is written on the 'go-as-you-please' principle, without beginning, middle or end ... There is no reason why the play should end when it does – except that Mr Shaw has had enough of it. We wish he had got tired a little sooner.

Beerbohm took it on himself to reply to the 'no play' brigade. 'Pray, why is this not to be called a play? Why should the modern "tightness" of technique be regarded as a sacred and essential part of dramaturgy?' Why indeed? 'Not a play' became, as Beerbohm said, the parrot cry. And then, when this had been said, in the manner of a vague genuflexion to one or other deity of 'pure drama', the tendency was to go back on one's protest and to confess to having greatly enjoyed the play that was not a play. Archer, Baughan and even Walkley executed about-turns in this way, Walkley declaring without a blush that the piece, though disappointing, was also a delight.

Looking back to this first production of *John Bull's Other Island*, one can perhaps understand why critics balked at it, for that matter at every one of Shaw's plays in the Edwardian years. *John Bull* was fundamentally different (as Shaw had promised) from what they were used to. Walkley was right in that it has no conventional 'plot' or 'story' with a beginning, middle and end. What 'happens' in the play is almost ostentatiously unspectacular in that the Englishman Broadbent and the expatriate Irishman Doyle, friends and partners in a civil engineering concern in London, go to Roscullen, Ireland, where, within a space of 24 hours or so, Broadbent becomes betrothed to Nora, an Irishwoman, sets himself up, more by accident than design, as a candidate for election to parliament and decides to develop Roscullen by building a golf course and hotel. This series of non-events is punctuated by several episodes, some amusing, some profoundly disturbing, all thought-provoking, but there is no sop to traditional plotting, not a 'reversal of fortune', no complication of plot, no twist in the tail. Indeed, Broadbent carries all before him, brooking no complications of plot or twists in the tail. Quite plainly, again as Shaw had promised, romantic Ireland has no chance of survival in this prosaic context: it is dead and gone, although Broadbent's courtship of Nora has charm. Given such an uncompromising mixture, the critics were baffled, but – on the whole – good-naturedly so.

Shaw found an opportunity to come back at the fault-finding in a self-drafted 'interview' in his friend Clement Shorter's *Tatler* a fortnight after the opening.[12] Shorter, the ostensible interviewer, cites the critics as all agreed that *John Bull* was not a play and says that Shaw has 'thrown all attempt at construction overboard. Even Walkley calls it a Shavian farrago'. Shaw replies that he 'delights in Walkley: he has the courage of his *esprit*; and it gives me a sense of power to play with him as I have done in a few Broadbent strokes which are taken straight from him.' As for the apparent lack of construction:

> My dear CKS, I never achieved such a feat of construction in my life. Just consider my subject – the destiny of nations! Consider my characters – personages who stalk on the stage incarnating millions of real, living, suffering men and women. Good heavens! I have had to get all England and Ireland into three hours and a quarter.

There is more along these lines, but Shaw does not really answer the question about 'construction'. He never discussed the specific dynamics of his plays.

Yet this is the point, for if the play was not a play by Walkleyan injunction (and if subsequent plays would similarly not be plays), *John Bull's Other Island* is as tightly constructed as the most traditional of stock romances. More so, for if the stock-in-trade of West End theatrical fare was held together by a loosely knit 'story' and little else, the coherence of *John Bull* is achieved by everything the laws of dramaturgy demand. The Aristotelian dicta relating to the unities – time, locale and plot – are firmly in place: an action that, following the prefatory first act, runs its course in about 24 hours, that takes place in or near Cornelius Doyle's dwelling in Roscullen and – most important of all, considering the primacy Aristotle (and his Edwardian disciple Walkley) placed on it – the plot focuses intently on, in Shaw's tell-little phrase, the 'destiny of nations', more specifically the destiny of Ireland in relation to Britain. For all its topicality, most of the jokes surrounding which have survived extraordinarily well, and its episodic apparently rambling progress, *John Bull* never wavers in its scrutiny of Ireland and the Irish, from 'the dreaming' with which Larry Doyle designates it, through Keegan's metaphysics and on to the foibles and egos of the Irish 'chorus' surrounding the principal characters. Render Shaw's airy generalities in particulars and his 'feat of construction' becomes a feat of dramaturgy that makes even the 'good' playwrights of the age – the Pineros, Joneses, Grundies and Sutros – seem like journeymen cobblers in comparison. But not Walkley, not any critic, sensed this unity of design; and that even Yeats, with his 'fundamentally ugly and shapeless', should have failed to intuit this says little for his acuity and a good deal for the way Shaw was distancing himself from contemporary stereotypes. As for the characters, they are all, the subordinate as much as the principal, as vividly realized and differentiated as one would want, representing a cross-section of rural Ireland with the fidelity that only a disillusioned expatriate Irishman, a Shaw or a Doyle for example, can bring to the task. One says nothing about Broadbent who, one of Shaw's happiest creations, bestrides the world of the play with heart-warming, baffle-headed amplitude.

Walkley's name keeps on cropping up. As the principal stumbling block in Shaw's Edwardian career, he should be appraised, despite the tendency nowadays to brush him aside as a Victorian-Edwardian irrelevance. Shaw never entertained such a thought, no matter how often he may have wished to consign Walkley to the other side of the moon. One sees how he foregrounds him in the

*Tatler* piece featured above; he addressed his epistolary preface to *Man and Superman* to him; he seems to have made a point of letting Walkley have the text of his plays before production, gave him a leading role (as the critic Trotter) in *Fanny's First Play* and generally treated him as an adversary worthy of respect and friendship.

They probably got to know each other in the late 1880s, when Shaw was music critic as 'Corno di Bassetto' and Walkley was drama critic as 'Spectator' on the *Star*. He reviewed Walkley's *Playhouse Impressions* (1892) in that paper on 9 January 1892 and was full of praise. Walkley was the best critic in London, he said. Archer used to be the best but Walkley had superseded him because Archer had a conscience whereas Walkley was absolutely unmoral. He, Shaw, was able to cut quite a figure as a critic in England, but place him next to Walkley and Shaw's greatest admirer would admit that he wrote like an auctioneer in comparison.

Walkley joined *The Times* as drama critic in 1900 and remained there until his death in 1926. The prestige of his position gave his utterances considerable weight; he added to this by bringing a cultivated mind – one markedly Frenchified – and a sophisticated and witty pen, an air of ineffable and unchallenged authority, to his criticism. Everyone interested in theatre took note of what Walkley had to say. 'Your critic', he wrote in an essay on criticism, 'is a sedentary person with a literary bias. His instinct is to bring to the play the calm lotus-eating mind with which he day-dreams over a book in his library. To this frame of mind the boisterous flesh-and-blood element of the actor comes as a rude distraction.' This was bad news for the likes of Shaw, for whom the boisterousness of the play, let alone that of the flesh-and-blood actor, was the spirit of the play made manifest on the stage. Walkley had certain blind spots: his defence of dramatic censorship points to one and his scepticism regarding a National Theatre to another; and he had certain obvious likes and dislikes. Writing in the *Nation* of 15 February 1908, an anonymous reviewer of a later collection of theatre pieces by Walkley, *Drama and Life* (1907), said that to Walkley the art of a dramatist was primarily the art of telling a story well; the most trivial detail seen on stage outweighed the most important philosophy deduced; the dramatist's ideas were not as important as his manner of conveying them; the play should not be a painful experience; and the dramatist had to persuade his audience that what was being witnessed was actually happening, or might happen. More bad news for the likes of Shaw because, as the reviewer put it, '[T]he reader will infer behind these critical principles a certain sceptical disdain for the work of philosophic artists, and a temperamental impatience of experimental or didactic realism ...' If it was Shaw's misfortune during the crucial Edwardian years to have to cope with Walkley, it was Walkley's tragedy that he could not cope with Shaw.

An often comical sideshow that grew out of critical reactions to Shaw's plays was the 'war of the critics', which was for opinion to become polarized into determined anti- and staunch pro-Shavians who, if they did not quite know how to react to the play in question, could always fall back on sniping at their fellows in the opposite camp. Beerbohm had no compunction in disposing of the 'no-play' scribes. He also called them, and theatre managers, 'dullards' for failing to recognize Shaw's abilities and commented, with unwitting prescience, that it would probably take ten years before London accorded him his due, not that Beerbohm himself could not be 'dull' on occasion. The polarization is well illustrated in the *Observer's* 'a political tract without the semblance of a policy ... a formless, aimless skit'[13] and the *Sketch's* 'the only real political play of our time ... remarkably luminous ... as a drama peculiarly interesting and diverting'.[14]

*John Bull's Other Island* made the Vedrenne-Barker venture an initial success, both financially and artistically. It appealed to that section of the public that took its playgoing seriously. It also appealed to politicians, who took its topicality seriously. The Prime Minister, A. J. Balfour, attended the performance on 10 November with his hostess Mrs Sidney Webb, who asked him whether the derision embodied in *John Bull's Other Island* unaccompanied by any positive faith or hope counted for good. Balfour seemed surprised by the question and suggested that humbug had to be cleared away at any cost.[15] He went again, taking the Leader of the Opposition, Campbell Bannerman, with him, and yet a third time with H.H. Asquith, and then a fourth and (according to some reports) a fifth time. A columnist of the *Sunday Times* remarked on the occasion of the second revival in May 1905: 'This week there is to be a full-dress debate at Westminster on that very problem i.e. the "eternal Irish problem." It will be a sheer waste of time ... How much better it would be if the House would adjourn for the nonce to the Court Theatre for a matinee of *John Bull's Other Island*.'[16] Short of actually adjourning the House, its leaders had set the desired example.

It is generally thought that this first production of *John Bull's Other Island* marked the turning point in Shaw's career in London. Yes – and no. A playwright who a few short years before had been dismissed as 'idiosyncratic' was suddenly and emphatically on the theatrical map of London, though still idiosyncratic. His plays could not be ignored any longer and after *John Bull*, for the next 45 years, they would never be ignored again. Yet this is not the whole picture. If public response during the first run of six matinees, and thereafter with revivals – there were six in all at the Court – proclaimed a resounding success, and if Shaw became fashionable after the special performance of the play early in 1905 for the King (Shaw refused to authorize a 'Royal Command' performance), it should be borne in mind that this particular public, venturing as it did beyond the West End proper to the wilds of Sloane Square, was scarcely representative of the mass of theatregoers of the time. Its mainstay became more than a coterie of dedicated first-generation Shavians, but not much more. The *Sketch* of 15 February 1905, for example, described the matinee audiences as being chiefly of the sex that dons stage-obscuring headgear. (The 'matinee hat' became quite an item of fashion at the time.) Moreover, when Shaw fell unambiguously foul of the critics, as he did with *Major Barbara*, or the play simply failed to rise to requisite heights, as happened with *Captain Brassbound's Conversion*, even the faithful proved infirm of purpose. Shaw certainly 'arrived' with *John Bull's Other Island*, but he was far from conquering London. Nor would he accomplish this, as he saw more clearly than anyone else, until the critics were, if not silenced, at least subdued sufficiently to acquiesce to Shavian 'farragoes' as legitimate dramaturgy.

This was a long way in the future.


## II


*Candida* came next. This was the play that had unofficially started the season at the Court in April 1904, and common sense dictated that it should be brought back immediately. It was possible to re-engage almost all the April players and, equally important, its immense success in Daly's New York production the year before pointed to its yet unexploited potential in London. It had led a fugitive provincial career in Britain since 1894, the year Shaw completed writing it, and came to London in a Stage Society production only in 1900, an important occasion, as we recall, because it brought Shaw and Barker together.

*Candida* had six matinees at the Court and, because of the demand for seats, four more performances were added, two in the evening. This was in spite of the extreme cold, which prompted Shaw to tell Vedrenne that 'Four cases of frostbite were treated at the Chelsea infirmary – one stall & three pits ... The Morning Post has lumbago for life. The Daily Mail threatens to head his article "A Frost at The Court."'[17]

Vedrenne took the hint. The theatre was closed for three weeks and such were the improvements that on its reopening it was claimed to be 'one of the cosiest and warmest in London'.[18]

The critics tended to treat *Candida* as a revival of the production earlier in the year and so passed it by with little or nothing to say. Purdom, who evidently saw the production, averred that it 'has never been equalled'.[19]

The failure of *Prunella* impelled Vedrenne and Barker to revive *John Bull's Other Island*. It was accordingly put on from 7 February for a run of nine matinees with substantially the same cast as before.

The performance for King Edward took place on the evening of 11 March. Shaw was less than enchanted. He told Vedrenne and Barker that, as this performance was 'unauthorised', he would be subject to heavy penalties for compounding a felony if he accepted royalties. 'Short of organising a revolution ... I have no remedy.'[20] If the submerged pun is intentional – no royalties from royalty – it is execrable. He returned the cheque, but of course such exalted patronage guaranteed emolument of another kind, that of impeccable prestige; what was more, the story that stout King Edward laughed so much during the performance that he broke the Royal chair guaranteed excellent box-office returns in the future. The Court and Shaw himself were suddenly fashionable.

### III

The triple bill that followed – nine matinees running from the end of February to mid-March – featured Yeats's *The Pot of Broth*, which the critics tolerated, Schnitzler's *In the Hospital*, which the critics loathed, and Shaw's *How He Lied to Her Husband*, which the critics rather liked, although they gave vent to several metaphorical whistles of amazement that an author should pen a skit of his own allegedly serious work, the serious work being *Candida*. Shaw wrote to Gertrude Kingston, who played Herself: '... you must forgive me for Mrs Bompas, which was rather an outrage, but perhaps was pardonable as a sordid matter of business.'[21] A sordid matter of business it may have been, but the playlet retains its freshness to this day. *How He Lied* did not save the triple bill, which scarcely paid its way, but it proved popular enough in its own right to be revived at the St James's Theatre in 1905 together with two plays by Alfred Sutro.

After this, Shaw 'rested' while Hauptmann's *The Thieves' Comedy* and Euripides-Murray's *The Trojan Women*, running in turn from 21 March to the end of April, threatened to plunge the enterprise into bankruptcy. *John Bull's Other Island* had to come to the rescue again, which it did on 1 May, inaugurating a new development: evening performances, with a matinee on Wednesdays.

As if to formalize the occasion, Vedrenne and Barker signed an agreement of partnership which bound them together for three years, entitled them to share equally in the profits and losses and to draw a salary of £20 a week. Actors' salaries and production costs were also regularized. Heretofore actors and actresses had been paid one guinea a performance; now, with the introduction of evening performances at the Court, a small stock company was engaged, members being paid a salary of £3 a week. The cost of any one production was not to exceed £200.

A third important event marked this revival of *John Bull's Other Island*. Shaw found his leading lady. Lillah McCarthy, instructed by Shaw some ten years before to go off and learn her business as an actress, had taken him at his word and then returned fully fledged, as far as Shaw was concerned, as a Shavian 'heroine'. She was to create several roles in Shaw's plays, notably that of Ann Whitefield in *Man and Superman* and Jennifer Dubedat in *The Doctor's Dilemma*, and would appear in one or two other productions at the Court. She was also to become Barker's wife. The marriage was to end in divorce after ten years, but it is worth remembering that she was his partner in the years of his theatrical supremacy.

Meanwhile rehearsals for *You Never Can Tell* were proceeding. The Shaw boom was gathering decibels by the day.

IV

Shaw completed *You Never Can Tell* before July 1896. 'I have finished a new play of such extraordinary cleverness that an eminent London manager, who once played Faust to the most beautiful of all Margarets, writes, after reading it, "when I got to the end, I had no more idea of what you meant by it than a tom cat".'[22] The eminent London manager was George Alexander and the most beautiful of all Margarets was Ellen Terry, to whom the letter was addressed. One sees the direction of Shaw's aims at the time: *You Never Can Tell* was an attempt to emulate Oscar Wilde's success with *The Importance of Being Earnest* the year before, that is to say, to take the commercial theatre by storm. Two months later Shaw appeared to have got his feet on a lower rung of the commercial ladder. He reported to Ellen Terry, 'The Haymarket people – Harrison, Cyril Maude & Co. – appear to be making up their minds to ruin themselves with it.'[23]

The story of how the Haymarket people avoided ruin by not putting the play on, as recounted by Shaw in Maude's book, *The Haymarket Theatre*, is well known and need not be repeated here, except to note that when Shaw withdrew the contract he in effect withdrew all hope of breaking into the commercial theatre, either then or subsequently. As Christopher St John observed, 'The breach thus made between the Shavian drama and the normal commercial theatre was never really healed.'[24] The breach would be plastered over on occasion in the years ahead – the hit of *Fanny's First Play* and the sensation of *Pygmalion* being two pre-war commercial successes – but these were the exceptions, and the belief that Shaw was a financial risk, especially the first time round, became entrenched in theatre lore.

*You Never Can Tell* began its stage life with the usual copyright performance, at the Bijou in Bayswater, London, in 1898. The Stage Society then put it on at the Royalty Theatre in London on 26 November 1899. Shaw's reaction to this production was of a wronged man vindicated. He told Archer, 'You didnt like You Never Can Tell, which happened to be an almost diabolically good play technically, and you solemnly assured the public that it was a tedious farce, and doubted whether even the most skilful acting could make it tolerable.'[25] Then, beginning on 2 May 1900, there were six matinees at the Strand Theatre. The occasion was important enough for the critics to criticize and for Shaw to retaliate, which he did by placing a self-drafted interview in the *Daily Mail*, where, under the headline '[G.B.S.] Tells how He Laughs at his Critics', he commented: 'The painful efforts the dramatic critics make to say kind things about any play that I write are very amusing. They do not in the least understand what I am driving at, and they are continually trying to read into my work some conventional meaning ... I ignore all their conventions.'[26]

Casting at the Court was again a problem. Discussing this with Barker, Shaw commented on the subtext of *You Never Can Tell* more explicitly than was his wont: 'It has always seemed merely a farce written round a waiter. It ought to be a very serious comedy, dancing gaily to a happy ending round the grim-earnest of Mrs Clandon's marriage & her XIX century George-Eliotism.'[27] As director, he would no doubt have emphasized this during rehearsal, but it seems that the production lacked cohesion, mainly because Barker as Valentine did not hit it off with his opposite, Tita Brand as Gloria. This was Shaw's opinion. As far as the public was concerned, the play was a hit and it soon became one of the favourites at the Court, being revived three times with occasional changes to the cast and achieving 149 performances by the end of the season.

As soon as *John Bull's Other Island* ended its run of evening performances, *Candida* took its place, also for three weeks, beginning on 22 May. The day before, on Sunday 21 May in the afternoon and again in the evening, the Stage Society was treated to the first two performances of *Man and Superman*. Two days later, it opened to the public for a series of 12 matinees. With this, the first production of *Man and Superman*, the first year at the Court and Shaw's headlong career of the past seven months rushed to its climax.

V

The critical reaction to the publication of *Man and Superman* in 1903 had friend and foe agreeing that Shaw had made a brilliant ass of himself. No one had bothered to consider its theatrical possibilities, except to assume that it would fail horrendously if Shaw was ever so presumptuous as to foist it on the theatregoing public.

Yet Shaw himself – and Barker – had thought otherwise from the very beginning. Barker wanted it as the first production at the Court but Shaw held back; the play was too big, the Court was not ready for it – and, although he had tried to persuade several actresses to take the part, he had not found his Ann Whitefield. Not found anyone, that is, until Lillah McCarthy arrived on the scene. He was also unsure of Barker as Tanner and flirted with the idea of enticing Herbert Beerbohm Tree to play the part, which was out of the question, given Tree's lofty eminence at His Majesty's Theatre; then he approached others, without success. Casting, as Shaw knew very well, was three-quarters of the battle and Barker – a superb Marchbanks in *Candida* – was not sufficiently expansive on stage to do full justice to Shaw's concept of Tanner. It was Barker who created the role in the end. To enable him to play out of himself, Shaw hit on the idea of having him made up to look like a younger version of himself, complete with red beard through which he was required to run his fingers *à la* Shaw.[28] A Jaeger suit was not included in the get-up.

A section of Act I and the whole of Act III – what came to be called *Don Juan in Hell* – were to be omitted. In explanation of this the *Stage Society News* of 30 March 1905 carried a statement, unsigned but by Shaw, in which members of the Society were assured that they would not be kept in the theatre for eight hours, the estimated running time of the entire printed drama. The omissions 'will not involve any mutilation of the author's work', they were told. 'The sections which will be omitted were designed from the first with that in view.' A similar, shorter statement was given out at the first public performance two days later.[29]

The critics left the Stage Society performances alone, but were at the Court on Tuesday afternoon in droves. One wonders whether Shaw nurtured any faint hope that *Man and Superman* would win at least a modicum of understanding from his detractors. Probably not; even *You Never Can Tell*, popular success though it proved to be, had earned him the usual brickbats. *Man and Superman* was a considerably bigger offering, Shaw's most ambitious theatrical piece yet, and it was crucial to his career. His *raison d'être* was invested in it and this was now in the hands of the critics who, he knew too well, made it their sacred duty to stand united in their misunderstanding of him.

Walkley's response should be cited first and at length.[30] He had 'inspired' *Man and Superman* by challenging Shaw to write a modern play about Don Juan, and the preface to the published work was dedicated to him. No sense of this emerges in what he wrote, not even a glimmer of a smile. Perhaps he disliked *Man and Superman* too comprehensively to allow himself a personal touch or two. The only compliments he paid, dubious ones at that, were that he felt bound to write a very long review and, by way of a preamble, to compare Shaw to Shakespeare, the upshot of which is a massive put-down for Shaw: 'On the one hand a born dramatist, and that the greatest; on the other a man who is no dramatist at all.' An oddity of this comparison is that the 'greatest' is called on to put down a nonentity. This nonentity is immediately and confusingly qualified, however:

> When I venture to say that Mr Shaw is no dramatist I do not mean that he fails to interest and stimulate and amuse us in the theatre. Many of us find him more entertaining than any other living writer for the stage. There are many things in his plays that give us far keener thrills of delight ... than many things in Shakespeare's plays.

This, again, is immediately qualified – Shaw is guilty of 'artistic waste' – and this is requalified – 'You forgive the waste for the sake of the pleasure' – while Walkley refines and re-refines his argument until he is in danger of losing himself and his reader in fine-spun sophistry. But he makes his point in the end, which is that the fundamental problem with *Man and Superman* is that its 'action-plot' does not sustain the 'ideas-plot', that the action-plot is warped and maimed in order to be a vehicle for the ideas-plot, that it becomes trivial, null, haphazard and unnatural.

This is the kernel of Walkley's criticism. What follows is a *reductio ad absurdum* of the action-plot and of the characters who are required to keep it moving. He could lay sarcasm on with a trowel when he wished. 'We see, first of all, a smug bald-headed old gentleman who proceeds, *à propos de bottes*, to spout the respectable middle-class Mill–Spencer–Cobden Liberalism of the mid-Victorian age.' This is Roebuck Ramsden who, whatever Walkley may have conceded about Shaw's talent to amuse, plainly does not amuse him. Neither does Tanner, when Walkley makes his acquaintance. He is a 'youngish, excitable, voluble gentleman who evidently stands for the latest intellectual "advance"'. Tanner tells the audience (and Walkley tells his readers in tones precisely calculated to set up a snooty response among them) that he is a product of Eton and Oxford, 'but' – Walkley sniffs – 'some of us who think we know that product will nourish the secret conviction that he is really like his *chauffeur*, a product of the Board School and the Polytechnic.' Tanner spends the *whole* of his time, Walkley says wearily, in 'spouting' – pretty well everyone in *Man and Superman* 'spouts' – the 'precious theories' of 'the fragments of the newest German philosophy which find their way into popular English translations'. Tanner 'does this, as he admits, because he has no sense of shame; to put it more simply, he is a young person of rather bad manners'.

So the notice goes on, primly reproving, rejecting, repudiating. Had Shaw depended on what Walkley had to say and on those who read him in *The Times Literary Supplement*, his career would have lain in ruins. Amazingly, he and Walkley remained friends.

The other reviews, and there were many, tend to pale into insignificance beside this grand dismissal. Archer gave the appearance of withdrawing the criticism he had been levelling at Shaw through the years. It was a withdrawal to defeat. He had given his friend up. 'Mr Shaw's ... wit is unique, personal, priceless. The wit, in fact, is the man ... He is not, and he never will be, a great dramatist; but he is something rarer, if not better – a philosophic humorist, with the art of expressing himself in dramatic form.'[31] The *Daily Telegraph* followed a similar line: there was no play, not really a story; a comedy of a sort. 'And now,' it concluded, '... let us frankly admit that it is one of the most amusing pieces of work which even the Court Theatre has ever put on the stage.'[32]

It was all rather weird: on the one hand the parrot cry and on the other the suggestion that the play was in some inscrutable way a major event in English drama. No critic, not even the most pro-Shaw, said it was a masterpiece. That would have been expecting too much.

The play ran for its allotted 12 matinees and was subsequently revived three times, reaching a total of 176 performances at the Court. The public loved it.

*You Never Can Tell* succeeded *Candida* on the evening bill on 12 June to 1 July. This concluded the spring season, after which there was the summer break of over two months.

Archer saw fit to commemorate the first nine months in a 'Record and a Commentary'. No 'outsider' was more keenly interested in the Vedrenne-Barker undertaking than he. He saw the beginning of a National Theatre in it and as producing work of first importance on its own account. He praised the Court management for its achievement, 'carried through without any subsidy, yet with perfect adequacy of scenic appointments, and with acting not only adequate, but in many cases extraordinarily brilliant'. All this held enormous promise for the future, both of English authorship and of

English acting. He added a reservation: 'the undue prominence of the works of Mr Bernard Shaw'. Not that this was a bad thing in itself; the disquieting aspect of the matter was that while his plays were well supported those by other playwrights were not.[33]

Commemoration of a different kind came from another, an altogether unexpected, source: from *Blackwood's*, whose periodic attacks on Shaw's 'vestryman' attitude to life have already received attention. On this occasion – July 1905 – 'Musings Without Method' sneers away for all he is worth, while allowing that Shaw has enjoyed a peculiar triumph in the theatrical season then ending. Shaw had become the fashion and 'henceforth there is no extravagance which will not be permitted to him'. He was continuing to clown it 'before the devout ... not scrupling to wrap up a genuine talent in the rags of charlatanry', the most recent and appalling being that *Man and Superman* was written 'under the inspiration of that demented professor', Nietzsche.

Then the about-face: 'Shaw, if he only knew it, is a dramatist first and last.' His characterization is of and for the stage, not in terms of dogma; he has a surpassing gift of construction, a far higher and rarer gift than traffic in false doctrines. 'But superstitions endure, and it will be long before the brethren of the cult [of Shaw] discover that their prophet is nothing better than a dramatist after all.' So the sneer remains to the end, but an important concession has been made.

By now even *Blackwood's* and other dedicated voices of conservatism had little option but to make concessions. There was no ignoring or stopping the force that was Shaw.

It would have filled *Blackwood's* with holy glee that with his next play, *Major Barbara*, Shaw seemed to try his utmost to stop himself.

# 9

# 1905–1906: Shavian Profanities

I

The new season started, predictably enough, with evening performances of *John Bull's Other Island*, which ran from 21 September and was as popular as ever, although Shaw professed to be disgusted, telling Vedrenne that the production had gone to pieces. 'An abominable, coarse, careless, play-for-laughs, third class suburban performance. Tell [the cast] so.'[1] *Man and Superman* followed from 23 October. No duration of run was indicated on the playbill but it evidently ran through November and for the greater part of December. Shaw continued to monopolize the evening bill.

The matinees were another matter, and here first St John Hankin's *The Return of the Prodigal*, then Ibsen's *The Wild Duck*, then Barker's *The Voysey Inheritance* put Shaw in a back seat. This was only temporary. While Hankin and Barker in particular were gratifying the demand for an indigenous drama consisting of more than one man, that one man was at work on and then rehearsing yet another *magnum opus* – his 'stiff dose of lecturing', *Major Barbara*.

He struggled to complete the play. His correspondence at the time testifies to his running the gamut of most un-Shavian emotions, from sullen desperation to the admission (to Murray) that he did not know how to end it. He even confessed to Eleanor Robson, the American actress he had particularly wanted for the part of Barbara but who resisted his blandishments, that the writing of the play was 'a fearful job: I did what I never have had to do before, threw the last act away and wrote it again. Brainwork comes natural to me; but this time I knew I was working.'[2] Murray's constructive suggestions and his family's contribution in providing models for some of the characters have been mentioned. He himself was the model for Cusins (though strenuously opposed to being called 'Adolphus'), his wife contributed some touches of her personality to Barbara, while his mother-in-law Lady Carlisle, a famous battleaxe of the day, was the model for Lady Britomart. Shaw admitted to Murray that the prospect of this lady, 'filled with idle rumors, contemplating Miss Filippi [who played Lady Britomart] and drawing conclusions as to my conception of her, terrifies me.'[3] Everyone was relieved when she appeared to enjoy watching herself on stage and refrained from punctuating the performance with her customary disparaging comments delivered, so the legend goes, in a voice that carried.

The text was passed on to the Lord Chamberlain for the usual licence. G. A. Redford, the reactionary Reader of Plays, expressed some doubts. Would the Salvation Army not be affronted? And what about Barbara's 'My God: why hast thou forsaken me?' Barker assured Redford that the Salvation Army, so far from being affronted, would be delighted and had undertaken to advise on technical matters and lend uniforms for the production. As for Barbara's words, these were actually a quotation from the Psalms – Psalm 22:1, to be precise. This was good enough for Redford, who may well have been nodding, and the play was passed.

Meanwhile Shaw, casting doubt aside, was telling the newspapers in his usual serio-jocular way that romantic playgoers should keep away from *Major Barbara* because it contained 'no drama, no situations, no curtains, no feeling, no heart, no dramatic interest – in one word, no adultery'.[4] This put no one off. Shaw was the man of the hour, and a new play by him about which the most delicious rumours of 'blasphemy' were circulating would certainly attract attention. Shaw told Eleanor Robson in the letter cited above that the theatre was jam-packed and hundreds were turned away at the door, not only for the premiere, but for the entire run of six performances. The Court had never known such popularity, not even in the days of Pinero's farces. Beatrice Webb was there with Balfour (who would resign from the premiership a week later); Salvation Army leaders, conspicuous in their red uniforms, filled a box; fashionable London and bluestockinged London rubbed shoulders in the foyer and stalls. As the *Clarion* remarked, 'There were almost as many carriages and motor cars outside the theatre … as there are in the Mall on a Drawing-room day.'[5] All this happened, it should be remembered, at an afternoon performance. The matinees had their vindication here, the Vedrenne-Barker enterprise its finest hour.

The only notable absentees were Murray and his family, which was fortunate because it gave Shaw occasion to write to Murray about the performance. He praised Barker who surpassed himself in Murray's spectacles and was at his best as a drum virtuoso; Calvert, playing Undershaft, 'suddenly realised that his part was blasphemous, and that Balfour, glaring from a box, might order him to the stake at any moment. He collapsed hopelessly and said, in the last act, "They have to find their own drains; but I look after their dreams." The last act was consequently a hideous failure.'[6] Shaw also wrote to members of the cast, gently encouraging Annie Russell, who played Barbara, and telling Calvert that he was the most infamous amateur that ever disgraced the boards.

Private and public reaction to the play soon followed. Beatrice Webb gives an account in *Our Partnership* of her reaction:

> G.B.S.'s play turned out to be a dance of devils – amazingly clever, grimly powerful in the second act – but ending, as all his plays end (or at any rate most of them), in an intellectual and moral morass. A. J. B[alfour] was taken aback by the force, the horrible force of the Salvation Army scene, the unrelieved tragedy of degradation ... the triumph of the unmoral purpose ... I doubt the popular success of the play: it is hell tossed on the stage – with no hope of heaven.[7]

She told Shaw what she thought and he explained what he meant in the last act; to which she replied, 'But you don't get your meaning into the mind of the audience: the impression left is that Cusins and Barbara are neither of them convinced by Undershaft's argument, but that they are uttering words ...' She at least was prepared to give Shaw the benefit of a hearing and went so far as to admit that she was 'not clever enough to tell' whether the fault she perceived was in the acting or in some lack of proportion to Undershaft's argument.[8] She was a shrewd woman, if lacking in appreciation of the arts, and it may well have been such a comment as hers (plus Shaw's own continuing uncertainty about the last act) that prompted him to go on tinkering with the text. In fact, he only put it aside finally some 25 years later when it went into the Collected Edition; and he tinkered with it again in 1939 when preparing the text for Gabriel Pascal's film of the play.

The critics had none of Beatrice Webb's scruples. Shaw had been severely criticized before, but nothing of the past 15 years approached the storm of abuse that followed the opening of *Major*

*Barbara*. It was quintessentially the reaction that the present work has been highlighting: that of a highly conservative world, its icons grounded in the verities of the past hundred and more years, to the hammer blows of a powerful iconoclast. All the standard ingredients were there: incomprehension, resentment, fear – in a word, massive resistance. In this instance the resistance was to the way Shaw confronts the question of religious salvation in an evil social dispensation, in the process savaging conventional piety and pointing the way of authentic salvation through (it seemed) the very gates of hell. He did not pull his punches in depicting the viciously squalid and amoral existence of the poor and flaunting the unashamed munitions manufacturer, Undershaft, as an agent of individual and social redemption, and the comfortably well-off middle-class men and women of Edwardian England were genuinely shocked by this, not noticing, as they should have, that their shock was nothing to the spiritual deprivation inflicted by Undershaft on his daughter, Barbara. But Barbara, quick, intelligent woman that she is, swiftly comes to terms with her loss, while audiences continued to flounder in the midst of the 'dance of devils'. To be fair, it was (and remains) difficult to reconcile salvation with the production of armaments and it needed uncommon insight, more perhaps than the average Edwardian could summon to his assistance, given the strict conventionality of his upbringing, to probe to the quick of Shaw's stark paradox with its declaration that salvation could be achieved only by violent purgation of social and personal iniquity, by waging war on war itself.

The *Morning Post* best testified to the shock, although some other papers were not far behind it in the intensity of their reaction.[9] Its anonymous critic had a field day 'disposing' of both Shaw and the play, beginning with a general denunciation of the 'lack of straightforward intelligible purpose', the 'deliberate perversity' and 'self-contradictory insincerity' of Shaw's work, before turning on *Major Barbara*. He touched on the 'pseudo-realism' of the characters, dwelt on Shaw's 'bad taste' in resorting to biblical phrases in his text – 'it is so bad that we wonder at its escaping the notice of the censorship' – and denounced him as jeering at everyone: he 'keeps up his bitter gibes to the last' and Barbara and the others 'fall easy victims of the long-winded logic of the cynical capitalist'. All in all, 'its offences of bad taste and good feeling are of a kind not readily to be forgiven'.

Beatrice Webb records that Shaw was greatly upset by this attack.

Not so upset as to be incapable of defending himself in the pages of the *Morning Post*:

> Gross and profound as is the insult to myself ... I can see that your critic is not only quite unconscious that he has overstepped his function and is simply slandering me, but also so naively incapable of appreciating religious sentiment that he regards the use of the stage of the classical English expression of the tragedy of the human soul when its faith fails it at a supreme moment as a 'display of distressingly bad taste.'

There was a standing joke about the existence of Vedrenne. Beerbohm once hinted that there was no such person, and that 'Vedrenne' was one of Barker's pseudonyms. Now 'J. E. Vedrenne' wrote to the *Morning Post*, taking exception to that paper's statement that the Court Theatre was still subsisting on matinee performances alone. 'Does your dramatic critic not know that regular performances of Mr Bernard Shaw's plays have been given since the beginning of September at this theatre ...?' The shadowy business manager was most annoyed.

By this time, 2 December, the paper was carrying a full column of correspondence on the play. There was another letter from Shaw, in which he defended his use of quotations from the Bible. There was a letter from 'Manners Maketh Man' who, among various expressions of censure, ventured to predict that it would not be long before Mr Shaw was found to be 'tinkling brass and a sounding cymbal'. There was a letter from 'A Healthy-Minded Britisher' whose healthy-mindedness exercised itself in such phrases as 'the caustic ridicule of Mr Shaw's pen ... his mischievous plays ... the Divine gift of faith is not a fit subject for a coarse jest ... corrupt the minds of the young ... moral poison.'

Shaw was back on 4 December, replying to a leading article of 1 December which mentioned his 'slanderous depreciation' of Henry Irving, who had died in October 1905. *Major Barbara* was put aside; Shaw defended his article, commissioned and printed by *Die Neue Freie Presse*, and spoke bitterly of the way it had been misrepresented in the London papers. He had the original article typeset and distributed in galleys to the entire London press during November, authorizing editors to reproduce it in full without payment. That not one editor initially felt morally bound to take up the offer is an indication of the hostility with which he had to contend. A man of his kidney did not deserve fair play. However, one good thing grew out of the altercation with the *Morning Post*: publicly invited by Shaw to do so, the paper had no option but to publish the original article, which it did on 5 December.

Meanwhile the argument over *Major Barbara* had spread over two columns. 'A Kentish Vicar' asked the *Morning Post*, in the name of religion, to accept his grateful thanks for its bold criticism, while 'H' discoursed on Shaw's 'vulgar profanity'. Not every letter was against Shaw or his play. One or two souls went to see *Major Barbara* and these stoutly defended Shaw and the play.

The leading critics were less 'sensitive' to the alleged violence and blasphemy but they still found fault. Archer sighed as he said that Shaw's real daring in the play lay, not in his dispensing with plot, which one had grown to expect from him, but in his dispensing with character.[10] Shaw told him privately that he was a 'wretched atheist' and that *Major Barbara* was 'a MAGNIFICENT play, a summit in dramatic literature'.[11] Walkley said the play was – his favourite word again – a 'farrago'.[12]

The surprise – a notable about-turn – came from Beerbohm. His weekly feuilleton in the *Saturday Review* of 9 December, under the heading 'Mr Shaw's Position', was more a review of critical attitudes, his own included, than of *Major Barbara*. He noted how critics – mainly Shaw's personal friends – had patronized him initially; how, after the King had seen *John Bull's Other Island*, he had become fashionable and enjoyable – a galling thing to the critics, who had always resented Shaw, and now found themselves at odds with the public they were accustomed to 'voice'. Having slated previous plays, they faced a fearful dilemma in *Major Barbara*. Should they not 'climb down, and write moderate eulogies?' Stupidity as much as pride impelled them to go the other way. Unable to make head or tail of the play, they decided that Shaw had really come a cropper this time, adding to their repertoire of such stock phrases as 'no dramatist', 'laughing at his audience' and so on the charges of 'brute' and 'blasphemer'. The critics who reacted in this way would have to submit to one of two verdicts – insanity or hypocrisy. Beerbohm had no doubt they would prefer the latter. It was more typically British.

As for the 'superior critics' – Beerbohm does not mention them by name, but he plainly has Archer, Walkley and a few others such as Baughan of the *Daily News* in mind – they insist that Shaw cannot draw life, that he is but a theorist, that his characters are incarnations of himself, that, above all, he cannot write plays –

> while all the time the fact is staring them in the face that Mr Shaw has created in *Major Barbara* two characters – Barbara and her father – who live with intense vitality; a crowd of minor characters that are accurately observed ... from life; and one act – the second – which is as cunningly and closely-knit a piece of craftsmanship as any conventional playwright could achieve, and a cumulative appeal to emotions which no other living playwright has touched.

After this, the incomparable Max himself 'climbed down', owning to his errors of the past when judging Shaw and asking that his should be seen to be a 'sympathetic' part in 'Mr Shaw's Position'.

Beerbohm's contribution to the controversy provided some counter-balance to the bigotries of the *Morning Post* and other papers; but it did not actually say much about the play itself, least of all about the spiritual conflict that underpins the action. This would be noted by the young critic of the *Speaker*, Desmond MacCarthy, who saw *Major Barbara* as 'the first English play which has for its theme the struggle between two religions in one mind'. What was more, '*Major Barbara* was ... one of the most remarkable plays put upon the English stage; ... it is the first play in which religious passion has been fully presented.'[13] Shaw would have appreciated this lone voice crying in the wilderness.

The matinee performances of *Major Barbara* ended on 15 December and went on to the evening bill two weeks later with one or two changes in the cast. Such immediate promotion indicates that the play aroused considerable interest, but it did not become a popular success like *You Never Can Tell* and *Man and Superman*, earning Shaw comparatively modest royalties, and it was not revived at the Court. Time would be needed for the public to realize that the play was indeed a summit in dramatic literature.

## II

The evening performances of *Major Barbara* kept Shaw a presence at the Court during January and the first two weeks of February, but his name fell away from the billboards for the matinees, while

Murray-Euripides' the *Electra*, R. V. Harcourt's *A Question of Age*, Fenn's *The Convict on the Hearth* and Hewlett's *Pan and the Young Shepherd* and *The Youngest of the Angels* were allowed to stake their claims for attention. It was only towards the end of March that Shaw returned to the matinees with the seven-year-old *Captain Brassbound's Conversion*, 'rejected', as we may recall, by Ellen Terry in 1899. That did not matter any longer, for she had agreed at last to play Lady Cicely Waynflete; what was more, the play would be produced during her fiftieth jubilee year *and*, so it was planned, it would be running at the Court when the jubilee was celebrated at the Drury Lane Theatre. Everything pointed to a considerable theatrical coup.

Shaw could barely hide his glee when the arrangements were being concluded in August 1905. 'I am looking forward with malicious glee to the rehearsals,' he told Ellen Terry. 'I shall have my revenge then. I will not leave a rag, not a wink, not a flippertyflop of that tiresome Ellen Terry who wouldnt do my play.'[14] Later he told her that she had to allow him to teach her the part. 'You can learn it easily as a child learns hush-a-by-baby if only you hear it *rightly* read to you. But that can only be done by another Ellen Terry or by me.'[15] Barker, who was not taking part, appears to have had a hand in the directing; but Shaw was also present during rehearsals and, true to his intention, instructed Ellen Terry on her phrasing and stresses by means of postcards, the gentle good humour of which may well have masked his growing anxiety about her apparent difficulty in coping with the part. A letter to Barker underscores this anxiety. He advised Barker not to let her repeat any scene because she 'always goes to pieces the second time & discourages & demoralizes herself ... She has just strength enough to get through the play once without tiring herself ...'[16] In her *The Story of My Life* Ellen Terry records that Shaw was unfailingly courteous and considerate at rehearsal. She responded as well as she could, feeling that a good performance was the only thing in her power she could do for him.

In spite of the excellent auguries, the production was a comparative failure. Ellen Terry was nervous and missed her lines; the rest of the company, affected by her uncertainty, did not attain their usual high level of performance. Barker told MacCarthy some time later that portions of Lady Cicely's part had to be written out on pieces of paper which were stuck about the set. Ellen Terry improved, as she was bound to. Even so, she remained unsure of herself.

Dearest G.B.S. – I think we are nearly all of us going astray in your play, some way or another. Wont you come one evening and give us a little gentle chiding? Or a whack! I dont do it 'on purpose' but I am sure to have gone wrong, and should be tremendously obliged by corrections from you, if you will spare the time.[17]

Shaw told her briefly, '*You* are all right.' He would remain unshakeably loyal to her, but he was far from satisfied with other members of the cast.[18] And, now that the play had been put to the test at last, he was far from sure about it. He wrote to Vedrenne: 'I am bound to say that I dont think the lukewarmness of the C.P. (Court public) towards Brassbound is Miss Terry's fault ... It may be my fault ... Sometimes I think the play is no good. Sometimes I wonder whether the cast just misses the mark.'[19]

It may have been more Shaw's than Ellen Terry's fault. One wonders whether Lady Cicely was modelled too closely on Ellen Terry herself: the resemblance between the character in the play and the personality that emerges in the letters to Shaw is striking. Shaw insisted that she had only to be herself to make the part a success, yet this went against an acting maxim he had once repeated to her: 'Is it not curious that the one thing not forgivable in an actor is *being* the part instead of playing it?'[20] She quite rightly protested, in the beginning at any rate, that Lady Cicely gave her no chance to act. On the other hand, *Brassbound* is not among Shaw's more accomplished plays. It is entertaining and has plenty of exotic colour, but it is comparatively thin in intellectual content (by Shavian standards) and structurally weak, tending to sag in the middle of the first and second acts.

There was almost no critical reaction, possibly because the play was not new, or because the critics thought it kind not to notice a production in which the honoured leading lady was performing below her best. MacCarthy's retrospect in his *The Court Theatre* amounts to a kindly dismissal: 'The Court Theatre performance was well below the usual mark ... Miss Ellen Terry contributed some delightful touches ... and all her own charm; but there was an absence of sureness in her acting sometimes, which spoilt its effect.'[21]

Two weeks after its run of matinee performances, on 16 April, *Captain Brassbound's Conversion* went onto the evening bill for 12 weeks. It was during this run (on 12 June) that Ellen Terry celebrated her jubilee with a matinee at Drury Lane. The Court was closed the evening before and provided a special commemorative programme for the evening performance on the day of the jubilee.

This account of *Captain Brassbound's Conversion* has gone ahead of the chronology of the seasons and it is necessary to backtrack slightly to pick up the threads. Barker's *The Voysey Inheritance*, received with acclaim during its run of matinees towards the end of 1905, succeeded *Major Barbara* on the evening bill from 12 February for four weeks, the first play by someone other than Shaw to be revived in this way. A season of Euripides-Murray followed, first with *The Electra* for two weeks from 12 March, then with *The Hippolytus* also for two weeks from 26 March. This took the evening bill to the opening of *Captain Brassbound's Conversion* on 16 April.

The matinees went into partial eclipse. There was nothing after *Brassbound* for over two weeks, then *Prunella* came back on 24 April for a series of 12 performances, twice the number usually given to matinee runs. It was a risk which events justified. It became increasingly popular, with each performance establishing it more firmly in the English dramatic repertoire.

This was the last matinee production of the spring season. There were no 'Tuesday afternoons', for that matter any afternoons, at the Court for nearly four months.

The evening bills continued. *You Never Can Tell* succeeded *Captain Brassbound's Conversion* on 9 July. It was advertised to run for a limited number of weeks and ran for ten. Barker had undertaken rehearsals during Shaw's absence abroad. He went to see a performance as soon as he could and wrote to Barker asking for the name of the author of 'that play': 'The first half of the performance attained a degree of infamy which took away my breath ... the second act ... moved like an unskilfully galvanised lay figure, not even like a corpse.'[22] He was being hypercritical; the general public saw no such deterioration and kept the box office busy. And Vedrenne-Barker were able to remain solvent.

No one, least of all the critics, would have realized that Vedrenne and Barker attained a high plateau in English drama during the first half of the theatrical year. *Major Barbara* brought 1905 to an end in a fury of controversy; its immediate forerunner, *The Voysey Inheritance*, confirmed beyond question what *The Return of the Prodigal* had hinted at: the rise of a purposeful 'new' English drama. All at once it was not only Shaw, but a body of dramatists. A very small body, but it gave the months and years ahead a more solid foundation for development than the solitary genius of Shaw could give. If one adds to the three plays cited the quality of the revivals mounted during the period – *John Bull's Other Island, Man and Superman,* also a new production of *The Wild Duck* and Murray's version of the *Hippolytus* – then there is some warrant for claiming a renascence of the English stage at the Court Theatre – the first in 200 years.

That was the winter season. The spring season lapsed. Failure and poor box-office returns marked most of the productions of these months and *You Never Can Tell* had to be brought in at the end to keep the enterprise afloat. One cannot reasonably expect unbroken success: failure sooner or later is bound to occur. Even so, something good was needed to restore some lustre to the image of the Court. Fortunately something good – still better, several good things were on their way.

# 10

# 1906–July 1907: Shavian Bad Taste

---

The new season opened – yet again – with *John Bull's Other Island*, which filled the evening bill for six weeks from 17 September 1906. This was the last revival at the Court of Shaw's Irish play, which reached 121 performances at the end of its run. It was followed on 27 October by *Man and Superman*, which ran through November and well into December. Meanwhile Galsworthy's *The Silver Box* launched the matinee season on 25 September; it was followed by Hankin's *The Charity That Began at Home* on 23 October. It was a crowded and exciting month, in spite of the disappointment of Hankin's *Charity*. More was to come. Shaw had completed a new play: *The Doctor's Dilemma*. It succeeded Hankin's play on the matinee bill on 20 November.

As usual, the genesis of the play lay scattered among Shaw's interests, campaigns and confrontations of the years and months before – in what he would have called his 'journalistic' activities and we may see as the topicality of his preoccupations: in his long-standing and abiding interest in medical matters and in his friendship with the eminent bacteriologist, Sir Almroth Wright, in whose hospital, St Mary's in Paddington, Shaw witnessed the incident that gave rise to the dilemma which triggers the action of the play. This dilemma was whether a patient's moral probity or otherwise should be a consideration when a medical practitioner had to select cases for treatment. A more literary 'influence' arose from an argument he and Archer had been conducting in the press. Then there was the bread and butter issue: Barker urgently needed a new play from Shaw to reverse the Court's flagging fortunes.

The argument with Archer had begun a month or two before, in June 1906, when Shaw wrote the obituary notice on Ibsen for the *Clarion* in which he charged Ibsen with a tendency to use death on

the stage for morbid, hence dishonourable, reasons. Archer leapt to
Ibsen's defence and levelled a counter-charge, that Shaw's criticism
characterized 'the aestheticism of the fox without a tail – the
instinctive self-justification of the dramatist fatally at the mercy of
his impish sense of humour ... [Shaw] shrinks from that affirmation
and confirmation of destiny which only death can bring.'[1] The fox
without a tail immediately began to grow one, evidently hugging
himself with delight at the fine specimen he would cultivate for
himself. He wrote to Barker:

> You will have a deathbed scene (to please Archer) which will,
> both in sublimity and blasphemy, surpass anything that ever
> gave Redford a nightmare. The spectacle of a hopeless black-
> guard dying a beautiful and imposing death, with his wife
> adoring him, and everyone else in the room knowing the truth
> about him, will satisfy my soul completely.[2]

When the time came, Archer's paper, the *Tribune* (he had moved
from the *World*), was given a special press release which announced
that Shaw had written a new play while on holiday in Cornwall.
This play was Shaw's answer to Archer's charge that he could not
claim the highest rank as a dramatist until he had faced the King of
Terrors on the stage. 'Stung by this reproach from his old friend, Mr
Shaw is writing a play all about Death, which he declares will be
the most amusing play ever written ...'[3]

He wrote the play in a month, beginning on 11 August and
completing the first draft on 12 September. There was some rewrit-
ing and revision, but the play was ready before the end of
November, when he began directing rehearsals. It was a remarkable feat, the more so because he had to contend with a number of
crises and commitments which had him engaged on all Shavian
fronts – 11 public lectures between 20 October and 29 November,
H.G. Wells's 'rebellion' in the Fabian Society, the controversy in the
Society of Authors brought about by *The Times* Book Club and, to
top it all, revision of Augustin Hamon's French translation of
*Candida*. As he admitted to Hamon, 'Each of these singly was work
enough for one man: the whole together has knocked me almost
to pieces.'[4]

It may have been this pressure that made him relatively perfunctory about casting the play. All he really wanted was Lillah
McCarthy to play Jennifer Dubedat. 'Never mind the cast: I have

had enough of casting: we can pick up a cast in a week provided we are sure of Lillah.' Not only 'sure of Lillah' but sure as well that Vedrenne would agree to the cost of her gowns, about which Shaw was equally insistent: 'This means that there will not be much change out of £100 so let Vedrenne look to it.'[5]

Years later Shaw would describe Vedrenne as the business manager who, 'made prudent by a wife and family, was like a man trying to ride two runaway horses simultaneously',[6] the runaway horses being Barker and Shaw. On this occasion the horses were two Shaws, one the playwright, the other the director, one of whom knew what the play needed and the other that the play had to get what it needed. He wrote to Vedrenne justifying the expense of the gowns, which had risen to £170: 'I am deliberately spoiling Lillah to get the best out of her for this play; for it will depend on her getting as much enchantment into it as possible. The alternative is Mrs Patrick Campbell ... So cheer up: it might be worse.'[7] Shaw was not deliberately spoiling Lillah; he was spoiling himself, the play rather, which calls for strong visual focus – the 'enchantment' – to fall on Mrs Dubedat to balance and enhance both the theatrical effect and the quality of her confrontations with the medical fraternity, Ridgeon in particular. As Shaw was to remark on another occasion, it was the women's clothes that provided colour in generally drab Edwardian settings.

A week before the opening, on 14 November, Shaw had a set-to with the *Daily Express*, which published a detailed summary of the plot and portions of the dialogue. He wrote to the editor, Ralph P. Blumenfeld. 'Somebody who has had access to the rehearsals has sold his information. This, I need not tell you, is the grossest breach of confidence that can be committed in a theatre ...' Would the editor let him know whether he claimed the right to reproduce the dialogue and disclose the plot of a play without the author's sanction before first performance; and would he communicate to Shaw the name of the person who gave the information? The editor's reply was unsatisfactory. Shaw wrote again. The matter of the violation of copyright would be at an end if the editor inserted a disclaimer in his paper under the same heading as his notice of his play. Shaw helpfully provided the disclaimer, which Blumenfeld, no doubt feeling that it amounted to grovelling, refused to print.[8] He tried to make oblique amends, however. *The Doctor's Dilemma* was given a eulogistic notice in the *Daily Express* on 21 November on the front page. 'In "The Doctor's Dilemma,"' the notice concludes, 'there is art, wisdom, real drama and real humanity.' There was also a large glamorous photograph of Lillah McCarthy as Mrs Dubedat, but not on the front page. Shaw, fearing loss of copyright by this kind of piracy, refused to be mollified and pursued the matter further, letting it drop only when advised that legal action would take a year and result in substantial costs.

The other critics, having no cause to ingratiate themselves, were considerably less fulsome. Archer thought that up to the end of the second act, the play was the 'most brilliant' thing Shaw had ever done; after that the themes dribbled out and the pleasure of the audience likewise dribbled away. Speaking of the death scene, which he felt bound to discuss at length, he insisted that it was in no sense a rebuttal of his charge against Shaw: '... it is not with a straight face that he sets about suppressing ... Dubedat.' Being Archer, he had naturally expected a straight-faced death scene; also, because he was Archer, he qualified this: 'At the same time, the death scene is enormously clever in an uncanny fashion. Dubedat dies in an odour of aestheticism ... Some people, I fancy, were shocked, but there are people who will be shocked at anything.'[9]

Most of the critics were, if not shocked, offended, or they said they were, Walkley in *The Times* adding a characteristic thrust about 'bad taste' and 'cheap art'. It is worth noting how the *Morning Post* reacted. A year had passed since its attack on *Major Barbara*; here now was the first new play by that paper's *bête noir* and a renewal of the attack was a distinct possibility. The critic, apparently the same as the year before, deciding on this occasion that discretion was the better part of valour, opted to join the rank and file of Shaw-bashers. Thus, Shaw was 'interesting' because he was 'original', 'amusing' because he had an 'inexhaustible store of intellectual fun', but he was also 'annoying' because he was 'unintelligible' (the same charge levelled at *Major Barbara*). *The Doctor's Dilemma* was decidedly unpleasant; the death on stage was accompanied by a 'good deal of conversation calculated to offend persons with a disposition for reverence' (more echoes of *Major Barbara*); and the final act 'annoys the audience' because the identity of Jennifer Dubedat's new husband is not disclosed. These less than penetrating comments lead to an admission of special interest: the critics quarrel with Shaw, the *Morning Post* critic said, because 'They go to the theatre expecting a particular kind of product. Mr Bernard Shaw gives them something quite different, to which the canons by which they are accustomed to test the works submitted to them have no reference.'[10] Here is a classic encapsulation of critical bewilderment when faced with something new, where the work in question goes beyond the horizon of expectations established by custom.

The critics found fault, the Court public its pleasure and Shaw himself the greatest pleasure of all in writing to the *Standard* to point out that he had cribbed Dubedat's artist's creed, uttered on his deathbed, from Wagner's short story 'An End in Paris'. *The Doctor's Dilemma* had good houses throughout its run of eight matinees and further six weeks in the evenings in the new year. It promised to inaugurate the last phase on a high note.

The matinees, on the other hand, seemed to augur disaster in the new year. The double bill of Cyril Harcourt's *The Reformer* and Masefield's *The Campden Wonder* was shouted down by the critics and avoided by the public. When this was followed on 5 February 1907 by *The Philanderer* everyone except Shaw believed another failure was in the offing.

No one liked the play: not Grein when given the opportunity to produce it in the 1890s, not Archer who, when inviting Shaw to submit plays for the New Century Theatre, told him, 'NO PHILANDERERS NEED APPLY!',[11] not the Stage Society who 'strongly objected to [its] morals and tone',[12] not Lillah McCarthy who 'loathed the play like hell'.[13] and not – least of all – Barker, from whom Shaw had to wring unwilling consent for its production.

Shaw himself seems to have had ambivalent feelings, or his opinion may have depended on his motives when mentioning the play. To Ellen Terry in 1896 he described it as 'a combination of mechanical farce with realistic filth';[14] to Gertrude Elliott (Mrs Johnston Forbes Robertson) in 1903 he called it a 'detestable thing';[15] to Trebitsch in the same year he suspected it would make money if properly handled: 'it is the little plays that pay for the great ones in actual theatrical business';[16] then in a startling about-face in 1907 he told Barker that he was proud of it: 'It is the best of my plays; and when I work it up with a little extra horse play it will go like mad.'[17]

The critics tended to be indulgent rather than condemnatory. Walkley, as usual, was amusing at Shaw's expense, saying that he, Shaw, never shirked a challenge. A friend had challenged him to write a play about Don Juan and he produced *Man and Superman*, another friend had challenged him to write about death and he produced *The Doctor's Dilemma*: 'Has he no friend who will challenge him to write a wordless play?'[18]

It ran for its allotted eight matinees and that ended it. Shaw tried to get it onto the evening bill and argued quite plausibly – while it was still failing to draw audiences in the afternoons – that it could be turned into a financial success:

> I have got that balance sheet badly on my mind; and it is becoming more and more apparent ... that now that the ... anti-boom has arrived, we must fight the press and whilst defying them by playing all the pieces they slate as if they were aces of trumps, take great care that the said pieces are highly entertaining as variety shows. With Lillah and Loraine we could make The Philanderer a humming success.[19]

But Vedrenne and Barker would gamble no further. They had been proved right and Shaw wrong. So it was not this play but that assured money-spinner, *You Never Can Tell*, which came on in the evening after *The Doctor's Dilemma*. It ran for seven weeks, from 11 February to 6 April, and the hard-pressed management began to breathe a little more easily after a while. 'Always Shaw!' a critic had complained some time before: he had monopolized the evening bill for nine months. It was time for a change, and Galsworthy's *The Silver Box* succeeded *You Never Can Tell* on 8 April for three weeks. But if the run of Galsworthy's play managed at least to keep insolvency at bay, Hankin's *The Return of the Prodigal*, which came next on 29 April for four weeks, failed miserably.

Shaw was similarly banished from the matinees. *Hedda Gabler* with Mrs Patrick Campbell followed *The Philanderer* here, and was in turn succeeded by Elizabeth Robins's *Votes for Women!*, which was rushed into the evening bill to salvage something from the Hankin shipwreck.

Shaw was anxious, annoyed about this avoidable failure and increasingly critical of Barker. In the letter of 26 February to Vedrenne, cited above, and in the context of the failure of Hankin's play he spoke scathingly about Barker as a man who for months past had been fit only for a padded room. Such outspokenness has to be taken whence it came – from an affectionate mentor cum father-figure administering salutary correctives to a moody, self-willed youngster – but he had good cause for anxiety. The financial situation at the Court during the last phase was bad, if not critical;

Barker was overworked and this was affecting his judgment; rela-
tionships were becoming strained. Overall there was exhaustion: it
had been an enormous effort to get the enterprise going and to
keep it moving, and the fact was that, with Shaw's supply of plays
drying up, there was little that could be counted on to draw the
public. Shaw read the signs, including what he saw as the increasing hostility of the press, but his sniping commentaries from the
sideline did nothing to improve matters.

*Prunella* succeeded *Votes for Women*! for eight matinees on 7 May.
After this Shaw took over. *Man and Superman* came back on the
evening bill while *Don Juan in Hell* and *The Man of Destiny* went into
the matinees. If everything seemed to have been going badly
during the last phase, Vedrenne, Barker and Shaw were determined that with these their valedictory productions they would
leave the Court trailing clouds of glory.


II


With *Man and Superman* being played in the evenings it seemed
peculiarly right that for this, the last matinee at the Court, there
should be, not only a play (or plays) by Shaw, but the 'dream' from
*Man and Superman*, the stageworthiness of which Shaw had been
considering for some time. When Florence Farr asked him in 1905
whether she could stage it, with her as Ana, he put her off without
quite saying no – 'have you realised the size of the job?' – but he had
clearly been mulling over its theatrical – more correctly, operatic –
possibilities: '[U]nless there is a really artistic fantastic picture, with
top lighting in the manner of Craig, and cunning costumes – a
violet velvet Don Juan (horribly expensive), a crimson scarlet
Mephistopheles, a masterpiece of white marble sculpture, and a
radiant female (will you radiate?), the thing will be unendurable.'[20]
Florence Farr abandoned the idea, so leaving the part to the actress
who, in Shaw's eyes, was pre-eminently suited for his heroines –
Lillah McCarthy. Barker did not have a part in any of the plays,
much to his undisguised relief, and the American, Robert Loraine,
took over as Tanner. Having played Tanner some 500 times in the
United States, he may well have imagined he knew his business
better than Shaw himself. Shaw thought otherwise. He wrote
amusingly to Barker of Loraine's perplexity and discomfiture when
he – Shaw – began to urge him out of the groove those 500

performances had caused him to slip into, but he was equally ready
to praise him. 'He acts extremely well in the style of Wyndham. His
vigour is apparently inexhaustible ... He has got all the comedy side
of the part capitally and does it quite in my old-fashioned way, with
a relish and not under protest, like you.'[21] The other two members
of the operatic quartet – Michael Sherbrooke, who played the
Statue, and Norman McKinnel, who played the Devil, were both
experienced and accomplished.

Charles Ricketts designed the sets and costumes. A many-sided
artist, he had only recently turned to stage designing, but his flair
was already evident. By general consent his staging of *Don Juan in
Hell* was magnificent. Walkley said:

> Though the lectures [that is, Shaw's dialogue] are too long-
> winded, they are delightful to look at. Mr Charles Ricketts is
> stated to have 'designed' the costumes; we should rather
> suppose him to have judiciously selected them from famous old
> Masters. Don Juan (in blue) and the (crimson) devil suggest Paola
> Veronese; Dona Ana is an authentic Velasquez.[22]

This was a rave notice by Walkley's standards. Henderson
described the scene: 'The costumes ... were gorgeous; and there
was little movement, the characters being like jewelled figures
pinned against a black velvet back drop.'[23] 'Gorgeous' Loraine may
have been, but his costume, which was so heavy he was afraid to
move in it, made him even more miserable than Shaw's direction
had made him. But 'Loraine was charming' Ricketts told Lillah
McCarthy,[24] and the actor, a professional to the backbone,
suppressed his personal feelings for the sake of the production.

Shaw thought his performance the most extraordinary histrionic
and verbal feat by any actor of the time; nor should it be forgotten
that, having played in *Don Juan in Hell* on eight occasions in the
afternoon, he would go on in the evening for *Man and Superman*.
The other players supported him well and, notwithstanding the
usual carping remarks of many of the critics, the production
amounted to a vivid and memorable display of Shavian fireworks.

Shaw gave Barker an analytical programme which was distributed before performances. 'There is no use in leaving the wretched
critics to discredit the whole affair by their misunderstanding.'[25] It
is an intimidatingly long programme note and initial remarks about
'modern theology' would probably have put the average playgoer

off. The wretched critics as well, who probably did not bother to read it before or after the performance. A pity, because the note offers a helpful analysis of the concepts personified in the four characters on stage: the devil, whose kingdom is frankly based on idle pleasure-seeking; Don Gonzalo (the Statue), bored to distraction by heaven and wishing to settle in hell; Don Juan, suffering amid the pleasure of hell in an agony of tedium, wishing to settle in heaven; and Dona Ana, unable as a woman and mother to choose either heaven or hell, in the end assuming the role of Woman Immortal and declaring her readiness to bear the Superman to the Eternal Father.

The second play in the matinee bill, *The Man of Destiny*, was not an anticlimax, but it was a let-down. The acting was inferior to that which had preceded it, although the two principals, Dion Boucicault and Irene Vanbrugh, were highly regarded players, and the play itself, even if it is perhaps more than (as it was billed) 'a trifle', scarcely matches its companion for verbal brilliance and intellectual substance. 'This is not one of my great plays, you must know: it is only a display of my knowledge of stage tricks,' Shaw modestly informed Ellen Terry in 1895.[26] The critics tended to agree with him.

The last matinee performance was held on 28 June, the last evening performance a day later. The season was over. It did not pass without a celebration. A week later, on 7 July, a testimonial dinner in honour of Vedrenne and Barker was held at the Criterion Restaurant. A number of toasts were proposed and replied to; a number of toasts and replies were intended but the lateness of the hour prevented these from being heard. Fortunately the proceedings – what was said and what would have been said – were recorded in a 'Souvenir' book, published shortly afterwards.[27] It provides invaluable insights into contemporary attitudes to and opinions about the Court seasons – given that the occasion was to praise, not to bury, Vedrenne and Barker.

An important chapter in the history of English drama had ended, so important that an overall assessment of the 'price and value' of the venture is called for.

# 11

# 1904–1907: Price and Value

I

In an article, 'Theatrical Finance', in *The Green Room Book* of 1907 a pseudonymous 'Member of the Stock Exchange' spoke in glowing terms of the financial success of the Vedrenne-Barker management of the Court. 'Art, with a capital A, can be made to pay on the stage,' said he.

> Here the productions and performances appeal to an exclusive and limited, though growing audience, but they have been almost uniformly successful from the box-office standpoint. The combination of the shrewd and able business manager, in the person of Mr Vedrenne, with the artistic and intellectual stage-manager, in that of Mr Granville Barker, has been completely satisfactory, and demonstrates that there is money in the drama in its most serious and thought-compelling forms.[1]

In the absence of the Vedrenne-Barker account books, which search has not brought to light, one cannot dogmatically refute or confirm this view. All there is to go on are stray remarks in Shaw's letters, mainly to Barker, other remarks in Barker's letters to Murray, and the impression, occasionally bolstered by figures, that one play did well while another did badly. And the picture this produces, if it does not flatly contradict the member of the Stock Exchange, is certainly less gilt-edged than his judgment allows.

The production budget of £200 was minimal even ninety years ago. It would have been Vedrenne and Barker's modest hope to cover such an outlay with every production. On the whole they managed to do this, and show a profit besides, with Shaw's plays. 'I might call him the goose that has laid the golden eggs,' Barker said, 'if I could find another more suitable metaphor by thinking of him as our Ugly Duckling.'[2] It is possible to estimate overall takings for his plays from the amounts recorded in his Receipt Book and

167

the biggest golden eggs were *Man and Superman*, *You Never Can Tell* and *John Bull's Other Island*, which made handsome profits. Without them the undertaking would probably have collapsed.

Apart from Shaw's three big golden eggs, there were some others – silver-plated ones – which would have paid their way. *Major Barbara* and *The Doctor's Dilemma* undoubtedly did satisfactorily (although *Captain Brassbound's Conversion* and *The Philanderer* did not). In a statement shortly to be cited, Shaw mentions but does not name two other playwrights whose plays edged their way into the black in the end: these were probably Galsworthy's *The Silver Box* and Barker's *The Voysey Inheritance*. After this, one runs up against a phalanx of plays which either managed to break even, which was probably the fate of Elizabeth Robins's *Votes for Women!*, the production costs of which would have been in excess of £200, or plays which lost money, which was certainly the fate of Euripides-Murray and the contingent from the Continent, Maeterlinck, Hauptmann and Schnitzler.

Barker was to recollect that it 'was a pretty precarious enter-prise'.[3] Shaw put the matter less casually in a statement written for Archer and Dame Edith Lyttleton in 1909:

> … From April 1904 to June 1907 at the Court Theatre in London – a small outlying theatre holding £160 when full – the private and unbacked firm of Vedrenne and Barker tried the experiment of running an unendowed theatre in the interests of public culture alone … Its artistic success, and its beneficial reaction on the theatre generally have been admitted on all hands. It was even commercially successful in the sense that the managers, though they did not get the commercial value of their time, skill, and labor, at least scraped a living and made a considerable reputation …
>
> Even the very remarkable measure of pecuniary success which the Vedrenne-Barker experiment achieved at the Court Theatre will not bear close examination from the public point of view. The vogue of my own plays, helped at a critical moment by the patronage of the King, made the Court Theatre and its principal author fashionable; and as in addition to the four plays which I wrote expressly for the enterprise, I was able to place at its disposal no less than eight others which were virtually new to the public, it was really trading on a windfall unprecedented in the commercial history of the stage … Only two other living

authors paid their way, although four of the seventeen were dramatists of European celebrity, six are highly distinguished English writers, and the remaining three, who were comparative novices, quite justified the opportunity afforded them. Yet it was impossible to give these authors their fair share of the performances. Incomparably the noblest play produced at the Court Theatre was *The Trojan Women of Euripides* in the beautiful translation of Professor Gilbert Murray. When I say it was performed only eight times, whilst my amusing but hackneyed comedy, *You Never Can Tell*, was performed 149 times (not counting the later performances at the Savoy), it will be seen how utterly unable the Court managers were to pursue an impartial artistic and educational policy. Having no regular endowment, they were compelled to use the popularity of my plays as a financial [word omitted]. It was by a quite uncommercial accident that I shared their aims and, having an independent income, could afford to let them make extraordinary sacrifices of their commercial opportunities by repeatedly withdrawing my plays at the height of their success to produce equally deserving new ones with the certainty of changing a handsome nightly profit into a loss.[4]

As far as Barker was concerned, there was one insurmountable impediment to financial success: rent. In his address at the testimonial dinner he spoke strongly against the strangling effects of the long-run system, stressed the need of a repertory system and pointed an accusing finger – shades of *Widowers' Houses* – at the main hindrance, the ground landlord. No theatre manager, least of all the manager of a repertory system, could stand up against him.

This is good Socialist doctrine, but the really interesting inference to be drawn from these remarks is not that the ground rent was exorbitant but that it was inimical to the system Vedrenne and Barker had adapted for the Court. Comparatively low returns were expected as a matter of course, it was the drama that really mattered; but still Lickcheese would be round at the end of every month to collect Sartorius's unholy dues.

Barker defended the short-run system they had adopted. He conceded that it had many disadvantages, but it kept the plays fresh and was perfectly justified from a business point of view. Vedrenne could well have interrupted Barker at this point with an emphatic 'No!' The short-run system was economically unsound, in fact. Every production was a risk against which no insurance was possible. If the play failed to draw audiences, it continued to run for its advertised duration, losing money all the time. One could either then hope that its successor would make good the loss or, as Vedrenne and Barker were twice obliged to do, scramble a substitute on to the bill. In addition, as Archer pointed out[5] and as Shaw implies in the statement quoted above, the impetus of an original success could be lost by taking it off and reviving it later. Shaw's frequent dissatisfaction with revivals of his own plays is proof of this.

Still, at the conclusion of the seasons, the overall picture was reasonably satisfying, good enough to encourage the managers to move into the West End proper. Shaw made something of this when it was his turn to speak. He assured his audience that the guests of the evening (Vedrenne and Barker) owed him nothing.

> They are perfectly solvent ... They have paid me my fees to the uttermost farthing; and they have had nothing else to pay or repay me ... The Court Theatre has had to cut its coat according to its cloth; and it has never really had cloth enough. But it has paid its way and made a living wage for its workers; and it has produced an effect on dramatic art and public taste in this country which is out of all proportion to the mere physical and financial bulk of its achievements.[6]

II

An assessment of the Court seasons would be incomplete without a broad evaluation of Barker and Shaw as directors, even though both have been fairly extensively discussed, Shaw perhaps definitively,[7] in previous publications.

When Barker took over the Court with Vedrenne, his productions, mainly for the Stage Society, had earned him the respect of a few discerning critics but no wide recognition. The Court made his reputation and by the outbreak of the First World War he was acknowledged as the leading director in the English-speaking world. Today, some 75 years after his renunciation of the theatre, and partly no doubt because this renunciation has tended to cast a halo round his 15 short years as a director, he is a legend.

The earliest influence was his mother, then later two Germans, Andreson and Behrend, taught him the value of teamwork and the importance of significant detail. William Poel, who directed him in two Shakespearean roles, revealed to him the potential range and quality of the human voice; and Shaw, whose contribution to Barker's 'education' was various and wide, was perhaps chiefly influential in his emphasis on rhythm and form. As a trained and experienced actor Barker could bring all this together in being able to tell and show his players what he wanted from them. In addition, as a practising playwright, he was that virtual exception in the theatre of the day, a man to whom the author's intentions were paramount.

There were these formative influences, but Barker was an original, an individualist; and his productions were individualistic, the realization of a disinterest and dedication which his actors and actresses would remember with an emotion amounting to reverence.

To him the theatre had a social responsibility – to be mentally and emotionally stimulating, also elevating, though not overtly didactic. This applied as much to actors as to the public. 'Our actors – and worse still our actresses – are becoming demoralized by lack of intellectual work – the continual demand for nothing but smartness and prettiness,' he once remarked.[8] Barker's ideal theatre would serve all parties involved in the public presentation of a play, both sociologically and aesthetically.

The aesthetic effect, the work consummated on the stage before an audience as a work of art, was the final, overriding consideration. It was aesthetic failure that caused him to decry the customary commercial production done by a 'scratch' company of players.

The acting of the average play to-day is all superstructure – and mostly facade! ... [N]o wonder we rise in aesthetic rebellion against the theatre. For of that fine interplay of visualized character, of (shifting the metaphor) the living tapestry of pictured thought and emotion into which the stuff of a play can be woven in its acting, what have we seen? Hardly a beginning.[9]

The book containing these reflections – *The Exemplary Theatre* – was written 15 years after the Court Theatre seasons; the gospel he preached here had its genesis in his rejection of the commercial theatre in the early 1900s and in what he tried to achieve at the Court. If the lack of a true repertory system hindered the full development of 'the fine interplay of visualized character', something very close to this was achieved. And something very close to his aesthetic credo was also achieved:

To suggest, to criticise, to co-ordinate – that should be the limit of [the director's] function. The symphonic effect must be one made by the blending of the actors' natural voices and by the contrasts that spring from the conflicting emotions which their mutual study of the parts spontaneously engenders. Even over things that seem to need the exactitude of orchestration the scheme of the play's performance must still, as far as possible, grow healthily and naturally into being, or the diversity of the various actors will not become unity without loss of their individual force.[10]

This was Barker's ideal, given form and substance at the Court. 'The symphonic effect' is the crucial phrase. Like Shaw, he conceived of his productions in musical terms and gave them a rhythmical unity, for, as he repeatedly emphasized, it was the peculiar emotional effect of dramatic art that most mattered and it was in the patterns of sound and rhythm that this effect could best be gained.

At work on a production, he was reportedly inspirational. 'An odd, Puckish creature, dressed all anyhow, and much too deeply immersed in what he was doing to remember to eat, or to let his cast eat,' was how one witness described him. Lewis Casson adds to the picture:

> ... his greatest asset as an actor and director was the instant-aneous response of his whole being, body, and voice, and to his imagination in his interpretation of character and emotion. In speech especially he had an inspired knowledge of the exact melody and stress that would convey the precise meaning and emotion he wanted, and a power of so analyzing it in technical form that he could pass it on to others. And with this he had at his command all the devices of rhetoric with which the actor or speaker can rouse the curiosity, the attention, the tears or the laughter of an audience.[11]

As a disciple of naturalism Barker took on the box set which he adapted, modified and enlarged, bringing a high style, a sharpened focus to it – often gained by setting a scene at an unusual angle and always served by minute attention to detail. In the second act of *Votes for Women!*, for example, this turned a crowd scene into a sharply observed, fluid organic unit.

He seems to have had a predilection for fairy-tale, fantasy, myth – for plays that gave him scope to exercise an instinct for poetic impressionism. St John Ervine thought his production of *Twelfth Night* the most beautiful he had ever seen; critics during the days at the Court were usually highly complimentary of the staging of plays like *Aglavaine and Selysette*, *Prunella* and *Pan and the Young Shepherd*. Yet even in plays such as these, where one might suppose that 'atmosphere' for its own sake would gain the upper hand, Barker adhered firmly to dramatic intention, with every stage property and effect justified. Coming as he did in revolt against the gothic splendours of the nineteenth-century stage, he probably struck many contemporaries as reacting excessively. But here the austerity of production decreed by the Court's finances went in full accord with Barker's aesthetic intention.

Comparing his methods and aims with Barker's, Shaw said he was Verdi to Barker's Debussy. Debussy was hardly given to loud, resonant effects; neither was Barker, and in this, the muted quality of his productions, he was inclined most to err: while there could never be any denying the delicacy and subtlety of his work, it occasionally tended to be understated.

Shaw, who directed all his own plays, had never been more than an occasional amateur actor reading parts at copyright rehearsals. An exceptionally talented amateur by all accounts. Lillah McCarthy said that the cameo roles he would assume for the benefit of his players was a revelation.

> He would assume any role, any physical attitude, and make any inflection of his voice, whether the part was that of an old man or a young man, a budding girl or an ancient lady. With his amazing hands he would illustrate the mood of a line. We used to watch his hands in wonder. I learned as much from his hands, almost, as from his little notes of correction.[12]

Lewis Casson could similarly recall the 'miracle' of a man who, without any formal training or practice, could not be bettered in his ability to give a vivid half-minute sketch of a character.[13]

The best accounts of Shaw as a director come understandably enough from the actors and actresses who played under him. Cedric Hardwicke – Magnus in the first production of *The Apple Cart* – provides a vivid pen-picture of Shaw reading the play to the cast. On the first day the company gathered on the bare stage waiting for Shaw. 'He strode in, tall, lean, and upright, looking, as Karel Capek once described, "half like God and half like a very malicious satyr"':

The soft Irish tones began to roll, with the dash of Dublin that made every point as incisively as a scalpel. He read continuously, without faltering or reaching for the glass of water that stood at his elbow. From an actor's point of view, it was a compelling performance. He exemplified his own insistence on impeccable pronunciation, giving every word its full sense and weight ... Later he would chide us mercilessly whenever we were slipshod in handling his words.

Throughout the reading, he maintained the inflexions of voice by which he differentiated each character. We were awed by the magnitude of his achievement ...[14]

Casson takes the account on, describing Shaw at rehearsal:

The reading over, he plunged straight into rehearsal, including positions and moves, for which he always had a clear plan without any preliminary lectures or group discussions ... At this period of rehearsals G.B.S. would be on stage with the company, when he could talk freely to the actors, and interrupt and interpret. He was always patient, but quite persistent in getting eventually exactly what he wanted, so far as the actor was capable of it. I never remember his teaching an intonation parrot-like, but he had the power, the skill and the vitality to make his version seem obvious and the only one, and one can certainly say that by the time rehearsals were over every phrase and pause had been considered and deliberately passed ...

When the musical and intentional framework had thus been fixed, Shaw would retire to the back of the circle and let whole scenes run through without interruption, taking elaborate notes in exquisite handwriting on a large drawing pad, while the actors first floundered with their words and then gradually got the feel of the scene and 'lived' their parts.[15]

Many of Shaw's director's notes have survived. They underscore his commitment to the task and reflect in their details his conviction that the 'atoms of dust' that cumulatively added to the manifestation of genius and the making of an achieved work of dramatic art had meticulously to be set up in production as much as in composition. If these director's notes indicate the abstract discipline that went into the production of a play, the personal notes he wrote to his players indicate another facet of his work, his concern for the individual actor or actress in rehearsal.

Casson mentions but says practically nothing about the 'musical framework', that element of Shaw's drama by means of which he achieved spoken 'opera'. He wrote for and in his casting insisted on vocal contrasts with the leads being taken by the standard bass and tenor for men and mezzo and soprano for women. Subordinate roles would either supplement these voices or refine on them with, for example, counter tenors and baritones for the secondary males and a lyric soprano and contralto for the secondary females. *Man and Superman* is an obvious example of this kind of vocal casting, but all the other plays adhere to the rule in one recognized musical combination or another.

Once such casting was accomplished, at least as well as the availability of players permitted, Shaw would then proceed to initiate the actors and actresses in the music of their lines, frequently indicating melody, tempo, rhythm, tone and other musical effects by literally scoring the dialogue with a melodic line, complete with crotchets, quavers, semi-quavers and the rest. His players would then be required to 'sing' their lines accordingly, not in the bashful tradition of drawing room warblers but in the tradition of Italian opera – *con brio*. If Barker was sensitive about the musical effect of the plays he directed, Shaw – so much more steeped in music and more knowledgeable – was super-sensitive.

During the seasons at the Court almost all the critics, tone-deaf to a man, were dumb on the subject of the musicality of his lines. Perhaps this would have been asking too much of them, hard-pressed as they were to follow the intentional framework; but a moment's surrender on their parts to the vocal scoring may have brought some of them to appreciate how Shaw, that allegedly most coldly cerebral of men, charged his lines with the enchantment only music can convey.

For the rest, and this is implicit in the above, Shaw was mainly concerned with keeping the cast happy. Barker was backward in bestowing praise; Shaw was the opposite, and he earned the praise and gratitude of most players who came under his direction. Sybil Thorndike has written:

> The unexpected thing about G.B.S. was the way he hated hurting people's feelings – hated to make people feel small or lose their self respect. This sometimes made difficulties for those in charge, when strong criticism was really necessary, but I think it was his

good manners, for no one had better manners than he – it was his respect for other people's personality.[16]

During the Court days he had several experienced and accomplished players under him, none more so than Louis Calvert. Casson describes such a stalwart as 'not merely meekly, but enthusiastically accepting Shaw's detailed direction'.[17] Not only accepting it at the time, but as the following letter from Calvert to Shaw testifies, emerging from the experience with profound appreciation:

> I just want to write you a line thanking you for the chance you gave me of playing Broadbent. People little know that the praise I received for my performance was really due to you, who looked after your actor with a father's care, giving him the exact emphasis and accentuation that Louis Calvert would never have got on his own in the wide world – I speak this sincerely – do not think I flatter, I am not that sort of man – you made us all act as if we were living, breathing human beings and I have learnt a lot from you that will be of inestimable value to me in the future.[18]

Calvert may have felt differently after *Major Barbara*, when Shaw described his playing in memorably scathing terms, but even then he knuckled under and turned in a vastly improved Undershaft in ensuing performances. To move from this big reputation to a relatively modest one, Ellen O'Malley, who played Nora in *John Bull's Other Island* in the first season, wrote to Shaw: 'If actors were often given such lines to speak, acting would become an easy matter, and I think that artists would have very little excuse for being anything but patient and good humoured with such a stage manager as yourself. You have just been too kind to us.'[19]

One or two prominent later actors and actresses have had reservations about Shaw's directing. Michael Redgrave thought he gave his actors insufficient scope for personal creativity and Edith Evans – Orinthia in the first production of *The Apple Cart* – said he acted like an 'old ham', forgetting perhaps that Shaw 'hammed' his demonstrations on purpose. When asked whether Shaw tended to inhibit players, Sybil Thorndike and Lewis Casson replied with an emphatic no. However, Casson said Shaw tended to make his productions move unnecessarily slowly and overemphasized the comedy, and Sybil Thorndike thought he became so engrossed in the 'word music' of his dialogue that he neglected movement.[20] It is likely that both were here speaking from their memory of the rehearsals of *Saint Joan* in 1924, when Casson in particular – he co-directed the play – had a rather trying time with his 'associate director' Shaw.

Shaw's 'Rules for Directors' came in for rather patronizing criticism by American directors when it was published in 1949.[21] 'These are rules for beginners', they said in effect, ignoring the fact that one 'beginner' had successfully applied them himself for half a century. 'It is absurd to pretend it doesn't matter if a player does not understand his part,' they said, again seeming to forget that the author of this opinion had often had to deal with players who did not understand Shavian ideas or drama and yet made successes of their parts by dint of carefully rehearsed vocal scoring.

Christopher Newton, Director-in-Chief of the Shaw Festival at Niagara-on-the-Lake, steeped as he has become in the tradition founded at the Court, says, 'Shaw knew how to make an effect. His directorial notes are exceptionally perceptive, but only from the outside. Granville Barker knew from inside the playing space; Shaw knew only from the stalls.'[22] Does this make Barker the 'better' of the two? Perhaps it does. There is no record of what each thought of the other as director, yet we may guess that they perceived their likeness and unlikeness and had their reservations about each other. Verdi would probably not have cared much for Debussy, and vice versa. Whatever their differences, Shaw and Barker were a unique complementary force and together they achieved a theatrical revolution in their productions at the Court.

## III

Barker touched on one aspect of this revolution in his address at the complimentary dinner. He spoke about the actor-managers.

> I do not believe that it is possible for a man to play his best and produce his best at the same time. The actor manager is a victim of what is, to my mind, a vicious system. The wind was sown long ago when productions were not perhaps the complicated things they are now, and in our times the whirlwind is being reaped.[23]

Perhaps he knew he was reciting the epitaph over the actor-manager, prematurely perhaps, but his and Shaw's productions at the Court amounted to the actor-manager's death knell.

What they began the 1914–18 war completed. The actor-manager died out. The playwright-director took his place. Pinero, Barrie, Jones and others undoubtedly forced the trend but it was Shaw and Barker who established the authority of the author. When, as often happened, the playwright was not able to direct his own play, then an independent director, ideally someone like a Barker to whom the text was sacrosanct, would take over. The fact that the Court had two playwright-directors, each in his way a man of genius, established a system which continues with only slight modification to the present day.

The revolution did not end here. It included the actors and actresses, and it happened with almost monotonous regularity that the critics praised the acting, regardless of what they thought of the play they had watched. There were occasions when the acting failed to rise to requisite heights, but even Walkley, even in such sweepingly dismissive critiques as that for *Man and Superman*, would usually pause for a paragraph or two to compliment the players, always by name, on their performance.

Max Beerbohm discussed this in the course of his review of *The Voysey Inheritance*:

> People often ask ... why the acting at the Court Theatre seems so infinitely better than in so many other theatres where the same mimes are to be seen. I should have thought that the reasons were obvious. One is that the mimes at the Court are very carefully stage-managed, every one of them being kept in such relation to his fellows as is demanded by the relation in which the various parts stand to one another – no one mime getting more, or less, of a chance than the playwright has intended him to have. The other reason is that at the Court Theatre are produced only plays written by clever persons who have a sense of character, and who are thus enabled to create characters which are human, and which, therefore, repay the trouble that the mimes take in playing them.[24]

Desmond MacCarthy goes further in his account of the Vedrenne-Barker seasons.[25] The management, in their endeavours to present dramatic truth rather than spurious effects, took a good deal of trouble over casting, the idea being that a player rightly cast would react with emotional and intellectual sympathy to the part and so be able to act naturally. MacCarthy cites two examples of how two very minor roles, being well cast, were so played as to 'diffuse reality all around them' and add their measure of resonance to the production.

One is tempted to pause on some of the names and careers of individual players, yet Barker himself, one of the leading actors at the Court, would have none of this. He said in his address at the complimentary dinner:

> ... as to the actors, if I once began about them, I should find it difficult to stop. If they will allow me one remark, I would rather think of them as a company than as individuals, brilliant individually as they may be, for I feel very strongly that it is the playing together of a good company which makes good performances.

This is Barker's credo as director in embryonic form: unity of production achieved by subordinating the individual parts to the requirements of the whole. One respects this and consigns – not without regret – the abstract and brief chroniclers of the Court, in so far as they were individuals, to oblivion.


## IV

Shaw's address at Vedrenne and Barker's testimonial dinner was remarkable for two things: the tribute to John Masefield and the attack on the critics. This attack was a climactic moment in Shaw's war against the critics. Their antagonism to the Court enterprise had featured in his letters to Vedrenne in 1906–7 and we may be sure that he had given the matter considerable thought before rising to reply to the toast 'the authors of the Court Theatre':

> The difficulties of the enterprise have been labours of love, except in one unfortunate and very trying respect. There has been no sort of satisfaction in the unremitting struggle with the London press, which from first to last has done what in it lay to crush the enterprise.

This uncompromising statement, he said, would surprise some of his listeners because every current newspaper report was full of praise of Vedrenne and Barker, of the Court Theatre acting and the most frequently played Court author. But, he said, 'this has become the fashion' and the praise being bestowed was done as a matter of fashion rather than of real appreciation. He invited his audience to turn back to notices of first nights of first productions and a different story would emerge:

> There you will find a chronicle of failure, a sulky protest against this new and troublesome sort of entertainment that calls for knowledge and thought instead of the usual *clichés*. Take for example the fate of Mr Masefield.

Shaw then praised *The Campden Wonder* in terms already noted. 'And what had the press to say?' he asked. In the presence of some of London's leading critics, he proceeded to tell the company what the press had said:

> They fell on it with howls of mere Philistine discomfort, and persuaded the public that it was a dull and disgusting failure. They complained of its horror … as if it was not their business to face horror on the tragic stage as much as it is a soldier's duty to face danger in the field … And what they did brutally to the *Campden Wonder* they did more or less to every other play … The mischief done was very considerable in the cases of new authors; and the discouragement to our actors must have had its effect, bravely as they concealed it.

Shaw wound up his attack by asserting that it was the first notice that did the damage; the revivals were usually well received. He asked critics to plan their work the other way round – to praise the new play and damn the revival: 'Praise comes too late to help plays that have already helped themselves. If the press wishes to befriend us, let it befriend us in need, instead of throwing stones at us whilst we are struggling in the waves and pressing life-belts on us when we have swum to shore.'

Quite plainly, in Shaw's view, the revolution initiated at the Court had failed in one major respect: it had failed to convert the critics. In the months ahead, with Vedrenne and Barker moving to the Savoy Theatre in the West End proper, that enemy would still have to be engaged, the incessant skirmishing and the by now 15-year-old confrontation with the guardians of the citadel would have to continue.

# 1907–1910
# Confront

# 12

# 1907–1908: Storming the Citadel

## I

Successful though the Court seasons had been, momentous even in the eyes of a few discerning spirits, they amounted to a small rather backwaterish splash in the very big pond that constituted theatrical London. Yet there had been several triumphs and Vedrenne and Barker, subduing the still small voice of caution and excited by the prospect of repeating such triumphs in the heart of the citadel, may be excused for allowing their hopes to run away with them. A theatre in the West End proper: this would surely consolidate their reputations and their fortunes.

They aimed high at first, thinking of building their own theatre and pursuing this idea to the extent of composing and quite possibly circularizing a letter to potential investors. Written on 8 March 1907 and signed by both Vedrenne and Barker, this letter mentions the intention of the management of the Court to move to a more central house. Prohibitive rentals (£8000 to £10 000 a year) and structural inconveniences of available theatres had persuaded them that the economical plan would be to build a theatre. A satisfactory site was available; ground rent was £3000; the option they favoured was a long lease of 80 years; their architect had advised them that they could build and equip a new theatre for £40 000. Details followed regarding the formation of a syndicate and the issue of debentures. 'If this appeals to you as an investment' – the letter ends – 'we shall be most happy to give you further particulars in due course.'[1] Barker may well have seen this as a means of setting up his National Theatre – funded, not by the state, but by private investment. It was a pipe dream: the scheme came to nothing and other avenues had to be explored. Luck seemed to favour them. The Savoy Theatre, home of the D'Oyly Carte Opera Company, would be available on a one-year lease at the ridiculous rental of £37 for the year. The opportunity could not be passed over.

Shaw thought the enterprise a foolish business at first. He discerned waning public interest. Society had had enough of brilliant cerebration and was returning to frivolous celebration; the critics, put out of countenance by plays they had slashed and the public liked, would assuredly sharpen their spears and await Shaw's invasion with every intention of hurling him back to the desolation of Sloane Square.

But he acquiesced in spite of his foreboding and, having done so, committed himself wholly to the enterprise, physically by involving himself with his customary thoroughness in all aspects of production, financially by putting up £2000. This was all he could guarantee, he told Vedrenne. 'I have barely £3000 loose at the bank; and I cannot get on with less than £1000 under my hand to produce the necessary effect of being a millionaire.'[2] It was agreed that the managers would each receive £1000 a year as salaries and Shaw the same amount 'in moral superiority'.

Even he eventually grew to have great expectations of the Savoy, but as matters turned out, he had repeatedly to advance further amounts, £500 here and £350 there, until by the end the firm of Vedrenne and Barker owed him over £5000. Vedrenne would punctiliously write to acknowledge these additional loans. He does not give much of himself away in these letters; even so, they reflect something of his growing despondency as first the Savoy, then the Queen's, then the Haymarket seasons plunged the management into ever-deepening debt. In the beginning, when hopes ran high, he would 'beg to thank' Shaw for the additional loan and affix a 1d revenue stamp cancelled by his signature; later, after repeated box-office failures, he dispensed with the revenue stamp and opened his cheque-book heart, so to speak, to tell Shaw how much he personally regretted having had to borrow yet more from him (on this occasion it was an additional £450), to agonize over the failure of the Haymarket season, which he had hoped would be to the advantage of Shaw, Barker and Vedrenne, and to express 'once more my deep gratitude for helping us in the way you have'.[3] This, coming from Vedrenne, said a good deal.

The management was to continue with the system established at the Court: a series of special matinees on Tuesdays, Thursdays and Fridays, and a play for short runs in the evening with matinees on Wednesdays and Saturdays. Shaw had the evening bill throughout, beginning with *You Never Can Tell* on 16 September 1907, followed by *The Devil's Disciple* on 14 October, followed in turn by Forbes Robertson's *Caesar and Cleopatra* on 25 November (when *The Devil's Disciple* was transferred to the Queen's Theatre, where Vedrenne had taken an additional lease) and ending with *Arms and the Man* on 30 December, which ran until 14 March 1908. The special matinees were intended to be more representative of the new drama, but there were only two new plays, the first Galsworthy's *Joy* (24 September), then Gilbert Murray's translation of Euripides' *Medea* (22 October). A third play, Barker's *Waste*, would have succeeded the *Medea* on 19 November, but it was refused a licence. There was no replacement. *Arms and the Man* came off at the termination of the tenancy of the Savoy, when it was perfectly clear that the enterprise had failed.

It is a primary maxim of military operations that when a citadel is to be stormed and breached the attacking force should be issued with a good supply of superior weapons. Vedrenne and Barker (and Shaw to a certain extent) used an extraordinarily ineffective assortment of weapons. Their programme would barely have retained the old Court audience, let alone attracted a new, larger one; in fact, the old Court audiences found the Savoy uncongenial and they tended to stay away. *You Never Can Tell* as a 'starter' was probably a sensible choice, although it was scarcely adventurous and must have been perilously close to exhaustion after its 149 performances at the Court. Galsworthy's *Joy* was a flop; it deserved to be. *The Devil's Disciple*, kept out of the Court by Shaw, who considered the facilities too limiting for a successful production, could conceivably have been a success at the Savoy. It had done very well in America and was virtually unknown in London. Yet it was only a qualified success, partly because Barker, who directed, failed to bring out the rumbustiousness the play demands. As Shaw told Murray, 'The D's D. revolts Barker's soul; he tries to crush the cast and get a delicate galsworthy result. Then I sail in and turn the whole thing into a blatant Richardson's Show.'[4] The production aroused sufficient interest to be included in the Royal itinerary of play- and opera-going, as *The Times* of 29 October 1907 recorded in its Court Circular: 'The King and Queen, the Queen of Norway and Princess Victoria were present at the performance of *The Devil's Disciple* at the Savoy Theatre last night.' This was not a Royal Command Performance; but the attendance of royalty conferred prestige and social acceptability on the production. Even so, during its initial six-week run at the Savoy it earned Shaw a fairly modest £275 augmented by £143 for the four or so weeks at the Queen's, which scarcely indicates a run on the box office. The *Medea* restored the management's reputation after the failure of *Joy*: it was not as fine as the Court productions of Murray-Euripides but the critics were respectful. Barker's *Waste* may well have saved the enterprise: it is one of Barker's finest plays, as incisive a scrutiny of Edwardian political man as *The Voysey Inheritance* is of Edwardian professional middle-class man; and it projects the personal tragedy of the central figure with remarkable force. It is hard to imagine its not having been a success in 1907. But the Examiner of Plays, Redford, was a reactionary and a fool, and Barker suffered for it. It goes without saying that Shaw and others did not take Redford's rejection lying down.

*Caesar and Cleopatra* was nominally a Vedrenne-Barker promotion, 'by arrangement with Forbes Robertson'. It was also a Shaw promotion, of course, and he naturally wanted this, his 'big' 1890s play, to succeed. Berlin had seen it in March 1906 in a Trebitsch translation and a Max Reinhardt production; New York had seen it in October 1906 in a Forbes Robertson production, where it had been a great success – the fifth Shaw 'hit' in that city since Mansfield's production of *The Devil's Disciple*. The *New York Times* called *Caesar and Cleopatra* an 'artistic triumph', doling out praise in equal proportion to Forbes Robertson, his wife Gertrude Elliott (as Cleopatra) and, 'last but not least', Shaw.[5] London had lagged, as usual, but it was now time to awaken this comatose monster to the fact of a major dramatic work and that the lead would be taken by the celebrated actor for whom Shaw had written the part. This would have meant a good deal to him, as much as Ellen Terry's playing of Lady Cicely Waynflete had meant a good deal to him. As he said in a comment in *Play Pictorial*, '[Forbes Robertson] is the classic actor of our day ... the only actor I know who can find out the feeling of a speech from its cadence ... Without him *Caesar and Cleopatra* would not have been written.'[6]

Forbes Roberston, like Ellen Terry, took a long time to act on the compliment, but when he finally did he must have been suitably appreciative. It served him well; but not in England, least of all in London, not in 1907. He and Gertrude Elliott were welcomed back from their travels with cries of delight from the critics; the play with which they had been travelling was not. *Caesar and Cleopatra* opened in Leeds on 16 September 1907 and the critic of the

*Yorkshire Post*, sedulously emulating his London *confrères*, wondered whether the play was not a prostitution of Forbes Robertson's splendid talents. Granted that Shaw's out-and-out admirers could find no fault, but others could not help but be startled if not shocked, the purist saddened even to indignation, at the sacrilege perpetrated on the altar of antiquity. The truth, as he saw it, was that the play ought to have been presented as comic opera.[7] It fared little better in London. Walkley also regretted the absence of a musical score: 'To see *Caesar and Cleopatra* is once again to regret Offenbach. None but the genius that set to lilting music the reckless wit of *Orphée aux Enfers* and *La Belle Hélène* could worthily "score" this Shavian extravaganza.'[8] Walkley could be a pretentious ass at times. E. A. Baughan of the *Daily News* thought the play 'dull and often downright foolish' but it was in some ways the finest drama Shaw had written; it had moments of 'something like greatness' and even a moment or two of passion, 'and with the passion comes drama'. Baughan was keen on 'passion'.

All this was not so much a drubbing as a snubbing. For once Shaw did not make a public issue of the critical reaction, possibly because the production and cast as a whole – Forbes Robertson and Gertrude Elliott excepted – did not measure up to the usual high Vedrenne-Barker standard. Barker had been against bringing the play to the Savoy, but Shaw had overruled him, telling Forbes Robertson, 'You are a sufficiently presentable actor to be able to appear without supervision in a theatre made classic by the illustrious traditions of Vedrenne-Barker and Bernard Shaw.'[9] Privately he resented the critical reaction. He told Gertrude Elliott that it required a deliberate and conscious effort of reason not to be furiously disgusted with the public and the press.

> They have not seen acting like that for Lord knows how many years ... And instead of appreciating it, they positively grumble at it ... I am sorry now that it was not possible to produce the play anonymously; for it is plain that the critics let their preconceived ideas of me get between themselves and the acting.[10]

One notes the remark about not having produced the play anonymously: not many years later Shaw would attempt this subterfuge with *Fanny's First Play*.

Everything now depended on *Arms and the Man*. The cast, which included Loraine, Lillah McCarthy, Barker and other experienced players of the Court years, was an indication of the importance the management attached to the production. Shaw told Daly that this was the charge of the old guard at Waterloo with Loraine leading the 'forlorn hope' and like Napoleon he could well be in for a defeat.[11] The play was fairly well received and it managed to keep going for 56 performances, but it was not a happy run, mainly because Lillah McCarthy as Raina did not enjoy playing opposite Loraine's Bluntschli and allowed her performance to suffer. Shaw did not mince his words in telling her so. This revival delivered too little too late; it was a forlorn hope indeed.

When the Savoy season ended on 14 March 1908, the management faced huge debts. Shaw had to dig deeply into his pocket, Barker had to pawn many of his possessions and was left virtually penniless; but every creditor, Shaw excepted, was paid in full.

The renascent drama seemed to have exhausted itself. This was not so in fact: apart from Barker's *Waste*, Galsworthy had completed one of his best plays, *Strife*, which Barker did not use; Hankin had at least two plays ready, *The Cassilis Engagement* and *The Last of the De Mullins*, both much superior to the two plays of his produced at the Court: Barker did not use them; Masefield had *The Tragedy of Nan* ready: Vedrenne would have nothing to do with it, at least initially. Shaw was the only one who did not have a new play and he, facing, as he explained, tremendous arrears of business to work through, could not consider anything for 1907.

Why were such fine plays passed over? There would have been practical problems. Writing to Shaw on 16 November 1907, Vedrenne was full of ideas about the Savoy season. *Man and Superman* could follow *Arms and the Man*; *The Philanderer*, which Shaw was eager to revive, could be included; Barker's *The Voysey Inheritance* could start a four-week run in May 1908; then there were also *John Bull's Other Island* and *Major Barbara* and so on and on. Vedrenne's only doubt was that two plays by Shaw at two theatres (the Savoy and the Queen's) would not be good for the firm.[12] Nothing came of these plans and one must assume that dwindling resources forced the management to abandon them.

Personal antagonism, envy and obscure principle can also cause theatrical enterprises to falter. These, in so far as they apply to the Vedrenne-Barker management, are not important any longer, except one – Barker's weariness and frustration. He was not the crusading spirit of four years before. Prone to moodiness, he was severely cast down by the banning of *Waste* and, following from this, the apparent fruitlessness of his mission. He would gladly have seen the partnership terminated; and, as though to underscore this sentiment, he went to New York, Archer accompanying him, as soon as the run of *Arms and the Man* had ended, to inspect the New Theatre which he had been invited to take over as director. He was soon back, having declined the offer.

However, as Shaw later reminded Vedrenne and Barker, the partnership remained in force. 'Vedrenne & Barker as individuals have created a Frankenstein's Monster (the firm of Vedrenne & Barker with a Goodwill for a soul) that they cannot easily slay, however much they may loathe it ... "Let me not to the marriage of true souls admit impediment" said Shakespear ...'[13] There must have been many occasions when the partners would have wished their playwright more curably light-hearted.

This letter was written shortly before 'Vedrenne-Barker' went out on its second tour of the provinces. The first began in late 1907, when *John Bull's Other Island* and *You Never Can Tell* went out, the second in mid-1908 with *Man and Superman* and *Arms and the Man*. It was hoped that these four plays, advertised as Vedrenne-Barker original productions and with many Court players in the casts, would make good the losses of the Savoy but, although the plays were well received, they did little beyond sustain themselves and eke out minuscule profits during the two years they were on the road.

The partnership was finally and formally dissolved in March 1911, by which time Vedrenne and Barker had gone their separate ways. Shaw's letter to Vedrenne, which concludes the matter, indicates how much he had ventured in the enterprise. The Phyllis in the letter was Vedrenne's wife, Phyllis Blair, a comedy actress of some standing; the Melville is either Walter or Frederick Melville, brothers who jointly owned the Lyceum and separately wrote a number of popular melodramas:

> ... Everything belongs to me, cash in bank, scenery, library, band parts, the Royalty Theatre, Circus Road, Phyllis, the boy, everything that you and Barker possess up to the value of £5,250 ...
>
> I attach some importance to the cash, and a great deal to Phyllis, whose consent, however, is (by an oversight in the law) necessary to her transfer to my household. If she refuses, I sweep away the house, the boy, the theatre, the furniture, plate, linen, and everything except what you stand in. To place her in the dilemma was my real object in lending the money and writing

plays for V. & B. The mask is now off: she must yield or bring about the ruin of all that is dear to her. Could Melville devise such a plot?[14]

## II

One Vedrenne-Barker production has not been mentioned yet: Shaw's *Getting Married*, which was put on at the Haymarket in association with Frederick Harrison after the Savoy season had ended. It came on as the first of three new Vedrenne-Barker productions, the other two being Masefield's *Tragedy of Nan* and a Housman-Moorat text-plus-music collaboration, *The Chinese Lantern*. Shaw had insisted that his play should not go on alone, '[S]o as to make the affair really a V.B. season and not a West End production of a play by me.'[15]

*Getting Married* was his first new play since *The Doctor's Dilemma*, written in 1906 under the sheltering wings of the Court Theatre where he would have expected and received the praise and applause of the converted, no matter what the critics said. That was all in the past; the Savoy incursion, also in the past, had shown that Fabian-style permeation was futile. The citadel remained unaffected and indifferent. It was time to bring a big gun to bear on the walls; time to breach them and to take the fight into the enemy's camp. Shaw began his assault with a preliminary barrage in the *Daily Telegraph* of 7 May 1908, and he let rip with a rhetorical salvo that would have taxed the breath control of Caruso. His new play, he told his fictional 'interviewer', was his revenge on the critics

> ... for their gross ingratitude to us, their arrant Philistinism, their shameless intellectual laziness, their low tastes, their hatred of good work, their puerile romanticism, their disloyalty to dramatic literature, their stupendous ignorance, their susceptibility to cheap sentiment, their insensibility to honour, virtue, intellectual honesty, and everything that constitutes strength and dignity in human character – in short, for all the vices and follies and weaknesses of which Vedrenne and Barker have been trying to cure them for four years past.

His play would last 150 minutes and consist only of talk, talk, talk, talk, talk – Shaw talk. The whole thing would be hideous, indescribable – an eternity of brain-racking dullness. And yet the critics would have to sit through it all. 'Well, serve them right! I am not a vindictive man; but there is such a thing as poetic justice; and on next Tuesday afternoon it will assume its sternest retributive form.'

But had he deliberately written a bad play?

> Good heavens, no; there is nothing [the critics] would like better. I have deliberately written a good play; that is the way to make the Press suffer. My play is the very best I can write, the cast is the very best available in London; and what is equally important, the audiences will be the best audiences in London ... But if we are to please such audiences, we cannot please everybody.

The play had no plot, no story: 'Surely nobody expects a play by me to have a plot. I am a dramatic poet, not a plot monger.'

In so far as this 'interview' is an attack on the critics for their refusal to grant Shaw his worth, it continues the campaign launched at the Criterion Restaurant the year before. Now with the critical failure of *The Devil's Disciple* and *Caesar and Cleopatra* as more ammunition for the Shavian artillery, he was forcing a confrontation with them by this extravagant display of loathing and, at the same time, trying to spike their guns beforehand, or at least pre-empt some of the damage he believed they would inflict on *Getting Married* in their by now predictable exhibitions of hostility.

There are several layers of subtext to this 'interview'. It is a 'puff-negative', by means of which Shaw hoped to elicit a positive reaction to the play from the public. One notices that he emphasizes the intelligence of the audience and at one point speaks of it as inhabiting the 'Beethoven plain' while the critics inhabit the 'Tivoli plain'. He was keenly aware of audience participation, audience response, audience reception – a more than ordinarily vital matter to him, considering his commitment to providing an 'advanced' kind of play to a relatively 'unadvanced' but, he would have hoped, an intelligent and open-minded, hence potentially sympathetic and appreciative, audience.

The subtext conveys something more, implicitly admitted by the extravagance of the 'interview', that Shaw had private doubts about *Getting Married*. Encouraged by the success of *Don Juan in Hell*, he would have been attracted to the idea of developing 'discussion drama'. It had worked once before, so why not again, where the 'talk, talk, talk' would be on a matter of great immediacy and relevance? But how would the critics and the audience react? – hence his targeting of these two entities in his 'interview'. For all the verbal and technical brilliance of the piece and its vaunted adherence to the classical unities, did it not venture too far from the tried and known formulae of drama? To what extent could a 'dramatic poet' abandon 'plot mongering'?

The play opened with a strong cast at the Haymarket (the theatre from which Shaw had once disgustedly withdrawn *You Never Can Tell*) on 12 May 1908. When the critics emerged late that Tuesday afternoon, they were unanimously of a mind to fulfil Shaw's prophecies to the letter and condemn the piece out of hand, which they did at length. All the characters talked like Shaw, and very prolixly; much of the play was wearisome, hackneyed, platitudinous, old, stale and soporific; whole scenes were dull to a degree in their straining after originality; the fun did not seem integral to the play, it had been foisted in lest the audience fidget; it was Plato's Symposium, to which the great conjurers with ideas always had to come.[16] One or two critics referred to the 'interview' Shaw had given the *Daily Telegraph* beforehand, Baughan grouchily conceding that if three hours in a hot theatre listening to detailed arguments on marriage is revenge, Shaw could be satisfied. 'He is beginning to hold his audiences too cheaply, and that is a pity,' Baughan added.

Quite the most scathing criticism came from the *Academy*, a literary weekly of small circulation but good standing. Shaw had contributed a few articles and letters to its pages in the previous ten or so years. His most recent contribution, on dramatic censorship, had appeared less than a year before, on 29 June 1907, when his well-known anti-censorship stance was supported by the new editor, Lord Alfred Douglas – Oscar Wilde's Bosie. Douglas had a high opinion of Shaw and made much of him and his work, particularly his plays. He went further than this on 15 June 1907 when his journal carried a light-hearted tribute to the principal author of the Court Theatre, a spoof of *Don Juan in Hell* – 'Shavians from Superman' by Robert Ross. It was quite possibly this that prompted Shaw to respond with a letter in which he congratulated Douglas on the rising circulation of the *Academy*.[17] Relations between the two were distant: they had met only once, during the famous lunch with Frank Harris at the Cafe Royal when Shaw, an unwilling witness, watched Douglas metaphorically tuck Oscar

Wilde under his arm and carry him off to his doom. There was some suggestion of angry resentment on Douglas's part on that occasion, but that was all long in the past; since then never the slightest hint of animosity.

Shaw could fairly have expected the *Academy* to return a favourable verdict on *Getting Married*, but by 1908 Douglas, married, the father of a son and determined to put his gilded past behind him, was becoming increasingly reactionary. The verdict the journal did return on 23 May 1907 must therefore have given him quite a jolt. It was unsigned but plainly written by Douglas himself. As an American commentator wrote: '[T]hough the article was unsigned, the hand of Douglas was plain from the signs … – the heavy writing and the light thinking.'[18] Shaw would certainly have seen this as well, but used his 'ignorance' of the authorship to his advantage when he responded. Headed 'For Shame, Mr Shaw!', Douglas's review of *Getting Married* tore into the play and Shaw himself in a way that went well beyond customary critical disparagement. Astonishingly, he admitted that the first act so got on his nerves that he left the theatre after 25 minutes. He was 'fed up' with the conversations of Shaw. The conversation in *Getting Married* was not only dull, but immoral. 'Frankly we do not think that the censorship should have passed the play.'

Douglas advised his readers to stay away from the Haymarket, unless they wanted to risk being bored to death – not his male readers, who would not be damaged either intellectually or morally by Shaw's impertinent treatment of serious subjects, but it was quite otherwise with the blameless British matrons and their young who had neither sufficient intellectual ability nor sense of humour to appreciate Shaw's pyrotechnics at their true value. 'They gape and they giggle, and, returning to their fastnesses in Bayswater or Balham, they take steps to render unbearable the lives of their blameless and respectable husbands …' Shaw was beginning to make serious inroads into the British home: '[I]f he had his own way he would break it up altogether.'

The prim old-maidishness of this must surely take the cake in an old-maidish age, and when it appeared, over ten days after the opening of *Getting Married*, Shaw would have been itching for a scrap with a critic, any critic. Douglas handed him his opportunity on a plate, practically inviting Shaw to mete out the treatment only Shaw could produce: firm correction dressed in comedy. His letter, which Douglas published the following week (30 May 1908) under the heading 'Can You Not Manage?' is simultaneously an indication of Douglas's failure of responsibility as a critic, reproof of this failure and a tease that goes so far as to suggest the possibility of litigation, a line of attack that must have been inspired by Douglas's notorious proneness to this kind of action. It is a retort courteous, with the refinement of avuncularity, which mercilessly exposes Douglas's callowness:

Dear Lord Alfred Douglas,–

Who on earth have you been handing over your dramatic criticism to? Your man, who must have been frightfully drunk, has achieved the following startling libel:

The waiter, disguised as a butler, told us, among other things, that his mother was very fond of men and was in the habit of bringing them home at night.

For that statement which I need hardly say is pure invention, you will have Vedrenne and Barker, Frederick Harrison, and Holman Clark (the actor concerned) demanding damages from 'The Academy' at the rate of about £2500 apiece ...

Can you not manage to *volunteer* in your next issue a withdrawal of the article? As a rule, I do not like asking an editor to throw his contributor over; but when the contributor throws over the editor so outrageously as in this case, I do not see what is to be done ...

I suggest that the best and friendliest thing to do is to state in your next issue that ... you feel bound to withdraw the whole article unreservedly. If you think well of this, or some equivalent course, you might let me have a line so that I may try to smooth matters.

This was a wasted exercise. Douglas did not have the wit to make a good fight of the issue. Shaw would have pricked his vanity and vain men are apt to resort to heavy-handed sarcasm or priggish self-justification. Douglas resorted to both. In his reply, also published in 'Can You Not Manage?', he 'strongly resented' the accusation of drunkenness brought against the writer of the article who, he admitted, was himself, adding that the part of the play he had heard teemed with indecencies. His *coup de grâce*: 'I confess that I am surprised that a man of your intellectual attainments should exhibit such pettiness.'

Shaw responded in a letter of 27 May, published in the *Academy* of 6 June in an article by Douglas headed 'The Shaving of Patshaw'. Shaw said he was enormously relieved to discover that Douglas had written the review and 'not some poor devil whom it would have been your duty to sack'. He thought that Douglas 'MUST have been drunk – frightfully drunk, or in some equivalent condition; no normal man behaves like that'. That Douglas did not realize Shaw was pulling his leg passes belief; all he could manage in response was a petulant 'Your letter is a piece of childish impertinence, but as it was evidently written in a fit of hysterical bad temper, I shall not count it against you.' The same article contained Shaw's response of 31 May:

> I asked for a friendly reparation: you have given me a savage revenge. However, perhaps it was the best way out. As you have owned up, we are satisfied; and the public will forgive you for the sake of your blazing boyishness.

That phrase, 'blazing boyishness', said it all. Shaw should have left the matter there, but he could not resist the temptation to add a paragraph of 'preaching' on the subject of 'Who is to edit the editor?' He signed himself off, 'sans rancune' and Douglas, relaxing a trifle in the remainder of the article, though not averse to indulging in preaching on his own account, signed himself off similarly: 'We have no reason to bear [Shaw] any malice; quite the contrary.'

This episode has a footnote: many years later, in 1931, when Shaw and Douglas were beginning the correspondence that would continue until shortly before Douglas's death in 1945, their quarrel in the *Academy* came up. Shaw said that he had honestly believed Douglas had not written the notice. One may disbelieve him; but the fiction gave him an opening for a couplet, telling Douglas:

> If boozy be bosie, as some folks miscall it
> Then Bosie is boozy, whatever befall it.
> You must have been as drunk as a boiled owl....[19]

Douglas insisted that he had not been, but 'I hated your play. It bored and exasperated me ...'[20] So 23 years later each was still sticking to his guns, but without rancour.

The galling thing was that *Getting Married* was well received by the public. Soon after it opened, Shaw told the *Daily Mail* that the result had more than justified his expectations. 'I said that I had written a good play, and I said also that the critics would not like it. You see now that I was quite right.' The critics should not have come to see it; they should have sent their wives – it was a play for women. Its only fault was that it was too short.[21] He adopted the same jaunty note when telling Vedrenne, 'All that play wants is £10,000 to nurse it into a full grown institution.'[22] A few weeks later, writing to McNulty, he spoke of the public response as a tremendous victory over the press. Whatever private doubts he may have entertained beforehand had been laid to rest. But there was the other problem, that of money. Shaw's royalties were good but he stood to lose because he had insisted that the management also produce two plays by young men, Masefield and Housman – 'plays without the slightest chance of paying their way. Result: I shall be out of pocket by the job.'[23] He was right. *Getting Married* could not sustain *The Tragedy of Nan* or *The Chinese Lantern* indefinitely and the Haymarket season soon ended.

This also ended Shaw's first assault on the citadel. On the whole it had not gone well for him and, although *Getting Married* enabled him to withdraw undefeated and capable of shaking a defiant fist at the critics, he would have known that he had still not established himself with any firmness in London. It would be two years before he returned with his next barrage of talk-talk-talk, in *Misalliance*. In the meantime there was another issue, coming rapidly to a head, which demanded his full attention: stage censorship. Everything pointed to an interesting confrontation.

# 13

# 1908–1909: Down with the Censor!

## I

On 27 December 1907 and 2 January 1908 *The Times* published two long articles on 'The Office of Examiner of Plays' in which the unnamed author, tracing the history of stage censorship since its introduction in 1737, raised the question of the rightness or wrongness of the practice in the new century. In the next year and a half this would become quite the burning issue of the day, if not to the public at large, certainly to playwrights, theatre managers, playgoers who took their excursions to the theatre seriously and, not least, those to whom censorship in whatever form denied the principle of freedom.

Shaw was involved from the beginning; he had been involved in a sporadic duel with the Lord Chamberlain's Examiner of Plays since his days as music critic for the *Star*. From his point of view, the turn of events at the end of 1907 had to be utilized to bring the issue to a head: the censorship of plays had to go, and he would use every means at his disposal – the press, plays liable to be handed the official veto, confrontation with the Joint Select Committee of Parliament appointed to look into the question, unremitting canvassing – argument, controversy, satire, ridicule – anything that would publicly expose the Examiner of Plays to the absurdity of his function and thus hasten the abolition of his office.

There would be others in the field on both sides of the question, but the principal adversaries were the Lord Chamberlain's inflexible Examiner of Plays, G. A. Redford, and Shaw, the most 'immoral' playwright of the time, each representing – it is not straining analogy to see the confrontation between them in these global terms – the polar opposites of the Edwardian world: Redford, the icon of conservatism, the defender of the old and established, and Shaw, the icon of radicalism, the champion of the new and revolutionary.

This confrontation would reach its climax in the future. At the end of 1907, as *The Times* realized, there was a muttering already growing to a rumbling, a taking of positions, a girding of loins. Hence these two articles which invited readers to acquaint themselves with the history of dramatic censorship in England, the better to assess the controversy. It is not an elevating history, but it is a perversely edifying one in the way it reveals the working of the censorial mind as, over the years, it established and applied shifting but inviolable criteria to dramatic presentations.

There had been control of the stage since the days of Henry VIII, but it had been *ad hoc* and non-statutory, left to the usually easy-going discretion of the Lord Chamberlain. Robert Walpole, Britain's first 'Prime Minister', changed this. Enraged by the way his administration, a notoriously corrupt one, was being exposed and satirized on the stage, particularly by Henry Fielding, he forced the Licensing Act through Parliament in 1737. There was strongly voiced opposition, memorably from Lord Chesterfield, whose speech in defence of the liberty of the stage would be echoed by other opponents of dramatic censorship for the next century and a half. The restraints which would be imposed on the stage amounted to an attack on the liberty of the press, he urged. The power to be entrusted to the Lord Chamberlain was 'more absolute than that which we would extend to the Monarch himself' and there was already a remedy at law for the abuses aimed at. A noble plea but the Act went through and the Lord Chamberlain became the statutory arbiter of the stage, his function delegated to an Examiner of Plays with the authority to grant or refuse licences to dramatic representations. Fielding, thus curbed, turned to writing novels, to the vast enrichment of literature. Topical political satire, thus curbed, vanished from the stage.

During the next hundred years social values underwent some reshuffling, and in 1832, when Bulwer Lord Lytton, the popular novelist and playwright, raised the question of stage censorship in Parliament, it emerged that political considerations had fallen away in importance while religious and moral ones had superseded them. No woman could be called an angel on stage; even a man could not be said to play the fiddle like an angel (angels were Scriptural beings); the mildest oath was expunged; obscene expressions, among them 'thighs', were not permitted. Attempts by Bulwer Lytton and others to liberalize the Act came to nothing and in 1843 – a watershed year – the Theatre Regulation Bill brought all theatres in Great Britain under the control of the Lord Chamberlain and authorized the Examiner to prohibit the performance of any play which endangered 'the promotion of good manners and decorum, or of the public peace', terms which the lawmakers in their wisdom did not define, thus opening the way for a succession of Examiners to read and interpret the Act as waywardly as they wished. The sensibility of Thomas Bowdler settled like a blight on the nineteenth-century stage.

Two subsequent Select Committees, in 1853 and 1866, served to confirm the Examiner's stranglehold on the theatre. Then in 1892, another Select Committee, on Theatres and Plays, was appointed. In the intervening years, as *The Times* reminded its readers, a good deal had happened to the drama: 'Ibsen had reached England; and he had reached it because there was coming into existence a body, earnest if small, of lovers of drama ... who wished to see the theatre the scene of some kind of "criticism of life."' The principal adversaries in 1892 were the Examiner E. F. Smyth Pigott and William Archer. Smyth Pigott had a lot to say in his defence. Was Shakespeare not a member of the Lord Chamberlain's Company? The censorship was a check on 'the two besetting sins of the stage in all times and all countries – licentiousness and scurrility'. He had refused a licence to the Oberammergau Passion Play in London, but he had licensed some of Ibsen's plays because he considered them 'too absurd altogether' to be dangerous. (No doubt he licensed *Arms and the Man* in 1894 on the same excellent grounds.) When he died in 1895, Shaw, then drama critic for the *Saturday Review*, remembered all this in his 'obituary' notice, as we shall see.

*The Times* reported that Archer gave his evidence with 'a clearness and decision which the masterly stupidity (or cleverness) of his examiners did little to shake', but his was the only voice raised in serious opposition, while the pro-censorship lobby, which included such powerful figures as Irving, presented an almost overwhelming case for the preservation of the censor; so, once again, nothing was done. Smyth Pigott was succeeded by G. A. Redford; change but no change continued as though by perpetual non-motion, except that by the late 1890s and on into the early 1900s the forces of change were generating a more concerted and vigorous challenge to the system. As *The Times* said in summing up: the growth of a 'serious' drama in England and the increase in the body of interested playgoers had brought the 'function of the censor into notoriety'.

An implicit theme of this account of stage censorship is the changing function of the playwright in theatrical history. For most of the time between 1737 and 1892 he had been a hack. As Nicholas Nickleby discovered when Mr Vincent Crummles engaged him as resident scribbler, he was required to produce texts to order – 'pieces' that would 'bring out the whole strength of the company' and incorporate whatever stage properties were to hand, in Nicholas's case a real pump and two washing tubs. 'That's the London plan,' Crummles tells Nicholas. 'They look up some dresses and properties, and have a piece written to fit them. Most of the theatres keep an author on purpose.' On purpose, that is, to do the actor-manager's bidding. And if Nicholas was not required to produce an 'original' piece, he would be translating and freely adapting French plays to bring out the strengths, such as they were, of Crummles's hopeful band of Thespians. Dickens knew that Shakespeare's occupation had degenerated to improvization and anecdotage.

But with the rise of the serious drama during the 1890s there was the concomitant rise of the serious dramatist, who was seriously determined not to be the lackey of a dictatorial actor-manager in the production of his plays. The rise of this new breed of playwright-director and the commensurate decline of the actor-manager has already been noted; one may now add that as far as the serious playwright was concerned the actor-manager was only half the battle: the other half was with the censor.

Two prime examples of the censor's repression occurred in 1906 and 1907 – two proscriptions that individually and in combination contributed substantially to the mounting crisis. The first victim was *The Breaking Point* by Edward Garnett. *The Breaking Point* was not a good play and, according to Purdom, Barker turned it down for the Court, but Frederick Harrison accepted it for the Haymarket. Redford rejected it. A year later, when Garnett published the play and included in his preface an account of Redford's high-handed action plus his retaliatory 'Letter to the Censor', the public could see for itself how arbitrarily the censorship operated. The plot of Garnett's play was 'modern' in that the heroine has an affair with a married man whose wife has left him, her lover quarrels with her father over control of her and she, fearing that she is pregnant, throws herself into the river and drowns. But if this challenged prevailing mores, it went no further than – to cite three examples at random from the major commercial playwrights of the time – Jones's *The Liars*, Pinero's *Gay Lord Quex* and Sutro's *John Glade's Honour*, in all of which adultery flirted with, seriously contemplated or committed (and condoned) is the overriding theme. What is more, the woman's suicide in Garnett's play follows honoured precedent, that of sinful Paula Tanqueray, the virtue of whose self-inflicted punishment had earned the dewy-eyed approval of thousands of playgoers and Shaw's undying scorn. But Redford objected to something in *The Breaking Point*, precisely what he refused to say, and this was final.

The second example was Barker's *Waste*. In this, the protagonist, Henry Trebell MP, a politician of the future, a statesman in the making, has a casual affair. The woman becomes pregnant, procures an abortion, and dies. An enemy manoeuvres Trebell's dismissal from the Shadow Cabinet and he commits suicide. As in Garnett's play, the 'wicked' are punished for their 'sin', yet Redford refused to grant *Waste* a licence, thereby contributing in his unique way to the failure of the Vedrenne-Barker campaign at the Savoy.

Barker had the right as director to demand an explanation and Redford told him that he had found the 'extremely outspoken references to sexual relations' and the references to 'an illegal operation' objectionable.[1] All references to this illegal operation, said Redford, would have to be expunged from the text before he would reconsider his decision. As Samuel Hynes comments, '[S]ince the plot turns on the abortion, Redford's demand [was] rather like asking the producer of *Hamlet* kindly to remove all mention of regicide.'[2]

When giving evidence before the Joint Select Committee on Censorship in 1909, Redford testified that in his time he had, he thought, recommended 43 refusals out of a total of some 7000 plays submitted for licensing; of those 43 'at least' 13 or 14 had been reconsidered and issued with a licence.[3] This is a minuscule proportion and, to the extent that a statistic can be taken to reflect the whole truth of a situation, scarcely an indication that the Examiner was a capricious tyrant. But this evaded the point, which was the kind of play regularly being vetoed: Maeterlinck's *Monna Vanna*, Brieux's *Maternité* and *Les Troix Filles de M. Dupont*, Shaw's *Mrs Warren's Profession*, Ibsen's *Ghosts* and Housman's *Bethlehem*, all of which had been privately produced. In other words, the most challenging pieces by some of the best modern dramatists plus, occasionally, the best of classical drama when *Oedipus Tyrannus* was also refused a licence. When Garnett's and Barker's plays joined this elect band, it was like a long-awaited signal. Redford had over-reached himself; concerted action was now imperative. As Shaw told Lena Ashwell, 'Pinero, Barrie and the rest of us are working like Trojans to get at the Censorship from above'[4] and representation was made immediately for a delegation of playwrights to meet the Prime Minister to voice their objections. At the same time, on 29 October 1907 and pending the meeting with the Prime Minister, a letter of protest signed by 71 playwrights was placed in *The Times*.

As one would expect, it is a good letter – measured, all-embracing and cogent. This, the playwrights announced, was a formal protest against the office of censor, instituted for political, not for so-called moral ends to which that office had been perverted. They protested against the power in the hands of a single official, who judged without a public hearing and against whose dictum there was no appeal; whose power was such that he could cast a slur on the good name and destroy the means of livelihood of any member of an honourable calling. The censorship was not being exercised in the interests of morality; it was relieving the public of moral judgment instead. The playwrights asked to have their art placed on the same footing as every other art, that they as dramatists be placed in the same position enjoyed under the law by every citizen. To achieve this, the licensing of plays had to be abolished.

The names among the 'one-and-seventy' included well-known and less well-known playwrights; also eminent men of letters whose calling was not primarily (if ever) to the stage, but who obviously felt that a show of solidarity was essential: Conrad, Hardy, James, Meredith and Wells catch the eye. It is an impressive list; those who, like Barrie, Pinero and Sutro, would not ever come within a mile of offending the censor add the weight of their respectable reputations to that of the disreputable radical element like Barker, Housman and Shaw, who had already been found grossly lacking in the proprieties prescribed by Redford. Writing to Murray a few weeks before, Shaw had said of the projected letter to *The Times*: 'We shall get in one blow, and one only; and it must be a smasher.'[5] This was the 'smasher'. In the event it did not do as much smashing as perhaps Shaw expected, but it certainly had an effect. No politician could afford to ignore such a formidable list, still less when, four months later, on 24 February 1908, on the eve of the meeting with the Home Secretary, Gladstone (not the Premier Campbell-Bannerman, who was ill), *The Times* published another letter, a statement of solidarity with the playwrights, signed by a galaxy of public personalities – 72 in all – ranging from Baring, Belloc and Beerbohm through Churchill, Gosse, Haggard and Lytton to a strong Fabian line-up at the end of the alphabet in Walker, the Webbs and Whelen. There can be no doubt that these letters contributed to the process that would culminate in 1909 in the setting up of the Joint Select Committee to look into the question of stage censorship.

More immediately, these letters got people to think and take up positions pro and con. *The Times* appended a special leading article to the letter of 29 October, in which it argued mainly against the anomalies regarding the performance of religious works; Galsworthy wrote to the same paper on 1 November stressing the claim of dramatists for their rightful freedom, not – he insisted – the licence, of the pen; Oliver Lodge resuscitated Milton's *Areopagitica*. The cons were not idle. On 15 November the Theatrical Managers' Association passed a resolution that the censorship should not only be retained but made more far-reaching, and on 18 November the celebrated author of *Dracula*, Irving's former secretary Bram Stoker, told the Authors' Club that the cry for the abolition of the censor was not the cry of the honest citizen. To the credit of the Authors' Club, he was not enthusiastically received.

The deputation of dramatists met the Home Secretary, Herbert Gladstone, on 25 February 1908. Shaw was a glaring absentee. One wonders whether his colleagues had tactfully prevailed on him to stay away, or whether he had decided on his own that his presence – and his inevitable contribution to the discussion – would be a distraction. Barrie introduced the deputation, Pinero delivered the principal argument in favour of the abolition of the censorship, Gilbert offered an alternative measure involving a court of appeal: all in all, their message amounted to a substantial restatement of the letter to *The Times*.

In replying, Gladstone was as speciously sympathetic and non-committal and woolly as only a politician can be. He felt diffident about handling the matter; the censorship was a complex matter, being one of those curious questions operating under the law although no executive branch of the government had as its duty to administer that law. He had made a note of the proposals as to a court of appeal and would convey this suggestion to the Prime Minister when he reported to him on the proceedings.

That ended the meeting. Barker had written to Murray a few days before, complaining that it was a nuisance to appear before

Gladstone, who was an ass. Gilbert and Pinero as the designated spokesmen should be left to do the job as best they could – except that they, especially Gilbert, '[A]re so terrified at being mixed up with the disreputable drama that, at the word "Shaw" so to speak they perform evolutions suggestive of flight.'[6] After the meeting, Barker would have been confirmed in his opinion of Gladstone and felt that he and his associates had accomplished very little, if anything.

One man was determined not to perform evolutions suggestive of flight. Shaw. His confrontation with the censor had scarcely begun.

## II

Shaw's first apparent reference in print to the dramatic censorship was in 1889 when, as Corno di Bassetto, he contributed to a public discussion about the 'want' of a censor of comic songs in music halls. He invited his readers to hear him gnash his teeth over the question. '[The censor] will, I hope, excuse me if, in the exercise of my duty as a critic, I describe his function as an unmitigated nuisance. I repeat, an unmitigated nuisance.'[7] Six years later, when drama critic for the *Saturday Review* and the author of several plays, he would go well beyond such facetiousness and regularly typify the censorship in the person of E. F. Smyth Pigott as an object of surpassing ridiculousness; and when Smyth Pigott died in February 1895, he exceeded his customary sarcasm to commemorate his passing with a swingeing attack on his career as Examiner and the function he had fulfilled. Entitled 'Down with the Censorship!', the feuilleton appeared in the *Saturday Review* of 2 March 1895; it was an impassioned yet cold (many would have said heartless) demolition job, patently calculated to shock readers into awareness of the iniquity of a system that maintained the censorship. 'His official career in relation to the higher drama was one long folly and panic.' As for his evidence to the 1892 Commission of Enquiry, it was 'one of the most irresponsible occasions of his official career'. In conclusion:

It is a frightful thing to see the greatest thinkers, poets, and authors of modern Europe – men like Ibsen, Wagner, Tolstoi, and the leaders of our own literature – delivered helpless into the vulgar hands of such a noodle as this amiable old gentleman – this despised and incapable official – most notoriously was.[8]

Strong stuff and Shaw knew it: '[T]he most abusive article ever written on a recently dead man,' he told Charles Charrington,[9] which was as much as to assert, with rather obvious bravado, that the proprieties could go hang when the question of the dramatic censorship arose.

He looked ahead to the appointment of the new Examiner. The Lord Chamberlain would have to appoint somebody like Smyth Pigott, 'a nobody whose qualifications, being unknown, can be imagined by foolish people to be infinite.'[10] The truth of this paradox was soon borne out. Shaw and other playwrights got their nobody in George Alexander Redford, a former bank manager and friend of Smyth Pigott's – qualifications enough in the Lord Chamberlain's view.

He and Shaw were bound to cross swords sooner or later. The duel began with *Mrs Warren's Profession*, which Shaw wished to license for a copyright performance pending publication of *Plays Pleasant and Unpleasant*. He did not expect the play to be passed, but he expected at least a response that would guide him in 'cleaning' the text, a legitimate expectation. He said as much to Janet Achurch, 'If Redford objects to Mrs W. I shall ask him to blue pencil what he objects to, or make Mrs W. a washerwoman or a pickpocket or whatever will enable him to licence enough of the text to protect me.'[11] As expected, Redford rejected the play. Shaw wrote to Redford. He had anticipated the refusal of the licence but could the case not be dealt with by a blue pencil? He then suggested where blue-pencilling could be applied. Such a 'drastic expurgation' as he was suggesting would be less objectionable from the Lord Chamberlain's point of view and his own than an uncompromising veto.[12] His letter was courteous, sensible and not remotely confrontational. Redford's reply was neither courteous nor sensible, and it was confrontational. He had already issued 'an uncompromising Veto' to *Mrs Warren's Profession*, he told Shaw. 'Most certainly it is not for me to attempt any 'dramatic [sic] expurgation' with the blue pencil, as you appear to suggest. It is for you to submit, or cause to be submitted, a licensable play, and if you do this I will endeavour to forget that I ever read the original.'[13]

Shaw's heavily sarcastic public response appeared on 2 April 1898 in his *Saturday Review* feuilleton. He praised the Examiner's business capacity, because, having already paid two guineas for the first refusal, he, Shaw, now had no option but to 'debauch [his] own play with [his] own hands' and then to resubmit it together with another two guineas. And yet more two-guinea handouts would be demanded were he reluctant to obliterate every syllable that gave moral purpose to the play and reduce it to mere sensational brutality. So Shaw had 'expurgated' *Mrs Warren's Profession* until it was 'as gratuitous an offence against good manners as any dramatist was ever guilty of' and Redford, presumably managing to 'forget' the original, had licensed it. This travesty had then been given its copyright performance; the original version would soon be published (as it was, in *Plays Pleasant and Unpleasant*, on 19 April 1898) 'without the omission of a single comma'. Shaw continued:

> And for the life of me, absurd and extortionate and obscurantist and indecent and hypocritical and purposely tyrannical and evil as the whole institution of the Censorship is, I do not see what else Mr Redford could have done, or why he should expurgate any play when he has the power to make the author do it himself, in addition to paying twice over for having it done by somebody else.[14]

The dramatic censorship had always been an important but comparatively remote issue to Shaw. Redford's treatment of *Mrs Warren's Profession* made it immediate and personal. It was not the veto in itself, although this was galling enough, but the manner of Redford's refusal which would have bitten deeply. This was insolence of office, an impugning of artistic integrity, to which few people, least of all a man of Shaw's intellectual pride, could acquiesce. From then on, throughout the Edwardian years and until the end of his life, he would castigate the dramatic censorship (later the film censorship) with the intensity of one with a personal wrong to redress.

He did not keep the issue at boiling point all the time. This would have been bad tactics; but he kept it simmering and ready for use whenever occasion arose. There was a long letter in the *Topical Times* on 24 November 1900, in which he tore into a certain Charles Heneage for suggesting that the Examiner should be a 'nice respectable gentleman' who had written a book and dined out in good society. And there were one or two other occasions for similarly forthright criticism of the Examiner himself or those benighted souls who inscrutably expressed themselves in favour of his function. During these years, of course, several of Shaw's plays, referred to Redford by Barker for performance at the Court Theatre, were being licensed, a fact Shaw would come to acknowledge with appropriate expressions of surprise.[15] His manifold 'immoralities' thus escaping censorial objection (though not censorial query), he may well have decided to stay his hand, at least until Redford behaved really outrageously.

The first opportunity arose when the Lord Chamberlain (not Redford, ironically enough) temporarily banned *The Mikado*. Shaw used the occasion to contribute 'The Solution to the Censorship Problem' to the *Academy* on 29 June 1907. That he recognized a 'problem' indicates some shift of perspective, and in fact he shows himself less dogmatically inclined to debunk the censorship than previously and, most surprising of all, the looks he casts on Redford are almost benign. Something must have happened to bring this about, and of course something had happened – in the person of Anthony Comstock in censor-free America and Shaw's transatlantic set-to with him over *Mrs Warren's Profession*. Comstock had induced Shaw to revise his attitude. Accordingly: 'A wise control of the stage by the community is very much to be desired indeed,' he says, abolishing in one sentence the principle of total abolition on which he had staked his all for over a decade. But by whom should this 'wise control' be exercised? Not by the Examiner of Plays, whose rule, exercised in good faith though it might be, resulted in anomaly, inconsistency and contradiction, and not by unchecked Comstockery which in America resulted in the persecution of all the arts in the form of police raids. 'With respect to all those who vote for the abolition of the censorship *sans phrase*, I prefer Mr Redford to Mr Comstock, and the Lord Chamberlain to Holy Willie.' Shaw's solution then was 'the municipality as the best censor within reach'. What about Redford? Shaw banished him into retirement on a handsome pension with leisure to write the perfectly moral plays he had failed to extract from other playwrights.

The article reflected an unusually meliorative Shaw. The mood would not be allowed to last, however, and is in retrospect a Shavian aberration. The reason for this was that Redford, showing no inclination to retire, showing instead that he could and would out-Comstock Comstock himself when given the chance, refused to license Barker's *Waste*. Shaw, casting benignity to the winds, casting aside as well all thought of municipal control, unfurled and raised his 1890s banner of 'Down with the Censor!' and charged at his enemy.

The first article that declared his return to the colours – it was technically a letter of article length – appeared in the *Nation* on 16 November 1907, and it was the specific 'transgression' committed by *Waste* that formed the basis of a good deal of Shaw's argument. Redford had no option, being a mere mortal, than to legislate according to certain rules. What were these rules? The first and most intolerable rule, which Shaw would challenge 15 months later in *The Shewing-Up of Blanco Posnet*, was that dramatic art was too unclean a thing to be religious. Then there were three more rules (Shaw starts calling them 'taboos'), all dealing with the question of sex. A playwright must never mention an illegal obstetric operation; he must never mention incest; he must never mention venereal disease. Skirt such taboos and no matter how vicious the play, Redford would license it; flout such taboos and no matter how serious the play, Redford would veto it. *Waste* was a case in point; here Barker had flouted taboo number one, the illegal obstetric operation, and Shaw defended the play against the censor's veto in the strongest terms. Incest, the second taboo, had been an issue in *Mrs Warren's Profession*: the result, prohibition. Then, the third taboo, venereal disease, had earned Brieux the same distinction. Ibsen's *Ghosts* qualified for a double prohibition by flaunting both venereal disease and incest. The sensible course was obvious: 'Abolish the censorship of plays altogether, root and branch … [L]et the play be born and take its chance with the consciences of men just as it came from the conscience of the author.' There is no mention of Comstock here; apparently playwrights would have to take their chance with that public-spirited gentleman along with the rest.

Another letter followed in the *Nation* three months later, on 8 February 1908, in which Shaw defended the sexual taboos he had identified and pointed to the copyright performance of *Waste*, performed a week or two before, where the censor 'had the play altered for the worse, and then guaranteed it as being altered for the better'.

There the matter had to be left to rest. Public interest was waning, the playwrights were preparing for their meeting with Gladstone. Shaw fell silent. One would have to wait and see what the government did about the matter.

The government did not seem inclined to do anything at first, partly because Campbell-Bannerman, in ill-health when the deputation met Gladstone in late February 1908, resigned from office on 4 April (he died on 22 April), and his successor Asquith, working himself into the premiership, would not have been disposed to regard the dramatic censorship as a high priority in affairs of state. However, English playwrights (and Shaw in particular) had a friend in the House of Commons. This was the sometime playwright, the author of the ill-fated A *Question of Age* at the Court Theatre, Robert Vernon Harcourt. It will be recalled that Harcourt had been described as 'dramatically, Mr Shaw's godson'.[16] Given this cosy relationship, did Shaw privately egg this putative godson of his on to raise the question of the dramatic censorship in Parliament, while he, Shaw, simultaneously raised the question outside Parliament by writing and submitting to Redford two potentially censorable plays? Quite possibly: it is an attractive supposition.

The facts are that in April 1909 Harcourt introduced a Theatres and Music Halls Bill designed to abolish the dramatic censorship in Britain. He continued to ask questions about the censorship until in June Asquith agreed to appoint a Committee of the two Houses to consider the matter. Although nothing had come of previous joint committees, the playwrights of Britain had reason to hope that something would come of this one. They had protested long and vehemently; informed liberal opinion was strongly behind them; the Edwardian age cried out to be rid of those rusted shackles of eighteenth-century Whiggism. Or so the more progressive elements believed.

And the other facts are that at the time this was taking place in Parliament Shaw submitted two one-act plays, *The Shewing-Up of Blanco Posnet* and *Press Cuttings*, for licensing and Redford rejected them both.

III

Shaw wrote *The Shewing-Up of Blanco Posnet* between 16 February and 8 March 1909. It was intended for Beerbohm Tree for production at His Majesty's Theatre, where Tree was running an 'After Noon Theatre' programme of more or less advanced plays; as Shaw described Tree and this programme: '[T]he first of our successful West

End managers to step into the gap left by the retirement of Messrs Vedrenne and Barker from what may be called National Theatre ...'[17] High-sounding words, written after Redford had vetoed the play and Shaw was projecting an image of himself as a grievously injured victim of censorial persecution. This is genuine enough: Shaw *was* injured by the veto; so was Tree and his After Noon Theatre; so was the children's charity for which the matinee had been intended; so too, Shaw would have liked his readers to infer, the cause of the National Theatre. And his grievance was also genuine in that *Blanco Posnet*, though not a major play in the canon, is not trivial.

On the contrary, as a 'Sermon in Crude Melodrama', as Shaw subtitled the play, it is a serious enquiry into the nature of grace (and of the often inexplicable ways of God), but Redford, unmoved by this, demanded emendation or excision of two offending passages. One, where Blanco accuses the 'fair Euphemia of immoral relations with every man in this town', was 'obscene' in Redford's opinion; Shaw was prepared to emend this. The other was 'blasphemous' – a much more serious matter – and had to be cut. This is the exchange between Blanco and Elder Daniels where Blanco describes God as a 'sly one ... a mean one' who 'plays cat and mouse with you' and then, 'when you least expect it, He's got you ... The laugh is with Him as far as hanging me goes.'

Have these offences removed, Redford told Tree, and he would issue the licence. It was *Hamlet* without regicide all over again. Like Barker before him, Shaw refused the invitation.

A paradox, almost a contradiction, lurks here. Shaw knew he was treading proscribed ground with the play. *Blanco Posnet* palpably broke the rule that he himself had enunciated in the letter to the *Nation* already cited: 'First and most intolerable, the infamous rule that dramatic art is too unclean to be allowed to be religious.' Seeing this and knowing Redford as he did, would Shaw not have been able to predict the verdict? If he could, did he not use Tree as a means of baiting the censor?

The answer to both questions is no – and yes. Shaw's assurance to Tree that the play would be passed was not a calculated lie. He rather hoped it would be. He was never duplicitous; but he could be manipulative, and he used Tree as a powerful ally in manipulating Redford. Tree was the pre-eminent actor-manager of the day and on the fringe of receiving a knighthood, the exemplar of theatrical respectability. Shaw probably hoped Redford would succumb to the enormous prestige that underwrote Tree's application. If this were to happen, the dyke would be breached at its strongest point, the censorship would be seen to be giving way and, precedent established, the advanced drama would sweep in, sweep over the censor himself and cover the land.

A fond hope. Reputation and prestige meant nothing to Redford; the rules meant everything. Tree had to withdraw, probably embarrassed and vexed; also, quite likely, angry with the playwright responsible for his loss of face. But Shaw, the gamble having failed to pay off, proceeded immediately to capitalize on the setback with as much vigour as his propagandist skills could muster. Now was the time, now that the censor had declared himself, to bring things to a head, and the greater the publicity and comedy he could extract from the situation for himself and the greater the embarrassment and discomfiture he could inflict on Redford the better.

He began by issuing a statement to the press. The *Observer* took it up. Shaw went over Redford's head, to his royal master; here and in subsequent letters he played the royal theme with aplomb, modifying it only slightly after the noted jurist Sir Harry Poland pointed out that the Examiner of Plays received his powers from Parliament, not the King:

> The decision whether a play is morally fit to be performed or not rests with the King absolutely, and I am not in the King's confidence. To write a play too vile for public performance ... is as grave an offence as a man can commit, short of downright felony ... I presume the King would not hold up Mr Tree and myself before Europe and America as guilty of this disgraceful conduct unless he had the most entire confidence in his own judgment or that of his advisers.[18]

This was the beginning; thereafter, in contributions to *The Times* in particular, he pressed his case against the dramatic censorship with insistent, persistent urgency. 'I have no remedy except to state my grievance; and because this grievance happens to lie technically against the King, I am told that it would be in better taste for me to suffer in silence. I can only reply that suffering in silence does not agree with my temperament.'[19] No doubt there were many who muttered that he could say that again.

One of his intentions was to rekindle public awareness of an issue which had lain more or less dormant for over a year and galvanize his colleagues into supportive action. Harcourt was doing his bit in the House of Commons; the anti-censorship lobby outside Parliament had to be roused to add its voice to Shaw's. He did not get a revival of the storm of protest of December 1907, but responses showed continuing awareness of the need for change. Hankin wrote to *The Times*, so did Galsworthy, so did others.

Shaw meanwhile was rhetorically asking how

> a certain Mr George Alexander Redford, who describes himself as 'the King's Reader of Plays,' levies a play-tax of two guineas (or one guinea for a one-act play), and carries on his operations at St James's Palace, can be prevented from compromising the Crown in this manner, and from causing the public to believe that his conviction that I am a blackguard and a blasphemer is the King's conviction?[20]

Redford wrote in sniffily to inform Shaw that he was not the 'King's Reader of Plays' but the 'Examiner of Plays', but made no attempt to deny that he, or for that matter the King, thought Shaw a blackguard and blasphemer. Shaw apologized for his error and unabashed went on to say: 'Parliament can control [Mr Redford] only in the sense that Parliament can starve the King out by repealing the Civil List Act, which I understand it is not willing to do for the sake of getting Blanco licensed.'[21]

Meanwhile *Blanco* had crossed the Irish Channel to Dublin. Its adventures in that city were possibly even more hair-raising and hilarious than in London, but in the end, with Shaw on holiday in Parknasilla watching the goings-on in delight, his two redoubtable deputies, Lady Gregory and Yeats, won their way and the play was put on at the Abbey on 25 August. It was a theatrical triumph, a triumph over the Lord Lieutenant of Ireland, whose deputy had attempted to ban the performance, and – so Shaw would have thought – a triumph over Redford. He suggested to Annie Horniman in Manchester that she apply for a licence for *Blanco*, submitting the text that had been used at the Abbey Theatre. Redford turned it down.

In London, Shaw was continuing his campaign, switching from one issue – that of *Blanco Posnet* – to another – that of *Press Cuttings* – with fluent change of gear. He announced the new suppression in, as usual, a letter to *The Times*. The headline is 'The Censor's Revenge':

A few weeks ago one of the most popular of London actors and managers was found guilty by the Lord Chamberlain of attempted blasphemy, and mulcted and suppressed accordingly. To-day the King makes that manager a knight ... An hour after I read in *The Times* of Sir Herbert Beerbohm Tree's triumph the counterblow fell on me (the accomplice in Sir Herbert's blasphemy) in the shape of the Lord Chamberlain's refusal to licence my sketch entitled *Press Cuttings* ... It only remains for the King to make me a duke to complete the situation.[22]

This new suppression provided fuel of a fresh and different kind for Shaw. He wrote *Press Cuttings* between March and May 1909 for the London Society for Women's Suffrage. The censor's veto meant that public performances were out of the question, but the other option within the law, private performances, was available. A spurious but legal Civic and Dramatic Guild was hurriedly formed and two matinee performances of the play took place at the Court Theatre under the aegis of this Guild on 9 and 12 July. So as matters turned out the London Society for Women's Suffrage had its play, but it had been a tremendous bother and Shaw was in no mood to let Redford off the hook. Not when his adversary had again demonstrated his predilection for asinine decisions.

This time, Shaw told the *Observer* of 27 June, his offence was not blasphemy but, in Redford's words, 'personalities, expressed or understood', an allegation which was totally beyond comprehension or even conjecture. The presumed personalities in *Press Cuttings* – the Prime Minister Balsquith and the Army Chief, General Mitchener, who may or may not have been a composite of Balfour and Asquith in the first instance and Kitchener or Roberts in the second – had done duty time and again without offence in the pages of *Punch*. Redford had also drawn his attention to the rule 'No representation of living persons to be permitted on the stage.' Shaw himself had been represented on the stage, with the Lord Chamberlain's full approval, on more than one occasion.

Shaw mentions two such representations, the first a 'little fantasy' by Barrie, a 'very charming little sketch, "Punch and Judy",' which had featured 'a person called Superman, an unmistakable and confessedly humorous skit on myself.' Barrie's skit was actually entitled *Punch* and the person was called Superpunch; but Shaw was right in that Superpunch was an unmistakable take-off of himself. *Punch* was produced at the Comedy Theatre in 1906 in a triple bill that included another Barrie skit, *Josephine*.[23]

Another representation of Shaw on stage was the Court production of *Man and Superman*, in which Barker as Tanner was made up to look like Shaw.

A third occasion was a skit, *Shakespear v. Shaw!* by J. B. Fagan, presented as part of a benefit afternoon for the actor H. B. Conway at the Haymarket on 24 May 1905. Here Shakespeare sued Shaw for libel and was awarded damages of one farthing. Shaw and Shakespeare, played by Edmund Maurice and Cyril Maude respectively, contributed their measure of levity to what was evidently a very successful entertainment.[24]

These two skits, one in 1905 and the other in 1906, indicate the force of Shaw's impact on the theatre and on public awareness at the time. More to the point, they indicate that as far as Redford was concerned the theatrical profession could represent itself on stage to its heart's content without invoking his admonition; also, that if the personality represented happened to be Shaw, he would not lift his blue pencil by so much as a millimetre to protect the smiling victim.

Shaw's quarrel with Redford had little to do with the fact that he had permitted Fagan and Barrie to depict him, however; it had rather to do with the fact that one of the companion pieces to *Punch*, Barrie's *Josephine*, was pointedly political. Political personalities were quite a different matter from theatrical ones: political personalities were sacrosanct; even so, Redford had licensed *Josephine*, by doing which, in Shaw's eyes, he had set a precedent which would be applied to *Press Cuttings*. Considering that it was a piece of fun in which the personalities were conceived in such farcical and good-natured terms that the alleged originals would have been hard put to identify themselves, Shaw could justifiably expect such a decision.

So why did Redford veto *Press Cuttings*? He was not so stupid as to be unable to know when he was being baited. Censors are supposed to be impervious to criticism, armoured as they are by their conviction of absolute rightness, but Shaw's incessant attacks would eventually have penetrated even Redford's defence, particularly as Shaw's method was to eschew the abstract principle and go for the immediate and the particular, the Examiner of Plays in person, and make him look as foolish as a show of civility and the laws of libel allowed. Redford maintained a tight-lipped silence throughout Shaw's 1909 campaign, but when two technically censorable plays came from that vociferous source he could not but have seen them as yet more censor-baiting – and hit back in the only way he knew how, by vetoing both. Whelen was to confirm this when giving evidence to the Joint Select Committee: Redford, said Whelen, suspected Shaw of trying to bait him with *Blanco Posnet*. He would certainly have seen *Press Cuttings* in the same baleful light.

In the end Shaw got an even greater laugh out of the veto by renaming his two characters 'Johnson' (for Balsquith) and 'Bones' (for Mitchener), the clown and ringmaster of the Christy Minstrels. When Iden-Payne produced the play at the Gaiety Theatre in Manchester on 17 August – Redford having had no legitimate excuse for again refusing the licence – these two names raised a roar of laughter and loud ironic applause from the audience.

By this time Shaw had appeared before the Joint Select Committee on Censorship and suffered a rebuff beside which Redford's actions, infuriating and frustrating though they had been to him personally, paled into insignificance.

IV

The Joint Committee of the two Houses of Parliament appointed to look into the question of the dramatic censorship met in a committee room of the House of Lords to hear evidence on 29 July 1909. The full Committee was present. The chairman was Herbert Samuel; the Lords was represented by five members, the Commons by four. One would not have thought from the unemphatic and orotund way with which *The Times* announced the commencement of public proceedings that this was the culmination of a two-year-long agitation and the moment playwrights had been waiting for since 1737.[25] Here for the first time in 172 years the central question would be the dramatic censorship (although the role of the music halls *vis-à-vis* the legitimate theatre would receive attention), with, on one side, the Lord Chamberlain's Examiner of Plays backed by the vested interest of a large thriving industry in the persons of theatre managers, actors, actresses and others and, on the other side, the playwrights of England. It was an unequal contest on the face of it, but the playwrights were organized for the first time. As Shaw, drumming up support for concerted action, reminded members of the Dramatists' Club, in 1892, when the last Select

Committee was appointed, they had not been organized at all, whereas now they could be well represented and any author who wished to give evidence would be entitled to do so.[26]

Shaw would soon have occasion to make sour fun of the Committee, but it was probably as good a one as Parliament could muster. The Chairman, Herbert Samuel, though still comparatively young (he was born in 1870), had already begun to make a mark in public life – 'a spoilt child of fortune (quite unspoilt …)', as Shaw told him[27] – and he would hold office in several key positions, pre-eminently that of High Commissioner for Palestine in 1920–5, in his public career. He was also a philosophical writer of some distinction. The Lords on the Committee included a distinguished judge, Lord Gorell, and the Commons the popular novelist and former actor, A. E. W. Mason, a certain H. Law, who asked some probing questions, and the initiator of the proceedings, Shaw's 'godson' R. V. Harcourt. These five at least could be expected to bring practical experience and judicial impartiality to the enquiry, although there was also a Colonel Lockwood whose undisguised partiality to the status quo made him an Edwardian version of Colonel Blimp of a later era.

Officialdom spoke first: an Assistant Under-Secretary of State for the Home Office reported that his Office wanted no change, a bad augury for the playwrights. Redford was second. *The Times* did not, on this occasion, give the names of members of the public present, but it is possible to infer the attendance of a few play-wrights and other pro-abolitionists: Shaw was present, so was Archer, so, in all likelihood, was Barker. They would have listened to their adversary's responses with intense fascination; with mounting incredulity as well, no doubt, because if Redford revealed anything of himself in his evidence it was his ineptness.

He was asked about the principles on which he acted. Principles? He did not work by any set of principles; there were no 'principles' which could be defined. He simply brought the 'official view' to bear and kept up the 'standard', basing himself on 'custom' and following the 'precedents of former Examiners'. Yes, he would object to anything that might be offensive to religious sentiments or to crowned heads of other countries. When asked about other matters that might be offensive, he hedged while avoiding such specifics as sexual mores: 'These things are constantly changing. There is no limit to the number of subjects that may be dealt with on the stage.' He did not read a play as though he were a dramatic critic; authors were free to see him to discuss difficulties (Shaw and Garnett would have snorted at this); he treated religious plays on their merits (Housman, author of *Bethlehem*, which Redford had rejected out of hand without having read it, would have snorted at this); personally he did not think it a wholesome thing that politicians should be satirized on the stage (an opportunity for Shaw to snort again); he decided difficult questions mostly on his own authority; he thought a body of appeal against his decisions would be unworkable because such a body would be expensive and it would be difficult to get the right men.

He followed custom in deciding about French and other foreign plays and habitually allowed them a good deal of latitude. He had no knowledge of German, but his wife read plays in this language for him. Pressed to explain and justify this practice, he went on the defensive but Colonel Lockwood gallantly saved him with an interjection: 'You have an interpreter?' 'Precisely,' said a relieved Redford.

Redford continued with his evidence in the first session of the second day. Law questioned him on Maeterlinck's *Monna Vanna*, one of the notable plays on Redford's proscribed list. He had refused to license this on the principle (said the man who did not act on principles) of the immorality of the plot. But was not the whole idea of the play that love is not identical with, but the enemy, of lust? Did Redford call that immoral? 'I certainly consider it immoral from the point of view of the Examiner of Plays.' Garnett's *The Breaking Point* came up for discussion. Redford said the play was refused a licence, 'and when it was privately performed it was almost universally condemned'. Harcourt pursued him: 'Condemned as dull? You know the one scene that was objected to?' said he. 'I could not possibly allude to it here,' a squirming Redford replied. 'Oh, spare our blushes!' Law interjected amid laughter. Alluding to *Mrs Warren's Profession* and D'Annunzio's *La Città Morte*, which were both refused a licence, and Hall Caine's *Christian* and *Die Walkure*, which were passed, Law asked whether it was the Censor's rule that prostitution was not to be alluded to or a procuress introduced on the stage. Redford answered that these were certainly subjects which were against morality. 'Then why did you licence *The Christian*?' 'I am afraid I do not recollect even the plot.' 'Do you refuse a play when a certain subject is treated seriously, and grant it when it is treated in a light comedy fashion, or in a sentimental fashion?' 'I treat a case on its merits.'

The questioning continued on these lines and Redford fell back repeatedly on his stock responses, that he treated cases on their individual merits and was bound by precedents – the 'unwritten laws'.

He was then questioned on the words on the licence 'immoral or otherwise improper for the stage', words which were not in the Act. Redford had to admit that he had always thought they were and had further to admit that he had not investigated whether the rules regulating his decisions were not merely precedents and possibly *ultra vires* or under the authority of the Act of Parliament. This concluded his evidence.

He made an appalling witness. His inconsistencies, his failure to set out a clear-cut policy, the capriciousness of his adjudication, the suspect nature of his touchstones of acceptability, or for that matter the suspect nature of his touchstones of non-acceptability, his reliance on 'custom', 'merits', 'unwritten laws' and 'precedent' recited like a mystic catechism that warded off any possibility of error – all this emerged from his evidence. The playwrights would have seen it as amounting to a total exposure of the man and his function; Shaw said as much to Samuel: 'Redford … does not understand the simplest question'[28] and did not hesitate to knock him down with some well-aimed jabs when his turn came to give evidence, which is more than can be said about the other playwrights, all of whom, Barker included, tended to pull their punches when Redford's name came up.

Archer was the next witness. His evidence was what one would have expected: lucid, unambiguous, rational; as utterly opposed to the censorship as convinced that theatre managers were mistaken to fear the abolition of the function. He mentioned Shaw; many witnesses mentioned him. Among living authors to whom he, Archer, attached the greatest value, Shaw and Barker had suffered most from the action of the censor.

Then it was Shaw's turn. 'He was determined to be the star witness,' Dan H. Laurence comments.[29] Indeed, the public campaign reflected in these pages is not much more than the tip of the Shavian anti-censorship iceberg at this time. He did everything possible, with the untiring thoroughness one associates with all his activities, to muster and drill fellow playwrights, to elicit responses from his translators on the state of the censorship in their own countries, to solicit evidence from influential non-playwrights, to infiltrate the pro-censorship lobby and weaken it from within, to bend the Select Committee itself to his will by bombarding the chairman with advice.

And, working against time, he wrote an 11 000-word statement which he intended to submit to the Committee as part of his evidence. It would supersede Milton, he told Murray.[30] He published the text at his own expense and distributed it among fellow playwrights. He also distributed copies among members of the Select Committee two days before being called to give evidence.

Forearmed like this, he would have felt confident about obliterating Redford.

This confidence was shattered within minutes. He was massively snubbed – rebuffed – by the Committee, not once but twice. The Committee refused to accept his statement: this was the first rebuff. He was considerably taken aback but covered up well, continuing with his evidence and agreeing to appear again when the Committee convened the following Thursday. Later that first day, writing to Samuel, he complained mildly enough: the Committee's refusal to accept his statement was a 'grievance' – 'always a valuable property in an agitation like this'.[31] More than a grievance, however. It was a muzzling – a censorship – of the principal spokesman against the censorship, and Shaw would not, he could not, accept this put-down in dignified silence. Dignified protest was more his line. 'I shall fly to the last refuge of the oppressed: a letter to The Times,' he told Samuel.

This appeared on 2 August, two days after the Committee had refused to accept his statement. It was unlike most of his letters to the press in that he put his usual witticisms aside and presented an unsmilingly formal account of what had happened. His bitterness is apparent: he had asked leave to submit his statement in accordance with a precedent set in 1892; his request had been refused; he could only conclude that the Committee was discriminating against those who opposed the censorship; he had no more copies of his statement to hand out. 'I am sorry; but I cannot afford it. My printer's bill, incurred for the sake of an ungrateful country and a thankless committee, is quite heavy enough as it is.' He would say later that he wrote this letter with full awareness of the status of the Committee and the dignity and importance of the matter with which it had to deal. We may doubt this. Restrained though the letter may have been in Shaw's eyes, it said enough to invite a second rebuff, which came his way with exemplary promptness. The Committee reconvened on the morning of Thursday, 5 August.

Shaw, as had been expressly understood, presented himself for a continuance of his examination. The chairman spoke: 'The Committee desire me to say that as in their judgment your views have been very fully stated in answer to my examination, they have no further questions to ask.' That was that – a rebuff that amounted to a public rebuke. Shaw tried to make light of it, but he would have felt not only humiliated but cheated of his right to argue his case to the full. 'Oh,' he had lamented to Samuel in the letter already cited, 'if parliaments & committees would only do just what I tell them!' As he learnt here to his cost, parliaments and committees would impose a bleaker censorship than even a Redford could devise when they thought their integrity had been questioned, their dignity compromised by a man who was too clever by half.

He would have the last say in his Preface to *The Shewing-Up of Blanco Posnet* which, published with *The Doctor's Dilemma* and *Getting Married* in 1911, gave his version of the events and included the full text of 'The Rejected Statement'. This, his argument against censorship, though unevenly executed, is a classic of its kind; so is his recreation of the story behind the statement, including his racy characterization of individual members of the Committee, of Colonel Lockwood in particular, a bunch of carnations as large as a dinner plate in his buttonhole. All this remains as fresh as paint after ninety years, while the government Blue Book which records the proceedings has mouldered away in forgotten archives.

Nevertheless, it is this Blue Book one should turn to. Shaw's account in the Preface to *The Shewing-Up of Blanco Posnet* is true enough, but it is a retrospective and highly coloured – and biased – version, whereas the official transcript has the virtue of uncluttered verbatim reporting. This is Shaw at a climactic moment in his Edwardian career and it is worth observing him in action.[32]

Samuel began the cross-examination and virtually monopolized the first part of the session. After a few routine questions about the number of plays by Shaw that the censor had refused to license:

> Both as a result of your own experience and on broad considera-
> tions of general policy, do you think that the censorship ought to
> be abolished? – I think that the censorship ought to be abolished
> – I would not say so much on broad questions of general policy
> in the ordinary sense; but owing, if I may put it so, to my abhor-
> rence of anarchism, I want the drama to be brought under the

law and the author to be brought under the law. That is really my meaning. I only mention it because the words 'general policy' do not quite convey my feeling about it.

I notice in the statement of your evidence that you have been good enough to submit to the Committee the following passage: 'Accordingly there has risen among wise and farsighted men a perception of the need for setting certain departments of human activity entirely free from legal interference'? – Yes.

That is in reference especially to the drama and dramatists? – To liberty of the Press, liberty of speech, and liberty of conscience.

Is that not in some degree inconsistent with the doctrine that you desire to bring them under further control? – No, because I conceive law to be the guarantor of liberty …

This initial exchange indicates a desire on Samuel's part both to question Shaw as closely as possible and to accommodate him, while his reference to Shaw's printed statement suggests that he had privately made up his mind, before the request had been made, to accept it as evidence. Shaw on his part seemed to be at ease and at no loss for the cogent, brief response. He trembles on the verge of paradox with his remark about the law being the guarantor of liberty, but the sentiment is so palpably true that no one could conceivably have been confused by it, always excepting Colonel Lockwood. A short while later:

You consider that there should be some form of control in the social interest? – Yes, the law of the land.

We have to consider what the law of the land should be? – Well, I may say that I have gone into the question in the statement that I have made …

And Shaw, citing the precedent of the 1892 Committee, asked the Chairman to allow his statement to be taken up as part of the evidence, to be taken as read and to examine him on the basis of that text. Having refused the request (after discussing it with the Committee *in camera*), Samuel continued to question him. The transcript at this stage suggests that Samuel was embarrassed by the Committee's decision. His first question after the break shows him at a loss, whereas Shaw seems to take the setback in his stride and contradicts him firmly:

I think you were saying that the control that you contemplated
would be greater than that which now exists? – No, that is not so.
The control that now exists is of the most tyrannical and impossible character. Almost any lawful control that you could get
would be less so … [T]he control that at present exists is one
whereby the gentleman whom you have seen here this morning
has absolutely at his personal disposal my livelihood and my
good name without any law to administer behind him. That, it
appears to me, is a control past the very last pitch of despotism.

This was strongly and well put. Samuel continued, drawing his
questions from 'The Rejected Statement,' as though wishing to
allow at least some elements of that text through the back door. Did
Shaw think the present censorship unintentionally gave special
protection to certain forms of impropriety? In what way did the
censorship encourage impropriety? And –

You consider that if the methods of the censorship were
improved the position of the dramatist might be even worse than
it is now? – Yes, I am quite sure it would.
    Why is that? – Because at the present time a great many
extremely immoral plays (and I am using the word now in the
correct English sense; I had almost said in the sense in which it is
*not* used from one end of the Bible to the other) are now passed
and performed because the Censor (I do not know how to put
this quite politely) is not sufficiently an expert in moral questions
to know always when a play is moral and when it is immoral.
Accordingly, he has licensed a great many plays which he would
not have licensed if he had understood them. If you had a higher
class of censorship, if you had more highly qualified men to
censor plays, they would not pass these plays; and my
contention is that the reason why they would not pass them is
that you cannot license a play without really accepting the
responsibility for it … I contend that the more you improve [the
institution of the censorship], the more disastrous it will be,
because the more effectually will it stop the immoral play, which
from my point of view is the only play that is worth writing.

The reasoning is impeccable but one may wonder whether
members of the Committee, unversed in the ways of Shavian
paradox, would have been able to follow him here with first his use

of 'moral' in the customary and then in the non-customary sense. Law came in with a question, also based on the written statement, intended to prompt Shaw to explain his paradox:

By 'immoral' all through, you mean non-customary?
– Yes, I mean non-customary … [W]ith regard to myself as an immoral writer I need hardly say I claim to be a conscientiously immoral writer. I lay great stress on the distinction in the use of the word.

Samuel returned to the question of the law – 'What should the law be?' – and Shaw replied that the ordinary law dealing with obscenity or blasphemy would cover abuse in the theatre and that legal prosecution would be the logical course to follow, but these answers do not appear to have satisfied Samuel who pursued him across the spectrum of hypothetically extreme representations – sexual vice, religious outrage, political effrontery. It is not likely he wanted to force Shaw into a damaging admission, but possibly some members of the Committee thought he did so when Shaw replied that 'any outrage on religion' should be allowed on stage. But his point of view – and the logic underlying this – was crystal clear: he did not propose a substitute for the censorship; he proposed the bringing of the theatre under the ordinary law of the land, 'where there was nothing before but the chaos of the Censor's mind'.

Shaw's responses at this stage were generally fairly long, expressed, however, with customary lucidity. Samuel, on the other hand, though apparently prompted occasionally by his copy of 'The Rejected Statement', either could not or did not want to grasp fundamental issues and gives the impression of fumbling. But after worrying over the question of the law *vis-à-vis* the theatre for some time, he let the matter go and turned to the New York reception of *Mrs Warren's Profession*. Shaw's graphic and characteristically exaggerated account of what happened there leads to the forceful conclusion that the 'impression produced that I am an indecent and unconscientious author is one which will follow me to the very end of my career. I have suffered severe pecuniary loss and a great deal of discredit …'

Would it be possible for a court in England to take a different view of *Mrs Warren's Profession* from that taken by the American court of Special Sessions? Possibly, said Shaw: 'It is a profoundly immoral play ...' Responding to a question about greater or lesser certainty regarding performances of his plays under the law, he said emphatically that he would have greater certainty than now: 'At present I have almost a certainty that my best plays will run great risk of being censored, because I should like to say that the cases in which my plays have been finally refused a licence do not exhaust my dealings with the Censor. Refusal has been threatened in other cases.' If the matter of a dubious play were left to the courts: 'I think that, finally, I should at least have a judge with some sense of law and some public responsibility at his back. I would much rather have to deal with him than with a gentleman who has no legal qualification, and who sometimes has not even the faculty of apprehending what law means.'

Samuel then took Shaw into the territory covered largely by the second part of 'The Rejected Statement' – the attitude of theatre managers to the censorship, the fact that theatres were places where drink was sold and prostitutes gathered, that theatres should therefore be licensed annually by local bodies, but that local bodies should not act as censors in any way. Shaw spoke fluently and at length, but on issues which need not be resuscitated here.

Ibsen's plays came up for discussion. Had any of his plays been censored in England? *Ghosts* had been censored, not only censored, said Shaw, but he believed that Redford had stated it never would be licensed in England. Redford had said that morning that he would be prepared to reconsider plays. This had not been the case with *Mrs Warren's Profession* (or, by inference, *Ghosts*). 'So that apparently there are cases in which he reconsiders and there are other cases in which he refuses to reconsider. In that, as in other things, he has no consistent usage.'

This would be Shaw's last shy at Redford. Harcourt took over the cross-examination and guided Shaw back into territory already covered, but where he probably reckoned certain members of the Committee would have needed more elucidation. The exchange, regrettably brief because the session soon ended, has an almost conspiratorial air about it. Harcourt quoted the last censor Smyth Pigott on Ibsen's plays:

'They are too absurd for words altogether.' ... In your opinion are the plays of Ibsen merely ridiculous plays which can be dismissed in that way?' – Certainly not. They are plays of enormous importance.

From the point of view in which you have used the words 'morality' and 'immorality' you would call them immoral plays? – Exceedingly.

They set up entirely new standards of conduct, which may or may not be right but which certainly is not the accepted standard? – In particular they challenge the existing standard of morality.

Having thus emphasized by association that Shaw's 'immoralities' were in the tradition established by Ibsen, whose standing as a modern master could not be seriously disputed, not even in England any longer, Harcourt returned to the question of an enlightened censorship, and allowed Shaw to stress his belief that this would be worse than the present system of an unenlightened censorship; thence to a consideration of the disadvantage of the dramatic author in relation to a public man enunciating similar ideas:

Dealing with cases of that kind, let us take the case of an author putting forward, I will not say identical opinions, but opinions of the same kind on the same subject [as those put forward by a public man]. Under those circumstances you might reasonably anticipate that a censorship would interfere? – Yes.

A public man of a certain kind – namely a politician or a judge – would be in a better position than a dramatic author for putting forward the kind of subject in the manner which he uses? – Distinctly. And you think that operates detrimentally to dramatic authors? – Yes.

This concluded Shaw's evidence for the day and, as matters turned out, for good. Harcourt's cross-examination gave Shaw the opportunity to clarify two fundamental paradoxes in his argument, and the references at the end to a hypothetical politician or judge are clearly intended to imply a comparison between Shaw as a disadvantaged 'immoral' playwright and Lord Gorell on the Committee, to whose work on the divorce laws Shaw had earlier made an amusing reference, as an advantaged 'immoral' public man.

Why did the Committee reject Shaw's statement? Shaw's belief that he was the victim of discrimination imputes motives to the Committee which its standing and publicly documented efforts to hear all evidence impartially pro and con contradict. One can only guess what was said *in camera* when Shaw's request to submit the statement was being discussed, that some members of the Committee reacted against the inversions and paradoxes contained in, for instance, Shaw's description of himself as an 'immoral and heretical' playwright. If this was an objection, it would have been contested by others and it does not seem likely that such 'heresies' in themselves would have carried the day. Why, then?

The most likely answer seems to be contained in another paradox initiated by Shaw. Writing to Samuel after the rejection, he told him that all his plans for making the report a classical Blue Book, unlike the 'wretched business' of the 1892 Blue Book, were upset. He had got Lord Esher to 'fire off a statement', the Bishop of Birmingham was possibly also available, he wanted to ask the Chief Rabbi to 'weigh in' and Mrs Lyttleton as well. 'Surrounded with such a galaxy, your report would be one of the great successes ... Do you think there is any chance of the decision being rescinded?'[33]

The naivety is startling; and it points to what would surely have been a prime consideration among Committee members, that if Shaw's statement, all 11 000 words of it, were admitted there would be no stopping others, from Lord Esher down to every Tom, Dick and Harry in the theatre business, from inundating the hearings with printed statements. Precedent would have to go by the board if such a prospect threatened. As for Shaw's plans to make the 1909 Blue Book a classical Blue Book in *his* image, this, we may be sure, was discerned and resented by a Committee intent on making it a classical Blue Book in *its* image. The paradox is, then, that Shaw, doing everything possible to ensure the defeat of the Examiner, overplayed his bid for stardom. It was his besetting fault, many would have said, and it served him right for being so pushy.

All things considered, Shaw was given a fair if rather disjointed and repetitious hearing. The suggestion has been made that he 'indulged in a certain amount of paradox-making and foolery' while the tone of the recorded interrogation reflected a good deal of 'irritation' with his behaviour.[34] To the extent that one can determine tone from the transcript, irritation is not evident in Samuel's questions. Quite the opposite. As for other members of the Committee, it is possible that one or two noble Lords and Colonel Lockwood felt themselves being got at by Shaw's use of paradox, but this was instinct with him and one could as well have asked a leopard to change its spots as to ask him, please, to moderate his proneness to cerebral gymnastics of this confusing kind. He once gave Willoughby de Broke a short answer when that Lord asked a silly question, and he tended rather to lay it on with his description of the opening night of *Mrs Warren's Profession* in New York, but for these possible lapses of tone he was lucid, fluent and courteous throughout.

The second rebuff is easier to fathom. It is another guess, but a reasonably well grounded one, that Shaw's letter to *The Times* would have been seen as an abuse of privilege. Those on Shaw's side – Harcourt, Mason, Law and possibly Samuel – would have found it difficult to defend their man, more so when it was apparent that Samuel had taken Shaw through his catechism fairly thoroughly during the first session. So there was truth in the Chairman's dismissal of Shaw; his views *had* already been fairly adequately stated; but it was less than half the truth.

Colonel Lockwood may have imagined that he had done for Shaw when, his carnation blazing, he ceremoniously handed his copies of 'The Rejected Statement' back to the offending author. He hadn't, not by a long chalk. Shaw kept on bobbing up in the proceedings, like an irrepressible sprite. The solicitor representing the Society of West End Theatre Managers conjured up his name in vigorous protest against his allegation that theatre bars tended to be gathering places for prostitutes: an indictment against theatre managers, he spluttered. Frederick Whelen reported that Redford had suspected Shaw of writing *Blanco Posnet* as a blatant challenge to his authority. That, Whelen said firmly, was not so. Beerbohm Tree was ambiguous on the same subject: 'Supposing I had produced *The Shewing-Up of Blanco Posnet* at my theatre and the police had stepped in, it would have given a publicity to the occasion which would certainly have been very distasteful to Mr Bernard Shaw.' Very distasteful, more likely, to Beerbohm Tree; one cannot be certain about Shaw's reaction. W. S. Gilbert did not mention Shaw by name but identified him pointedly in: '... I think that the stage of a theatre is not the proper pulpit from which to disseminate doctrines, possibly of anarchism, of Socialism, or of agnosticism.' Chesterton had a good deal to say about the prohibition on *Blanco Posnet* and *Press Cuttings*. He had read and enjoyed them thoroughly. They were certainly the first two plays by Shaw that were thoroughly conventional. *Blanco Posnet* was suppressed because it was said that the backwoodsman was blasphemous, but what was the good of a backwoodsman if he was not blasphemous? The suppression of *Press Cuttings* was worse still, absolutely comic, beyond his comprehension.

After the drama offered by Redford and Shaw, the hearings tended to peter out into a grinding series of questions and answers, especially when the theatre managers gave evidence; but there were some highlights. The Bishop of Southwark, who argued strongly in favour of freedom of the stage, provided one. Then there was Barker's wearily laconic exchange with Lord Newton:

> Were you much shocked when *Waste* was refused? – It was a great disappointment.
>     You were not altogether surprised? – I am never surprised at the action of the Lord Chamberlain.

There was Galsworthy producing letters from Hardy, James, Wells, Zangwill, Bennett, Conrad and Hewlett, all of whom except Hewlett condemned the censorship, all of whom except James said so in contemptuously dismissive phrases. James's letter is a gem of orotundity in even the shortest sentence: 'We rub our eyes, we writers accustomed to freedom in all other walks, to think that the cause has still to be argued in England.' Then there was Gilbert's much quoted and silly distinction between representation on the stage and in a book: 'There is a very wide distinction. In a novel when you write that Eliza slipped off her dressing-gown and stepped into her bath there is no objection to it, but if that were represented on the stage it would be a different thing.' (Did Shaw, many years later, in the published augmented version of *Pygmalion*, remember Gilbert's remark and have his Eliza undressed and bathed – off-stage?) Finally, providing in his own inimitable way another morning of drama, there was Walkley coming out in favour of the censorship – 'a despot, an enlightened despot' – and arguing so perversely as to produce in at least one member of the Committee – Harcourt – the utmost consternation. Unable to believe his ears, Harcourt questioned him:

> – In general terms, you think the importance of the drama and of all art in this country is very greatly exaggerated. Do you really think, then, that the British nation are an excessively artistic nation? – Indeed, I do not. But I think there is a great deal of inflated talk, and more now than there used to be; that is partly cant and partly the author's own prepossession in favour of art, and these have created a false standard.
> – Do you feel any sense of humiliation in concerning yourself

as a critic with this unimportant art? – No, one must live. (Laughter.)

Walkley named no names, but the villain of his piece, the one most prone in his view to inflated talk and high-sounding cant, would only have been Shaw.

The Joint Select Committee sat for a little over three months and heard evidence from 49 witnesses representing virtually the entire spectrum of cultured thinking England: the government, the churches, academe, the 'audience' (in Chesterton) and, naturally enough, those engaged in the business of theatre. Its *Report from the Joint Select Committee of the House of Lords and the House of Commons on the Stage Plays (Censorship) together with the Proceedings of the Committee, Minutes of Evidence, and Appendices* was issued on 11 November, nine days after the last meeting. Its recommendations were, in brief, and in so far as they affected the status of the playwright, that the Lord Chamberlain should continue to license plays and the Examiner of Plays should be retained, but that it would no longer be compulsory to submit plays for licensing. Such unlicensed plays could, however, lead to prosecution against both the author and the theatre manager if the Director of Public Prosecutions considered them indecent.

No doubt members of the Committee saw themselves as having produced a document that nobly enshrined the English genius for compromise. It was in fact a huge let-down and Shaw was disgusted, saying so at length. The Report merely endorsed 1737 and 1843; not only this, he said darkly, there was the revival of the infamous Star Chamber in the recommendation that the Attorney-General could apply to a Committee of the Privy Council to suppress an unlicensed play thought to be indecent.[35]

If the Report exemplified the Dickensian formula for How Not to Do It, the government went one better and Did Nothing About It. The Report was submitted to Parliament and then shelved, while Redford, then late in 1911 his successor Brookfield, the author of a smutty (and successful) West End play, continued to uphold precedent, the unwritten laws and other secret ways of the office. The struggle would start up anew in 1912, when Barker would take the lead in protesting against the appointment of Brookfield and later against some of his prohibitions. There would be another letter to *The Times* signed by prominent writers. Nothing was done. Yet gradually, almost imperceptibly as the years slipped by and the twentieth century sloughed off the repressions of the Victorian and Edwardian ages – as the Great War violently signalled the break with the past – the Examiner's stranglehold over the theatre fell away. In 1925, nearly 30 years after Redford had issued his uncompromising veto, *Mrs Warren's Profession* was granted a licence. In 1968, 18 years after Shaw's death, stage censorship in England was abolished, the premise on which the 1843 Act was repealed being precisely that of Shaw's campaign sixty years before – that the common law was sufficient protection against abuse.

This was in the future. In the Edwardian years Shaw and his fellow abolitionists would have known only that the forces of reaction had defeated them. The struggle would have to continue.

# 14

# 1910: Shavian Nastiness

I

'I write plays,' Shaw told the Joint Select Committee on stage censorship in the statement the Committee refused officially to read, 'with the deliberate object of converting the nation to my opinions' – of converting the nation, that is to say, to his particular immoralities and heresies. What is more, he says, he would not write plays if prevented from using them for the dissemination of his ideas.[1] The didactic objective could not be more baldly stated. But, one has to ask, was there no other objective, nothing which defined Shaw as someone who wrote plays for performance and demanded at least a modicum of the discipline required by that craft? Shaw is silent on that subject in his 'Rejected Statement', obviously because the statement was not concerned with the art of playwriting; but – although he would discourse on the 'modern drama' and the 'problem play' and 'discussion drama' in broad terms – he was generally silent on the dynamics of the subject as applied to his work, leaving his stage representations to stand or fall on their merits. It does not follow that criticism should be equally reticent. The Shavian play as a play is a crucial consideration, no matter how stuffed with heresies, immoralities and other confrontational items from the Shavian menu it may be, and Shaw took himself seriously as a playwright; perhaps, and in spite of himself, more seriously than he took himself as a reformer.

He also told the Joint Select Committee that he was not an ordinary playwright in general practice. He meant by this that he was not a fabricator of the 'well-made play' intended for the commercial stage. His plays had a loftier purpose and he wrote to that end, disdaining Sardou-esque contrivance. 'Why do you still ... *construct* plays?' he asked Pinero. 'I never construct a play: I let myself rip.'[2] Pinero may well have thought that more construction and less 'rip' would have done Shaw's plays a world of good, and had he ever allowed himself to say so Shaw would have smiled and continued

231

on his way. The point is that Shaw saw infinitely greater scope for himself – for the missionary and artist in him – in what he described as organic growth, that is to say dramatic growth impelled by characters in conflict in a given situation. He put this in a nutshell in a scenario written for Chesterton: once the action has been set in motion, 'The rest of the play will consist of whatever ... people do when you once start them in your imagination. They are all to have fair play & to be taken from their own point of view.'[3] A consequence of this was that his plays, whether the product of the ripping method or of more considered means, set him miles apart from those in ordinary practice; the cloth and cut were different, as unlike the stylish reach-me-downs of the commercial stage as a Jaeger outfit was unlike an evening suit; they were unfashionable (until the Court Theatre made them fashionable for a season or two), nevertheless very consciously fashioned – loose and occasionally a trifle baggy – to accommodate the Shavian world.

Ever aware of the foolishness of throwing the baby out with the bath water, Shaw took care not to abandon the theatrical formulae set up by his nineteenth-century predecessors. His plays were rooted in the theatrical stock-in-trade of the immediate and often comparatively distant past, and in this sense at least he retained ingredients of the 'well-made' recipe, particularly in his early plays, where the situational clichés of comedy and melodrama, subverted to serve Shavian paradox and common sense, are the backbone of his drama. However, at the beginning of the Edwardian years a new impulse may be detected, as though the headlong proliferation of heresies and immoralities had imperatively to be accommodated in a format of increased range and scope, in a play which, if it was 'not a play' in the conventional sense, managed conspicuously well to serve Shaw's expanding needs. This impulse declares itself in the first of the Edwardian plays, *Man and Superman*, where the claptrap romantic situation may provide the situational vehicle but the philosophy urging the advent of the New Man for the new century in intense conflict with Everywoman underpins and gives unique urgency and resonance to the romance. Shavian discussion drama was being born. In the next play, *John Bull's Other Island*, discussion drama was taken a step further; and in the next, *Major Barbara*, it emerged in as stiff a dose of lecturing as a theatregoing public was likely to take at the time. The trend was obvious: a theatre of ideas in which a strong, indeed a gripping, dramatic situation involving groups of interested participants becomes the flashpoint for intense confrontation and argument which lead to a resolution affecting the personal destinies of the participants.

There were thus two imperatives: the one ideological, didactic (in the broadest sense of that often abused word); the other artistic, the play as play. Polarities of intent which Shaw had to find ways of reconciling. The question was, how far could he take the first without jeopardizing the second?

*Don Juan in Hell*, the debate at the heart of *Man and Superman*, seemed to give him his answer. The production at the Court was a triumph and he would have felt that it vindicated his 'new drama' in its most extreme form. That his next play, *Getting Married*, should follow a similar path was probably inevitable. As we have seen, Shaw anticipated and received a practically unanimous veto from the critics, but he was sufficiently encouraged by the public response to believe that discussion as drama could hold its own when buoyed up and propelled by an intriguing situation, vivid dialogue, a range of colourful characters, mastery of comedy and stagecraft and, not least, that submerged formal element of dramatic art about which he was usually reticent. *Misalliance*, his next major play, merely continued and developed this Shavian genre.

That it would also continue and develop critical resistance to the plays goes without saying. Indeed, critical resistance would reach a high point in 1910 in the general condemnation of *Misalliance* and Walkley's measured, magisterial dismissal of Shaw and his kind in *The Times* soon afterwards.

Shaw wrote *Misalliance* because Barrie had persuaded the American impresario Charles Frohman to present a season of 'advanced' drama in repertory at the Duke of York's, one of his London theatres, and Shaw – together with Barker and Galsworthy – was an obvious choice for a contribution. He leaped at the opportunity and seems initially to have had high hopes of the enterprise, telling Pinero that in the long run Frohman's 'batches of authors' would be stronger than any one playwright could be individually and that therefore Pinero should join the 'movement'. He himself, he said, would take care to ticket himself for the top compartment of the repertory plan.[4] But he must have wondered even at this early stage. Frohman, who seems to have laboured under the delusion that avant-garde drama meant *Peter Pan* and *Alice Sit-by-the-Fire*, could have had no premonition of the unrewarding fare, financially speaking, Shaw, Barker and Galsworthy would provide and, in the event, his incursion into repertory lasted only

17 weeks, being saved from disaster at the end by Pinero's *Trelawny of the 'Wells'*.

Shaw began writing *Misalliance*, originally titled *Just Exactly Nothing*, on 8 September 1909 and completed it about eight weeks later, on 4 November. Composition was swift, but he seems to have struggled and, as with *Getting Married*, to have had doubts about it. 'Nothing but endless patter,' he told Vedrenne. 'My bolt as a real playwright is shot.'[5] Then, as usual, after revision, he read it to groups of friends, among them the Webbs and, as usual, Beatrice confided her reaction to her Diary.

> It is amazingly brilliant – but the whole 'motive' is erotic, everyone wishes to have sexual intercourse with everyone else – though the proposals are 'matrimonial' for the most part, and therefore, I suppose, will not upset the Censor's mind. I don't see any good in the play except intellectual brilliancy ... Sidney and I were sorry to see G.B.S. reverting to his studies in anarchic lovemaking. Now cramming these episodes into *one scene* gives an almost farcical impression of the rabbit-warren as part of human life. I don't think a rabbit-warren would be much improved by intellectual brilliancy.

Later she remarked that G.B.S. was 'brilliant but disgusting'.[6] There is no indication whether these thoughts were conveyed to Shaw. If they were, and Beatrice Webb was not the kind of person not to speak her mind, one wonders how Shaw responded. Whatever he may or may not have said, he could well have wondered at the failure of his peers to rise above the man and the moment. To the Webbs, Shaw could be 'supremely clever' but, riddled with flaws as they could plainly see, not remotely a dramatic iconoclast of supreme ability.

The play went into rehearsal in the new year and Shaw's pre-production 'interview' in the *Daily Mail* of 8 February 1910 focused yet again on the critics, first on their denunciation of *Getting Married* and then on how they had been fooled by Shaw and his public. *Misalliance* was just like *Getting Married*, only more so. He had cherished, repeated and exaggerated every feature that the critics had denounced in *Getting Married*. He had gone back to classic form and there was not a scrap of what the critics called 'action'. 'Nothing but Shaw and some very good acting.' The critics would leave the theatre broken men.

When the play opened on 23 February 1910, the critics did suffer, making this plain in their disgruntled notices. Three critics, Walkley of *The Times*, Baughan of the *Daily News* and Cannan of the *Star*, should again be cited ahead of the ruck.[7] Walkley first. The play had prompted three 'thoughts' in him: the first was that it was the debating society of a lunatic asylum. The second thought was to question the first: was this madness after all, or was it rather a crowd of personages each individually labelled fool, brute, bounder, bully, cad, humbug and so forth, all talking? 'And they talk of everything – everything in all Mr Shaw's prefaces, and many things that are not there yet ... Their talk sometimes bores, sometimes irritates, sometimes disgusts – very often amuses, and very often gets home to the bosoms of their hearers.' This brings Walkley to his third thought:

> These people are mainly horrors ... They do not behave as 'people' actually do behave. But in the course of their talk do they not reveal an uncomfortable deal of things which in the silence of the night-time we know to be true to human nature ... do we not recognise – let us say our friends, a little distorted and magnified, but still very like?

The notice is dismissive for the good old Walkleyan reasons, yet it teeters on the edge of more acute perception. One nudge, one imagines, and Walkley would have tumbled half a century ahead of his time to the notion of the absurd in Shavian drama; not only this, but the very absurdities he noted were versions of truths no other playwright of the day could even guess at.

Baughan declared that he did not like *Misalliance* as much as he had *Getting Married*. He had said about *Getting Married* that it showed Shaw sending into the marketplace all kinds of inferior ware and that Shaw was beginning to hold his audiences too cheaply. Baughan had a fallible memory, or perhaps he was one of those critics mentioned by Shaw who routinely condemned him the first time round and then praised him afterwards. The trouble with *Misalliance*, said Baughan, was that Shaw drifted helplessly about among his Shawisms. Some of the wit was poor and cheap and there was too much 'thin talk'. However, if cut by at least a third, the play would be an exhilarating entertainment. Baughan did not say it in so many words, but the absence of 'passion' upset him.

Gilbert Cannan seems to have written most of his notice before-hand. It is a lengthy disquisition on Shaw's many faults, the most heinous of which was his 'deliberate and wicked ignorance of life'. The coda to this was a slashing attack on the play. Cannan wished the characters had drunk sloe gin and been inebriated, a condition he would have preferred to all the talk. The play had no wit, no central idea, the action was revolting, much of the dialogue disgusting. 'Those who run away', he says sententiously, 'are invariably nasty-minded about it. There is a nice way and a nasty way of thinking, doing, and talking about everything in this world, from the most private function of our bodies, to the moon shining on pine-woods and water. Mr Shaw chooses the nasty way. It is not polite.' One would not think from these less than polite comments that Cannan was the author of advanced plays thought to show considerable promise (which was never fulfilled); also, having run away with Barrie's wife not long before, he should, one imagines, have been proof against such 'nastiness' as a middle-aged Shaw dealt out. He may have nurtured a grudge against Shaw, who had rejected one of his plays for the Stage Society, and possibly hoped by this aggressive notice to rouse him to wrathful retaliation. But Shaw was silent, at least for the time being. Opportunity would present itself in due course.

Beerbohm – to touch on one or two of the other critics – said the play induced him to believe he was in Praed Street on a Sunday morning with a keen and unremitting northeast wind against his face.[8] Anyone acquainted with Praed Street even today, and not necessarily on a windy Sunday morning, will know with what 'distressing unloveliness' *Misalliance* struck him. The *Observer* said the play was 'rather horrible'[9] and J. T. Grein of the *Sunday Times*, who had been wringing his hands over his old friend Shaw since *Getting Married*, was brought near to tears.

My admiration for Mr Bernard Shaw and his fame, which I proclaimed in Germany and Holland years before Trebitsch became his translator, does not cow me into fear. I tell him now straight to his face that he is ruining his fame, his record ... that he ruins it in the egotism of mortal man who forgets he is but the image of God ... And now I find that his great mind goes astray, coerces the public at the *fetiche* of his name, to sit in the theatre in torture, to listen to tittle-tattle about everything, and about nothing.[10]

The quaintness of expression (it should be remembered that Grein was Dutch by birth) make this cry more, not less, heartfelt.

All in all, the critical response amounted to a signal to Shaw that this kind of play would not be tolerated. It was a nearly unanimous verdict – quite the most unambiguous rejection he had suffered in his 18 years as a playwright.

He tried to counter all this with a self-drafted interview in the *Daily Mail* of 28 February in which he asked audiences not to applaud and laugh during performances. 'I do not dole out solitary jokes. I fling them out by handfuls; so that if you laugh at the first you lose the next six.' It was his only public attempt to undo the damage done by the critics while the play was still in performance. One has the impression he was tiring of a game which had never been a game to him, although later, when *Misalliance* and *The Madras House* had been taken off after eleven and ten performances respectively, he spoke up again, not angrily so much as wearily, on how critical prejudices had to be lived down at each new production. The play would rise from the ashes of its initial disaster and the critics would change their minds.[11]

Brave words, but the failure of *Misalliance* could well have impelled him to reassess his career. He could not afford to defy immediate augury, not if he wanted to attract audiences to his plays. More than one critic had already said that he was beginning to alienate his audiences; that he had shot his bolt as a playwright (he had said it himself, perhaps not altogether in jest); and there was the undeniable fact that since 1907 his new plays had failed to approach the success of the Court Theatre productions. There was another consideration, underlined by the failure of the Savoy campaign and the Frohman repertory season, that in the absence of an endowed theatre, which is to say a National Theatre, he would find it increasingly difficult to find a stage, let alone audiences, for his new plays. And there were the critics. When every one of them, the hostile, the perplexed and the semi-favourable, condemned such a play as *Misalliance,* sweeping dismissal of their stupidity was no answer. It was self-defeating in the long run, doubly so when the playwright, an avowed propagandist, was subverting conventional dramaturgy in so advanced a way as to leave his audiences in a fog of bewilderment, no matter that they were also amused. Even amusement would turn to irritation if not attached, at least in part, to the known and comprehensible. All this boiled down to the question: had he taken his 'conversation pieces' too far?

The answer to this today would be no. *Misalliance* is now seen as a major play in the canon, an uproarious farce at one level, a densely textured morality underneath the handfuls of jokes. As a much-performed though perhaps not sufficiently or adequately discussed twentieth-century classic, it is perfectly understandable to sophisticated modern audiences, which makes it all the more difficult to understand quite what all the critical fuss was about ninety years ago. To encapsulate the opinions cited above, from Beatrice Webb's 'disgusting' to Cannan's 'nastiness' – and not forgetting Beerbohm's 'distressing unloveliness' – one may see that it offended certain rigidly held mores relating to the proprieties: sexual mores mainly, although other 'unmentionables' – pre-eminently the overriding joke of the play that Mr Tarleton's fortune is based on the manufacture and sale of 'unmentionable' articles of clothing – made the Shavian brew all too strong, too outrageously 'advanced' and 'modern', for the average Edwardian stomach. Then there is the confusing fact that, while nothing strictly 'happens' in the play, what does happen – an aeroplane crashing into the green house, the emergence of a Polish female acrobat possessed of capabilities as formidable as her name (Lina Szczepanowska, no less), the discovery of an irresolute would-be assassin in the turkish bath – is so surreal as to tear into the starched Edwardian imagination and leave it in shreds. Finally, as though to confound the confounded, there is the pace of the piece. One may quote Shaw in this respect, out of Edwardian context but still technically within it, in a 1929 letter to A. K. Ayliff:

> My plays are nothing if not impetuous; and that effect is produced not by hurrying or slurring, but by never letting the current of speech (which is the action) halt for a moment. The audience shouldnt have time to think and should never be kept waiting.[12]

As will be noted, Walkley would preach about Aristotle and Shaw would point out, quite correctly, that the play adheres to Aristotle's dicta in all respects, but the velocity of *Misalliance*, with the dozen or so seminal scenes succeeding one another with unceremonious swiftness, seems to have added to the bewilderment of our Edwardian audience, which subsided dazzled but confused before what seemed pell-mell, arbitrary and utterly without structural unity. As for recognizing that the 'current of speech' was the action, containing within itself the dynamic unity of the play, this was quite beyond its ability. 'Too many notes, Mr Mozart,' the Emperor Joseph II is alleged to have said to the composer of *Don Giovanni*. 'Too many words, Mr Shaw,' was the consensus in Edwardian England.

Walkley had the answer to Shaw's 'problem'. Or he thought he did. He would be beating Shaw over the head with it while *Misalliance* was still running.

## II

Walkley's first attack on Shavian drama appeared in *The Times* on 21 March 1910 under the heading 'Got and the New Dramaturgy', the second, 'Leaving Aristotle Out', on 20 June. Neither article has a by-line, but there is ample internal and external evidence to point to Walkley.[13] 'Got and the New Dramaturgy' launches into its criticism through a notice of the first volume of the French actor Edmond Got's *Diary* in which Got invoked Aristotle's dicta for the drama. How amusing it was, said Walkley, to find a young actor restating these ancient 'laws'. Mr Frohman, he said, ought to be particularly amused, for 'Mr Frohman derides, denies, and defies these "laws"' and wants plays that are not plays. To oblige him Mr Shaw and Mr Barker had each provided him with one for his opening repertory. 'Behold, then, the new theatrical school, our dramatic "intellectuals", dismissing the old "laws" of drama as obsolete, and roundly declaring for a new aesthetic of the stage.'

The objection was not to the introduction of 'ideas' into the theatre. Far from it. Shaw had probably contributed more ideas to the common stock than any of his contemporaries and Barker was also brimming over with them. But, Walkley said, 'the trouble with these many-idea'd gentlemen is that they will not be at the pains to convert their ideas into that organic whole which we call a play.' They distributed them pell-mell among a number of interlocutors who talked Shaw or Barker. 'Plays' were now to be superseded by 'debates'.

But Aristotle's 'laws' were grounded in real human considerations; as Walkley put it, 'in a few elementary principles of psychology relating to *attention*.' He trotted out Aristotle's dicta, or rather his interpretation of them: the attention must be concentrated ('unity of action'), held ('continuity of interest') and kept from flagging by increased stimulus ('cumulative interest'). It was these laws that the new dramatists were ignoring. And the penalty they would have to pay in the long run would be disastrous:

> Wandering attention, boredom, irritation that comes from unsatisfied expectation and a sense of wasted material – these effects are only gradually perceived. But in the end they will tell; and either the new dramaturgy will have to reabsorb what was vital in the old, or else 'debate' itself out to empty benches. But let us hope for the better fortune. Mr Shaw and his friends will, we believe, come to see that they are on the wrong tack. It would be a thousand pities if they allowed the real force which they represent in the theatre – their moral earnestness, their knowledge of actual life, their fresh current of ideas, their brilliant dialectic – to be frittered away through an error of direction.

The second article, 'Leaving Aristotle Out', based on a notice of the second volume of Edmond Got's *Diary*, repeated and insisted on what had been said in the first because Barker's response had been to wish critics would leave Aristotle out. The first article had been solemn and anxious; this one was tetchy, as though Walkley found it necessary to rebuke Barker for his irreverence. He firmly declined to leave Aristotle out. He was a reminder of a human institution of venerable antiquity and not, as some 'advanced' young ladies supposed, invented by Shaw and Barker. He commented on recent remarks by Shaw about the 'vituperation' of the press, adding that it seemed 'to point to a certain degree of real exasperation' which, Walkley thought, was excessive; he expressed the hope that both he and Barker would soon be again in full 'coruscation' – but not, he insisted, by leaving Aristotle out.

Shaw did not respond to the first article. But he replied to 'Leaving Aristotle Out' in a letter to *The Times* on 23 June. He was, he said, no party to Barker's demand for the omission of Aristotle. He took the greatest pains to secure 'unity of impression, continuity, and cumulative force of interest'. Such mastery as he had been able to achieve had led him finally to the Greek form of drama, in which the unities of time and place were strictly observed. He was quite aware that his phrase 'the vituperation of the Press' would be neither accurate nor grateful if the press consisted only of *The Times*, but the invariably damning verdict of the London press at large was such that it had been necessary to hold his plays back from Berlin until the verdict was forgotten. As for critical tributes, these consisted in praising the old plays in order to throw into greater relief the infamy of the new one. Shaw particularized, moving back from *Misalliance* to *Getting Married*, from that to *The Doctor's Dilemma*, and so on, showing how in each case the critics had panned the current play while praising the previous one (also panned in its time) – all the way back to *John Bull's Other Island* – 'poor old *John Bull*, which first established the tradition that my plays are not plays but mere talk!' This kind of treatment turned praise sour for him.

> [I]t is my steady and impenitent purpose to permit myself, whenever, like Mrs Gamp, I feel so disposed, to do with [Walkley's] unworthy colleagues what Heine reproached Lessing for doing – namely, not only to cut off their heads, but to hold them up on the scaffold to show the public that there is nothing in them.

One does not want to inflate the significance of Walkley's two articles disproportionately; neither should one minimize them, because they seem likely to have had some effect on Shaw. The articles were patently induced by the productions of *Misalliance* and *The Madras House* and by what Walkley saw as the critical and public failure of these two plays. One should similarly not be in a hurry to see anything significant in the fact that Shaw did not respond to the first article, 'Got and the New Dramaturgy'. Even so, his silence was uncharacteristic. He always responded; why not on this occasion? Was it because those observations about the limited human capacity for attention, not to mention those phrases about boredom, irritation and debating to empty benches, came uncomfortably close to a reality Shaw was being forced to confront? Quite possibly.

His reply, when it came, is interesting, first, because of his declaration that he took the greatest pains in constructing his plays – so much for the letting-things-rip theory of composition – in accordance with the dicta laid down by Walkley-Aristotle. The pains he took are not in question; what is in question is his success (or failure) to hold audience attention and involvement. This was what Walkley was going on about, what Shaw circumvented in his response. The question recurs: was he taking this kind of drama too far – too far, that is, for the audiences of his day? Was this – in Walkley's phrase – an error of direction?

The second interesting aspect of the letter is the way it focuses closely and fiercely on the critics. It is out of proportion to the immediate cause, Walkley's airy reflections on the subject, but not out of proportion to Shaw's conviction that the critics had hindered and impeded his playwriting career in England, at great cost to his public image and private pocket. One is reminded of the attack at the Criterion Restaurant three years before. During a public address Walkley gave at the time, he regaled his audience with an anecdote about Shaw. *The Times* report of 13 June ran:

> Some years ago he had invited that remarkable dramatist Mr Bernard Shaw to dinner, and when he came there was some delay in admitting him because the knocker was one of those suburban knockers that could be heard all down the street but not inside the house. They asked him why he had not rung the bell, and he answered, 'I would have if it hadn't been for the word Press on it.'

Walkley added that this distrust of the press was now happily a thing of the past. Not for Shaw, it wasn't. His distrust of the press had reached crisis proportions.

*Misalliance* was the last major play of Shaw's Edwardian career. It was followed in 1910 by the enduringly appealing but comparatively slight *The Dark Lady of the Sonnets*, written as a contribution to the National Theatre Movement. The playlet found Walkley in his usual sniffy mood and Baughan regretting, as usual, the absence of 'passion' in Shaw. Gilbert Cannan, the third of our trio of critics, had left the *Star*, but he had done his bit for posterity in that unforgivable notice of *Misalliance*.

III

Four days before the opening of *Misalliance* – on 19 February 1910 – Richard Strauss's *Elektra*, conducted by Thomas Beecham, was given its first British performance at Covent Garden. A coincidental confluence of events, but its occurrence prompted an interesting and rare display of Shaw engaging in unconscious transference, by making an innocent music critic his whipping boy for the theatre critics who had so summarily dismissed *Misalliance*.

*Elektra* aroused enormous interest before, during and after its production and quite overshadowed *Misalliance* as the artistic event of the week; of the month, as well. The critics were enthusiastic, except one, Ernest Newman, whose notice in the *Nation* of 26 February returned an unfavourable verdict. The same paper carried Shaw's response on 12 March in which he requested Massingham, the editor, to request Newman to give his readers something a little less 'ridiculous' and 'idiotic' about *Elektra*. This was the beginning of the famous epistolary duel between the two.

Had the critic been anyone other than Newman, Shaw would probably have ignored the notice. He was past wasting the treasures of his Miltonic mind on the unregenerate. But Newman was a critic of note by 1910, not yet the pundit on matters musical in England and the unchallenged authority on Hugo Wolf and Wagner that he would become, but a force to be reckoned with and perfectly capable of returning blow for blow. Shaw, professional confrontationist that he was, would have seen Newman's standing as making for a good fight, with the public crowding in on it, a prerequisite if his demolition of the man and the dull Philistinism he represented was to reap social and cultural benefits.

Newman's notice of the *Elektra* is thoughtful, considered, sensitive; and his verdict is delivered with evident reluctance and regret. Yet Shaw took violent exception to it. It is not difficult to see why; the offence went beyond music:

All but the Strauss fanatics will admit that, though he is undoubtedly the greatest living musician, there is a strong strain of foolishness and ugliness in him, that he is lacking in the sensitive feeling for the balance of a large work that some other great artists have, and that consequently there is not one large work of his ... that is not marred by some folly or some foolery.

Shaw had read this kind of thing before, time after time, virtually word for word, in critiques of his own work: 'Shaw fanatics ... greatest living playwright ... strong strain of ugliness and foolishness ... lacking in the sensitive feeling for the balance of a large work ... marred by some folly or some foolery.' How often had Archer not said this kind of thing about him; and Walkley; and Beerbohm; and Baughan; and the ragtag and bobtail of theatre critics who presumed to set themselves up as judges of his work? He would have picked up the echo in Newman; more than an echo, considering the clamour of similarly dismissive notices that was then assailing his ears over *Misalliance*; and having picked it up, he would have retaliated. It reveals his state of mind at the time. The New Drama (his own) and the New Music (Strauss's) were one and the same to him, assertions both, each in its own way, of the evolutionary urge to forge a new aesthetic, a new sensibility, for the new age; transference from the one to the other was as easy as winking; demolition of the one (a music critic) rather than the others (the theatre critics) a job to be undertaken with maximum bravura.

There is the opening salvo of 'ridiculous' and 'idiotic' cited above, then a side-swipe at the dullness and insolence of English criticism; then a brisk portrait of Newman as a respectable, if pathetic, figure; a reflection on the ill-breeding of English criticism; a paragraph on how Newman should have done his job; then the rhetorical climax in which he lashes out at

> this lazy petulance which has disgraced English journalism in the forms of anti-Wagnerism, anti-Ibsenism, and, long before that, anti-Handelism … this infatuated attempt of writers of modest local standing to talk *de haut en bas* to men of European reputation, and to dismiss them as intrusive lunatics, is an intolerable thing, an exploded thing, a foolish thing, a parochial boorish thing, a thing that should be dropped by all good critics and discouraged by all good editors as bad form, bad manners, bad sense, bad journalism, bad politics, and bad religion.

Newman, he concludes, is distinguished enough to make him worth powder and shot. 'I can stand almost anything from Mr Newman except his posing as Strauss's governess; and I hope he has sufficient sense of humour to see the absurdity of it himself, now that he has provoked a quite friendly colleague to this yell of remonstrance.'

Newman, as it turned out, did have a sense of humour, but this 'yell of remonstrance' affronted him initially. Shaw's manners were becoming almost as bad as his logic, he said in his response of 12 March. He appealed to Shaw not to talk so dogmatically and offensively of things he knew nothing about (Shaw had admitted to not having yet seen *Elektra*) and to control his bad temper and his vanity sufficiently to save himself from becoming too gross a parody of the case he was attacking. As he would say in a later letter (26 March): '[D]iscussion with Mr Shaw while he is merely yelling is too much like arguing with a locomotive whistle in full blast.'

Now, however, as Shaw's manner had lost something of its blend of 'patronising pedagogue' and 'swaggering bully', he felt more able to argue the matter with him, which he did, fluently, expertly and amusingly.

So the duel continued merrily on its way until, the issue exhausted, the adversaries exchanged words of mutual esteem and disengaged. On the whole Shaw took the honours because he urged Strauss's genius in *Elektra* with greater conviction than Newman could conscientiously deny it. A few years later, Newman would consciously draw Shaw into another public argument about Strauss, but this lacked the urgency of the original confrontation.

This was a not unfitting finale to the epistolary and other duels Shaw fought in these years, for a month after the two adversaries had laid down their pens, on 6 May, King Edward died. The nation went into mourning and Shaw felt compelled to add his elegiac cadences to the hundreds then being published. He wrote to *The Times*. We may recall the brash way with which he had dealt with Queen Victoria's death. It is a different, if not changed, Shaw one sees here. The letter is on behalf of the middle-class family man obliged to deck his three daughters out in full mourning – a calamitous expense, he says, for any man making ends meet on a small income and obliged to keep up a social position above that of the working classes. The remedy is to allow the wearing of a violet ribbon as the appropriate mourning for Royalty, a token that would be correct, inexpensive and pretty. Being Shaw, he had to add that he was among those who abhorred mourning, who had never worn it for their own nearest relatives and made it a point of honour to discourage what they regarded as a morbid attitude towards death. Nevertheless, '[We] are as susceptible as any of the mourning wearers to the sympathy which goes out quite naturally and spontaneously to those to whom the late King's death brings too intimate a loss to be felt for the moment otherwise than as a keen personal grief.'[14] The sumptuary requirement is deplored, the family's sense of bereavement respected.

The Edwardian Age was over.

# 15

# 1910: Edwardian Shaw

Halley's Comet reappeared in 1910, portentously and spectacularly. Shaw had been anticipating that celestial body in himself for some time by then. The author of over twenty plays, most of which had been successfully produced internationally, the author as well of several critical, exegetical, polemical non-dramatic works, a leader among the Fabians whose reputation stood higher at this time than at any time before, a public speaker and debater of consummate skill, many said the finest public speaker in the country, a controversialist, a wit, a polemicist, a man of notable parts, he could know that the challenge of January 1901 had been met and that he had fulfilled his destiny, at least to the extent that his significant presence on earth could not be denied any longer.

The world's press was not backward in conceding this. A self-publicist of supreme skill, Shaw had advanced to the stage where his every word, and there were many, made headlines, not only in London but in other capitals of the Western world. He was famous, he was notorious. He had a reputation.

Reputation is an elusive entity but worth trying to capture in Shaw's case because it was a major element of his career. He said he had no illusions about it, and he once complained to McNulty about the way the press reported him: 'Do you wonder that you cannot open a newspaper without finding some silly lie about me in it, the cumulative effect of all the lies being what you may call my reputation.'[1] Which is all very well, except that he could not have it both ways by disparaging the medium with which he broadcast his messages to the world. If the effulgence of his mind had to light up the dark places of Britain and elsewhere, then a reputation and all the falsehoods that went with it had to be borne as bravely as possible. He perceived the danger while flirting with it, of becoming personally more newsworthy to the public than the books published, the plays performed, the causes fought for.

The cult of the personality is commonplace these days. In the early years of the century, when popular journalism was still warming to its task of creating instant myths about public figures, the idea of personality as a thing-in-itself was almost untested as a commodity for public consumption, and its corollary the 'celebrity', as a being apart from the worth or worthlessness of the occupation, was virtually unknown. A few achieved this dubious distinction at this time. Oscar Wilde did for a few brilliant months in the 1890s. Shaw achieved it during the Edwardian years and retained it for the next forty. The favourite of the press that he became, he was a 'personality' in next to no time and a 'celebrity' the moment his plays pointed him out as a being of social 'significance'. We may recall Beatrice Webb's acidulous comment about his new-found status – 'the adored one of the smartest and most cynical set of English Society' – but she also said, his self-conceit being as complete as it was, he was proof against flattery. Thus armed, he allowed himself the luxury of being in the public eye, reported on, quoted, misquoted, misrepresented. It was all one to him.

The issue for us is whether his reputation and its attendant horrors became ends in themselves for the public at large; or whether the personality was subsumed in the larger issues that Shaw made his own. Once all the ballyhoo is eliminated what does one see, what measure of substance? Our first gauge is Shaw's Receipt Book, occasionally referred to in these pages, and now worth closer scrutiny as a measure of his success (or failure) as an author and practising playwright.

Shaw's advice to an American lady who had been treating him and his plays in an un-businesslike manner was a peremptory, 'You should never think of anything else but money: I never do.'[2] Not quite true: he found time to think of plays and productions and several dozen other things besides; but money was an important consideration to him. Understandably. He had earned little of it in the first three-and-a-half decades of his life and when finally in the late 1890s the sporadic 'dribble' (Shaw's word for his sales in the early years) became a rivulet which would later broaden into quite a merrily tinkling stream, he naturally kept a close eye on it, recording it in his Receipt Book in his fine and precise hand, entering all sums of money earned in the pursuit of his profession, down to the last penny. More carefree souls than his might call the painstaking detail of the entries obsessive. Perhaps it is, although scrupulousness might be nearer the mark (Shaw was painstaking and

scrupulous in all his dealings), and it is clear from periodic statements in the Receipt Book that he kept the records largely for
income tax purposes.

These records can help one to assess the success or otherwise of
his plays in performance; the success or otherwise of his books. We
begin with the plays, and the extent to which they reached and
impinged on the public mind; and these, when viewed through the
Receipt Book, show a steady increase of revenue through the
Edwardian years, thus of performance. As already noted, the years
1904–7 at the Court and in America and Germany-Austria reflect
growing recognition, considerable popularity at times. However,
the following three and a half years reflect a marked falling off of
public interest, hence something of a decline in his status as a playwright. This refers to first productions, that is to say to the
productions of *Getting Married*, *Misalliance* and his occasional
shorter plays of those years. At the same time, the book also reflects
the consolidation of his reputation in the English-speaking world
and a few European countries, Germany and Austria in particular,
in the performances of plays already established in the canon,
although even here, it may be noted, not all revivals were successful. A 1909 revival of *You Never Can Tell* in London was poorly
received and *The Admirable Bashville* at Beerbohm Tree's After Noon
Theatre ran for only six performances. Even so, scarcely a month
passes that does not have entries recording the payment of royalties from his American agent, Elizabeth Marbury, or from Trebitsch,
or from Vedrenne and Barker (the last derived from the provincial
tours of the 1904–7 Court productions). There are others, one or
two from distant parts, all denoting Shaw's impact worldwide. A
few samples from 1909, a lean year for Shaw as a playwright, are
offered below.

January begins with this entry: 'Alex. Hevesi for Joseph Teleki,
1/2 advance of 1000 kronen on a/c of fees on Capt. Brassbound by
the National Theatre, Budapest, as per contract.' International
Shaw was obviously making headway, which is confirmed by the
number of times Trebitsch is recorded; indeed, as the packed
entries under 'Trebitsch' indicate, Germany and Austria were
seeing at least as many plays by Shaw in 1908–9 as the entire
English-speaking world. A typical 1909 entry reads that performances of *Mrs Warren's Profession* in November 1908 and of *The
Philanderer* and *The Doctor's Dilemma* in December 1908 were held at
'various theatres in Germany'. In February Miss Horniman,

another name that recurs as she took Shaw's plays round and about the British provinces, produced *Candida* at what appears to be Blackburn and, as noted above, there were six performances of *The Admirable Bashville* at His Majesty's, London. Apropos of this last-mentioned production, Shaw remarked sardonically to Barker: 'The Afternoon Theatre has had to fall back on Bashville for the 6th [January]. Such is the end of the first attempt at a Shawless theatre.'[3] A Shawless theatre anywhere was rapidly becoming unlikely as, still in February 1909, Elizabeth Marbury reimbursed Shaw for an amateur performance of *Arms and the Man* in Stockpool and another in, not very precisely, 'America', while E. Taylor Platt, managing one of the Vedrenne-Barker touring companies, returned royalties for performances of *You Never Can Tell* in Torquay, and an entry mentioning Miss Katherine Pole (a peripatetic pioneer of those years) indicates that Shaw's name had reached as far afield as South Africa, where *Candida*, *Arms and the Man* and *Captain Brassbound's Conversion* were performed in Bloemfontein and Johannesburg. Meanwhile in Sweden, Hugo Vallentin, whose promotion of Shaw's plays on the Continent came second only to Trebitsch's, sent royalties for performances of *Mrs Warren's Profession* in the provinces; he would take the same production to Finland later in the year, while a Frau Lindroth, also in Sweden, was overseeing a production of *Man and Superman*. June records two performances of *The Philanderer* at the National Theatre in Prague, Karl Masek being the man behind this production and, nearer home, in Letchworth, C. B. Purdom, well-known in later years as the editor of the Shaw–Barker letters, the author of the first Barker biography and related publications, put on two performances of *Arms and the Man*.

These are a few examples from pages crammed with entries. The royalties are not usually large, ranging from 7s 6d for Vallentin's three performances of *Man and Superman* in the Swedish provinces to occasionally more substantial figures of £60 and more from Trebitsch, Marbury and the Vedrenne-Barker touring companies. The total figure for the year is not negligible, though less, as we shall see, than Shaw's royalties from his books. The real point is that Shaw's plays were being performed, and were obviously drawing audiences, in England and abroad.

The sale of his books shows a not dissimilar, perhaps more spectacular, pattern. Shaw had said in the statement rejected by the Censorship Committee that his livelihood did not depend on the writing and production of his plays. It is worth looking into this claim. As with the plays, one must scan Shaw's major publications since the turn of the century to see to what extent they contributed to his income and, by inference, to the growth and consolidation of his reputation.

One begins in January 1899, when Grant Richards was his English publisher and Herbert Stone his American. There is an entry that records net royalties for Shaw's first collection of plays, *Plays Pleasant and Unpleasant*, from the date of publication in April 1898 to 30 June of the same year: a gross figure of £75 12s for his income tax return, from which he allowed himself a net amount of £56 11s 2d. A year later, in February 1900, the royalties for the same volumes for the half-year ending 30 June 1899 were £6 14s 0d, with the American edition contributing an additional £27 15s 3d, and *The Perfect Wagnerite* (published in England in 1898 and in America in 1899) earning a combined royalty of £21 6s 1d. This produced a grand total of £55 15s 4d, which was slightly augmented three months later, in May, with £17 6s 7d. A year later, in July 1900, the same books earned him almost exactly £32. Shaw does not appear to have kept a record for 1901 and it is quite possible that there was no income to record from his books in this year, because in October 1902 Grant Richards disbursed him a total of £183 12s 4d for the previous 18 months. The list now included *Three Plays for Puritans* (published in January 1901), *Cashel Byron's Profession* (re-published in England and America in October 1901) and separate plays. This last was a new departure for Shaw. They began modestly, earning £4 3s 11d in the year following publication in February 1901, but would become the source of considerable revenue within a few years.

These figures are scarcely propitious. Even when adjusted to present-day values, they reflect a meagre return. Shaw would have found cause other than his personal unsaleability for the poor returns. One reason was that the format in which he offered his work to the public – a highly individualistic, often polemical preface, a text consisting not only of dialogue but of often lengthy authorial descriptions and interjections, in a word a play that looked like but was not a novel – was strange at first to a public not accustomed to purchasing the texts of plays. Another reason was Grant Richards. Shaw complained that he did not promote his books; these figures underscore this failure; he had every reason to get rid of Richards. However, the overriding fact is that at this stage of his career Shaw the author was like Shaw the playwright and scarcely worth a farthing's reputation in the marketplace or in the general consciousness of the age.

Constable then took over with Shaw seeing to the printing, with results that showed an immediate improvement. The sale of *Man and Superman* reflects both more vigorous marketing and Shaw's gradual emergence from relative obscurity. The first royalty figure given, in March 1904, shows a balance on part of the *Man and Superman* account of £279 2s 10d, from which payment of £130 had to be made to his printer, Clark of Edinburgh. In America as well the switch from Stone to Brentano's drew dividends: in January 1905 Shaw received £120 7s 8d 'being an instalment of half the $1173-75 due to 31st December'. A year later, in January and March 1906, Brentano's paid over £360 in settlement of royalties due to 31 December 1905.

By now Shaw's plays had been receiving considerable publicity at the Court and the improved sale of his books, including such minor non-dramatic pieces as *The Common Sense of Municipal Trading* (February 1904), reflected growing public awareness of and interest in what he had to say. In September 1906, in settlement for the year ending 30 June 1906, Constable, who had taken over all Shaw's work from Richards, imbursed him £1346 11s 11d. This was the first time Shaw's royalties rose above three figures, and it is interesting to note the relative popularity of the different volumes, even when allowance is made for the different prices of different works. *Man and Superman* was being sold at 6s 0d, for example, *Municipal Trading* at 2s 6d. *Man and Superman* remained far and away the most sought-after work, although *Plays Pleasant*, which regularly outsold *Plays Unpleasant*, was high on the list. *Three Plays for Puritans* came a bad fourth after *Plays Unpleasant*. It would never become a general favourite and on this occasion was nearly outsold by *Cashel Byron*. The item 'Separate plays' at £88 8s 10d shows a growing interest in this form of marketing, while *The Perfect Wagnerite* and *Municipal Trading*, maintained their viability at a not negligible £20 19s 4d and £21 0s 7d respectively.

The next major royalty statement from Constable is entered in April 1908 for the period 1 July 1906 to 31 December 1907. *John Bull's Other Island*, *Major Barbara* and *How He Lied to Her Husband* had been published as a single volume at 6s 0d in June 1907; sales for the first six months had obviously been excellent and the royalty of £750 19s 11d soared above that for *Man and Superman* at its more or less steady £469 18s 10d. The other works all showed a slight increase, with *The Perfect Wagnerite* suddenly outstripping *Cashel Byron* and 'Separate plays' rising spectacularly to £388 13s 7d. The total of £779 1s 11d is over double the previous figure.

In the same month of April – certainly not the cruellest month for Shaw – sales of the *John Bull* volume through *The Times* Book Club (a controversial enterprise Shaw vigorously supported) resulted in a gross figure of £430 17s 11d, less a 15 per cent publisher's discount of £60 2s 8d, which gave him a net receipt of £370 15s 3d. This brought his total income for the month from the sale of his books over the previous 18 months to over £3000, a considerable sum. Six months later Brentano's settlement for royalties for 1907 (Shaw lists *Three Plays for Puritans, Man and Superman* and *Plays Pleasant and Unpleasant*) amounted to over £1000.

A year later, 1909, royalties from the same two houses reflected a drop in sales, but the figure of over £2000 remained comfortable. It was in this year that Shaw claimed to be financially independent of the stage. He was right in a sense, except that he chose not to recognize the importance of the stage productions in promoting his reputation and the demand for his books. This specific impetus could not be ignored.

By 1910 the dribble sales of the early years were gone, in their place a stream of ready money, and in 1911 this became a deluge when *Man and Superman* and *John Bull's Other Island* were brought out by Constable as separate 'Sixpenny Specials' and sales of each rose to over 30 000. Thus did he become a best-selling author, perhaps not as spectacularly as others in his lifetime, but quite satisfactorily, provided, of course, he managed to meet public demand with a new challenging trio of plays every two or three years. Not even Shaw could afford to rest on his laurels, at least not at this stage of his career.

We return to the question whether he succeeded in giving body and legitimacy to his 'celebrity'. He would always be a good copy for news-hungry editors, regardless of his actual achievement, and many at the time (still today) continued to regard him as little more than this – good copy for an empty-headed press. It is as well to bear in mind that Shaw had not conquered England, nor would he ever manage quite to do so. But the question is rhetorical; the answer is implicit in the foregoing account. Revenue cannot be an absolute gauge, but it has the merit of concreteness, and this, pointing a solid finger to the number of plays performed and the number of books sold, indicates that to tens of thousands of men and women in Britain, Europe and the USA he had become a household name.

The books – those that went under the titles of plays – came complete with prefaces, occasional postscripts and augmented play texts. As this kind of publication was revolutionary in its way and as, singly and cumulatively, it affords an interesting perspective on Shaw's aims as artist and propagandist, it is necessary to say something about it. He had two fairly overt reasons for bringing his plays out in augmented form: first, to produce a book of reasonable substance to promote sales; second to make use of the platform afforded by publication for the more complete exposition of his views. Shaw indicates this second motive in his Preface to *Plays Unpleasant*. Here, while arguing his case for padding his dramatic texts – falling back, as he said, on 'his powers of literary expression, as other poets and fictionalists do' – he laments Shakespeare's failure to provide posterity with texts that conveyed more than the 'bare lines'. He continues:

> It is for want of this elaboration that Shakespear, unsurpassed as poet, storyteller, character draughtsman, humorist, and rhetorician, has left us no intellectually coherent drama, and could not afford to pursue a genuinely scientific method in his studies of character and society....[4]

The inference the reader is invited to draw is obvious: where Shakespeare had failed, Shaw would excel. Not only would his plays be stuffed with comments about the characters, the action and the conflicts, but his prefaces and postscripts would take the task further and convey by means of generalized argument the 'scientific method' underscoring the play and, above all, the intellectual coherence of the entire undertaking.

The kernel of each individual undertaking was the play. As for his role here, as artist as distinct from pamphleteer, he declared his position in his first preface, that to *Widowers' Houses*, in 1893:

> [Y]ou will please judge [the play], not as a pamphlet in dialogue, but as in intention a work of art as much as any comedy of Molière's is a work of art, and as pretending to be a better made play

for actual use and long wear on the boards than anything that has yet been turned out by the patent constructive machinery.[5]

He went further five years later in the preface to *Plays Pleasant*, saying that the dramatic art to which he aspired, which he firmly believed he had been achieving, no matter what the critics said, was no cheap indulgence in ethical absolutes but a coherent, an intelligible and prosaic explanation of the revolt against contemporary constraints and the prefiguring of a new age. 'Discernible at first only by the eyes of the man of genius, [the dawn of a new age] must be focussed by him on the speculum of the work of art, and flashed back from that into the eyes of the common man.'[6] It is the voice of prophecy embedded in the contemporary scene that Shaw attributes to the true artist, himself included.

Such plays as *Caesar and Cleopatra* and *Man and Superman* are easy to equate with this largeness of vision, both being cast in the epic mould and attempting to make 'big' contemporary issues the stuff of dramatic art. 'Prophecy' is built into them. The smaller plays may seem less likely candidates for this pantheon, yet here again Shaw's constant objective is to make them more than they appear to be, as though Bluntschli's entry into the Petkoff household, Marchbank's intrusion into the Morell marriage, Lady Cicely Waynflete's conversion of Captain Brassbound and so on, are local habitation and name for cosmic surges – a music of the spheres for those with the ears to hear the subtle distillation of tones. He gave hints a-plenty, sometimes more than hints, that these plays resonated with such overtones. What was *Captain Brassbound's Conversion*, he told Ellen Terry when she turned it down, but a rebuttal of the heroism of the filibuster, the punishment meted out by judges – a repudiation of the violence that goes with 'civilization' and 'Empire' and the victory of 'simple moral superiority'?[7] This was small fry compared to *Candida*, where, as he grandly informed the same sympathetic reader, his heroine was the Virgin Mother 'and nobody else'.[8] In *Arms and the Man* the satire on romantic folly does not seem to take one far on the cosmic pathway, but buried in the title – and in the delineation of Bluntschli – is a hint that Shaw saw his Swiss officer and Bulgarian family in larger terms than immediately strike the eye. The title is from the first line of Dryden's translation of the *Aeneid*: 'Arms and the man I sing …' This man Aeneas, Dryden relates in the opening lines, was forced by fate and 'haughty Juno's unrelenting hate' to leave Troy, to labour long by sea and land and in 'doubtful war' before winning the 'Latin realm' and building 'the destin'd town'. Here he restored the banished gods and

> ... settled sure succession in his line,
> From whence the race of Alban's fathers came,
> And the long glories of majestic Rome.

To see Bluntschli as Shaw's Aeneas – for that matter Raina as the mother of the race of a converted Alban[9] – seems a tall order, but Shaw, who knew his *Aeneid*, quite probably in Dryden's translation, and fashioned his soldier anti-hero on the lines of Virgil's, right down to his rejection of the false gods and aversion to war, undoubtedly had the parallel, and the resultant echoes, in mind.

Each individual work then – the play as art-work together with its non-dramatic commentary, the whole built up, to recall Shaw's phrase to Trebitsch, from 'atoms of dust' – each aspired to be 'scientifically' true, intellectually coherent and 'prophetic' on a large scale. This was the overt intention of the publication as a whole and quite enough, one may have thought, for any one writer to attempt. But Shaw seems to have come to nurture an even larger purpose. As one publication succeeded another in the 1890s and beyond, a body of essays and plays came into being which possess striking homogeneity; continuity, development, a larger coherence emerges. By 1910 the pattern is clear, if incomplete: the corpus of Shaw's work – the prefaces, the plays and the postscripts – amount cumulatively to a critical anatomy of the human comedy as played out in late nineteenth- and early twentieth-century England, grounded of course, as Shaw never tired of telling his ever-growing audience, in the most scientific of methods and sustained by the most comprehensive and coherent of philosophies.

A critical anatomy of the human comedy. It was an ambitious undertaking, grandiose. There had been others who had pursued things unattempted yet in prose or rhyme, of equally grandiose vision, and Shaw had no qualms about ranking himself with these giants, at least in design. His became a conscious, though undeclared, attempt to soar, if not above the Aonian Mount, at least above the rotten institutions of his time, to pick them out one by one and to expose the mendacity, the hypocrisy, the greed and the folly which supported them. More than this, if he did not quite set out to justify the ways of God to man, he certainly aimed at bringing man closer to the ways of God – his God, of course, who brought retribution on those who did not mend their ways and rewarded those who strove to realize the godhead within themselves.

He probably did not begin with this large scheme in mind. His first few plays are random in the sense that they were triggered by his work as a Fabian Socialist or, later, by his reaction against current theatrical practice, while the accompanying prefaces are devoted more or less single-mindedly to his telling his contemporaries that his was a voice they would be fools not to heed; but towards the end of the 1890s, when the short retrospect – two volumes containing seven plays – would have shown how effectively he had been selecting and dissecting sundry diseased organs of the body politic, he seems to have realized that the larger aim could profitably inform and direct his career. *Caesar and Cleopatra* is the watershed: here one of Shaw's abiding preoccupations, the question of Just and Good Leadership, to him the central issue of the modern commonwealth of man, is given its first airing and opens the way for further investigation. After this, the Edwardian plays follow an almost systematic pattern, each considering vital aspects of contemporary society, each contributing to the total anatomy Shaw hoped eventually to produce.

An abstract of each work and its function in the continuum will do Shaw's grand scheme less than justice, and will not be attempted. It will have to be enough to say that his works when seen in sequence, even those apparently random ones of the early 1890s, move from one social ill to another in a noticeably methodical way, considering and reconsidering in ever-increasing depth and complexity such perennially topical issues as the Economic Question, the Woman Question and the Leadership Question, the Question of Political Man, of Irish Man, of Empire, of Religion and Medicine and Marriage, and, as a finale to the period, the nuclear Question of the Edwardian Family – all in the context of the new 'modernism' literally crashing in on the closed world of the 'Glass Case Age'. This scrappy résumé fails to note the complexities and intermeshing of the plays and prefaces, the steadily widening canvas, the deepening vision, but it does suggest Shaw's capacity for variety and his skill in exposing Edwardian England to its multifarious and deep-rooted ills.

## II

A previous chapter – 'Transformation' – traces Shaw's rise to public eminence in the first five or so years of the century, as witnessed mainly by the popular press. Notice did not end here. Jogging along somewhat in the rear of the daily and weekly press, but always in sight of its quarry, was the more weighty commentary contained in monthly and quarterly journals and in comparatively lengthy monographs: the ostensibly avant-garde 'intellectual' press. There was the beginning of critical, if not strictly scholarly, appraisal and of biography; the beginning of the 'Shaw industry', possibly the most voluminous of secondary literary activities of the century. A survey of this literature is necessary to round off our picture of Edwardian Shaw.

It will be recalled that in 1900 the critic W. K. Tarpay writing on 'English Dramatists of To-day' consigned Shaw to a corner of his article where he worried over him like a dog with a bone. Tarpay excelled himself in noticing him. Others writing on the same theme, and there were quite a few of these instant historians at the time, bewailed the lack of literary quality, of commitment, of vigour in contemporary English drama, and did not so much as breathe Shaw's name.

Two years later, in 1903, the situation was beginning to change. One sees the signs in Volume I of the *Bibliography of Writing about Shaw*,[10] where the first year of the new age has nothing; then in 1902 the Danish philosopher Georg Brandes leads the assault on contemporary sluggishness in *Politikken* with 'Bernard Shaws Teater', the article that prompted Archer to speak out on Shaw's behalf. Then again, during these years of Shaw's consignment to the wilderness, there is nothing until late 1903 when, amazingly, as if to rebuke the indifference of the English-speaking world, the Spaniard Julio Brouta produces a 31-page report in *Revista Critica*, 'El Teatro de Bernard Shaw', Vladoje Dukat produces 'George Bernard Shaw' for the Croatian *Vienac* and the German K. Kraus writes an 11-page article 'Literatur' for *Die Fackel*, in which he discusses the controversy surrounding Trebitsch's translations of the plays. Business becomes more brisk in 1904, when – to cite only a few of the dozen or more entries – Elisabeth L. Cary writes her 'Apostles of the New Drama' for *Lamp*, Havelock Ellis writes 'The Prophet Shaw' for the *Weekly Critical Review* and Archibald Henderson, newly converted to Shavianism, weighs in with no fewer than six articles in a selection of American newspapers and journals. By now *Candida* had become the hit of the season in New York, which soon prompted every American scribbler to reach for a pen and scribble. Thenceforth the annual lists of the *Annotated Bibliography* continue for page after page, filled mainly with notices of productions of plays but inflated by the kind of article under present review.

The increasing recurrence of Shaw's name does not denote the beginning of approval. Far from it. But it does denote the admission that he had become 'significant', therefore a necessary object of appraisal in the more thoughtful periodicals. Just how thoughtful, more precisely how lacking in thoughtfulness, most of the articles may seem today is not a necessary reflection of the mediocrity of the critics of the time; it is rather a reminder that Shaw, when he finally impinged on his 'intellectual' contemporaries, did so with such force that he scattered their wits rather than consolidated them.

A survey of a few of the articles gives an idea of the range and force of his impact. E. L. Cary's 1904 article 'Apostles of the New Drama' sees Shaw and Yeats as the 'apostles' in that both had 'contributed new elements to the worthiest traditions of the English stage', while Stephen Gwynn's 'Mr G. B. Shaw and the British Public'[11] takes the lofty view that Shaw's plays were 'caviare to the general', nevertheless the source of untold pleasure to the thousands of intelligent people (like Gwynn himself) who had been attending performances by the Stage Society and at the Court. At this time – 1905 – the most intellectually substantial essay to appear was the chapter on Shaw in Chesterton's *Heretics*.[12] It is a comparatively small piece, Chesterton clearing his throat preparatory to writing his book on Shaw, but big enough for one to see the advantage he enjoyed over his contemporaries: he could set himself up as Shaw's intellectual equal and, master of the incisive paradox, deliver thrust upon thrust with consummate precision. One or two will have to suffice. Shaw was a

> standing monument to the advantage of being misunderstood ... The man who is really wild and whirling, the man who is really fantastic and incalculable, is not Mr Shaw, but the average Cabinet Minister ... He has based all his brilliancy and solidity upon the hackneyed, but yet forgotten, fact that truth is stranger than fiction. Truth, of course, must of necessity be stranger than fiction, for we have made fiction to suit ourselves.

Yet Chesterton had profound reservations and the truth about Shaw was that he, the exemplar of the search for truth, had never seen things as they really were.

After this scintillating display other commentaries sound like hens in a barnyard, particularly towards the end of 1905 when reaction set in and the anti-Shaw brigade began to set up their squawks. Their protest ranged from the allegation that Shaw went out of his way to insult his audiences to the conviction that he was a menace to morals. One critic summed it up by declaring that Shaw was 'simply a yellow journalist on the stage'[13] and a staff writer on the *Dramatic Mirror* confidently predicted that '[T]wenty years from now Shaw's works will rest on those shelves of literary accumulation where dust is most to be found and least frequently disturbed ...'[14]

A breath of fresh air disturbs this stale litany of denigration in Constance Barnicoat's 'Mr Bernard Shaw's Counterfeit Presentment of Women',[15] not because she has any time for Shaw but because she applies a touch of humour in putting him in his place: '[I]f anything could justify the drowning of female infants, it is the dreadful possibility that they might grow up to resemble Ann Whitefield, Julia Craven, Mrs Dudgeon, or Blanche Sartorius.' Of this group, 'Mr Shaw's darling', Ann Whitefield, takes the cake. 'Heaven preserve us from all "vital geniuses"!' Barnicoat's hope is that one of Ann's marked-down victims will be public-spirited enough to strangle her.

The most interesting of the literary controversies surrounding Shaw was instigated by a trio of poets, noted by a staff writer of *Current Literature* in July 1907 in 'The Case of the Poets Versus Shaw', the poets being Arthur Symons, Richard Le Gallienne and Alfred Noyes. To Symons, Shaw's logic was sterile and the difference between him and Tolstoy was the difference between Euclid and Christ. To Le Gallienne, Shaw was a 'farcical doctrinaire of stale sociological philosophy'. And to Noyes, he was everything that was rotten through and through. Noyes's attacks on Shaw provide a classic example of literary paranoia. He makes no attempt to moderate his loathing and his air of lofty disdain fails to hide his insecurity in the face of what he saw as Shaw's challenge to traditional values. The first attack came in the article cited by *Current Literature*, a review of Shaw's *Dramatic Opinions and Essays* in the May 1907 issue of the *Bookman*, in which Noyes points to Shaw's 'blatant self-puffery', the 'empty laughter of [his] mentally bankrupt admirers', his 'indecent familiarity with himself' and generally 'unmanly' and 'disgusting' conduct.

This was mild in comparison with what he would launch at Shaw in another publication – at least Archer said it was Noyes, and he was probably right. In the same month of May 1907, from Shaw's old enemy *Blackwood's Magazine*, in an article entitled 'Sham and Super-Sham' by a pseudonymous 'Z', there came a torrent of startling invective. A few choice phrases, many filched from the illustrious dead, may be quoted:

> ... a charlatan like Mr Shaw ... we are tired of watching him hop over the graves of the illustrious dead and skip like a blue-behinded ape upon the trees of paradise ... Decadence and perversion are writ large over everything that comes from his pen ... paws so dull and brutish as these ... this ignorant jackanapes ... Mr Shaw is being found out with the rest of the morbid and mediocre crew.

These two attacks so outraged Archer that he prepared a counterblast, a letter entitled 'The Revival of Billingsgate', which he intended placing in his paper, the *Tribune*. It had already been set up in type when he showed it to Shaw, who replied:

> I havnt read Z: I *have* read Noyes. It amused me and didnt strike me as beyond the bounds.
> > 'I like to see young heroes
> > Ambitioning like this.'
> *I* should say, let him alone; but of course do as you please. Why shouldnt I be blasphemed against?[16]

Archer withdrew his letter and the *Tribune* was consequently deprived of an opportunity to promote a first-rate literary fight, especially as Archer made no attempt to disguise his belief that 'Z' was Noyes.

There were many feeble essays on Shaw at the time, but a certain Carroll Brent Chilton's 'Shaw Contra Mundum' earns top marks as the most cheerfully confused of them all. The editor of the American *Independent* did not think so; he thought the piece so tremendous that he sent it to Shaw, inviting him to respond. Shaw did, on a postcard: 'At your request I have read Mr Chilton's article. It is certainly a very bad one; but it was hardly fair to set him a subject manifestly too difficult for him. Why not ask him for an article on Oliver Wendell Holmes? He would probably do it quite creditably.' This may sound unkind and perhaps it is to Oliver Wendell Holmes; certainly not to Carroll Brent Chilton, whose critical acumen tended to spread itself thin in effusions like this:

In Shawnee-land – what? only a newer and cruder 'transvaluation of all values' – gravitation goes upward, away from the centre of things, moral questions are immoral, the devil himself the father of morality, which again is not morality but immorality; the prurient is the chaste, which again is not chastity but pruriency; law and order a stupid system of violence and robbery; the woman courts the man; economics is theology and poetry ... and so all things are mixed.[17]

Not least, one has to say, Carroll Brent Chilton.

All in all, these early contributors emerge as less capable than the theatre critics of London or New York and probably confirmed Shaw's low opinion of the 'intellectual'. He once told the American actor, William Faversham, that the 'man I dread is the actor who thinks that Shaw is "intellectual drama," and that he must play it as if there were a sick person in the house, the result being that the whole audience presently consists of sick persons.'[18] He could have said much the same about the 'intellectual' critics and the 'sickness' they managed inscrutably to abstract from the wit and vivacity of his work.

There were exceptions to this rule: Barnicoat was one in a small way, Chesterton another in a big way and Archibald Henderson a third in a dedicated way. These two latter names introduce another category of criticism: the monographs on Shaw that appeared from 1905 onwards.

III

That year – 1905 – was a watershed year. Beginning then, and thereafter every year throughout the Edwardian era, as though it spontaneously became a required annual event, a book appeared on Shaw. There were seven in all, and most of these are distinguished mainly by the fact that they were pioneering efforts. Three of them, four at a pinch, got Shavian studies rolling and one of these, Chesterton's book, made it soar.

The first monograph was Henry L. Mencken's *Bernard Shaw: His Plays*.[19] Scarcely launched on what would become a long and distinguished career in letters, Mencken was already flexing his muscles as an independent-minded champion of the new and sardonic critic of the old. Shaw, as the very model of what the iconoclast should be, appealed to him at the time as the embodiment of the modern rebellious spirit, and well worth a promotional tootle on the Menckenian trumpet. He would change his mind about Shaw a few years later and, as though wanting to expunge the folly of his youth, would run him down whenever he could. In 1905, however, he could recognize him as a world figure and say quite a few wittily appreciative things about him, although, when he came to discuss the plays, he was callow and inept.

The next work, published in Finland in 1906, was *G. Bernard Shaw* by Gunnar Castron,[20] which the present writer is unable to appraise. External evidence suggests that it was prompted by Shaw's successes at the Court Theatre.

Holbrook Jackson's *Bernard Shaw* (1907)[21] is a conscientious attempt to categorize Shaw as 'The Man', 'The Fabian', 'The Playwright' and 'The Philosopher' – with the 'Philosopher' as the immanent and final cause of everything else that comprised Shaw. His plays provided the only consistently religious drama of the day and were 'philosophical' in the sense that they were dedicated to the creation of a will to live masterfully.

Jackson is positive and manages by his thoroughness to qualify as a comparatively important early critic. His successor, the Dutchman C. J. A. van Bruggen, is judiciously negative, prone to downplay his subject. His *George Bernard Shaw* (1908) was one in the series *Mannen en Vrouwen van Beteekenis in Onze Dagen* ('Eminent Men and Women of Our Time'),[22] which focused almost exclusively on Europe and included Shaw as the only Britisher among some 15 Continental figures, itself a measure of his impact across the Channel. Van Bruggen's conclusion, after making heavy weather of Shaw's career, is that he has written some spirited comedies but does not begin to count as a leader in modern thought. He was too individualistic to exert any artistic or social influence; worse still: 'The cart and the fanfare have destroyed him. The great enemy of the playwright Shaw is the impresario Shaw.'

Shaw studies were jogging along. Something was needed to galvanize them into life, and Chesterton obliged in 1909 with his version of the many-sided subject.[23]

He and Shaw became acquainted in the early years of the century; by 1905 this was beginning to ripen into a friendship strengthened by a unique compound of respect and disagreement on virtually all matters of importance and unimportance. This is Chesterton in 1936 on his adversary of old:

> My principal experience [of Shaw], from first to last, has been in argument with him. And it is worth remarking that I have learned to have a warmer admiration and affection out of all that argument than most people get out of agreement. Bernard Shaw … is seen at his best when he is antagonistic. I might say he is seen at his best when he is wrong. I might also add that he generally is wrong. Or rather, everything about him is wrong about him except himself.[24]

Shaw would have said much the same about Chesterton.

Chesterton's chapter on Shaw in his book of 1905, *Heretics*, already cited, was an early salvo in their series of confrontations. Shaw counter-attacked with 'The Chesterbelloc',[25] in which he depicted Chesterton and Belloc as a pantomime animal (Chesterton as the hind legs). Next came Chesterton's book on Shaw; and next the series of debates between them which began in 1911 and continued, formally and informally, until 1927. Hesketh Pearson called them the 'Debaters of the Century'. They probably were.

They were poles apart in almost all respects: in the clothes they wore, their physiques, their corporeal tastes – the one a very tun of a man, beer-toping and omnivorous, the other lean and hungry-looking, teetotal and herbivorous; in their metaphysics, in their concomitant spiritual stances (the one catholic if not yet a Catholic, the other puritan if not ever a Puritan). Where they met was in their high fineness of mind which when in conflict played with ideas with such panache that one could be forgiven for thinking it merely play and not what it really was, a clash of beliefs, convictions, faiths from the sparkle of which profundity of thought would flash forth like cerebral fireworks.

Shaw reviewed Chesterton's *Bernard Shaw* in the *Nation* and acknowledged that 'Everything about me which Mr Chesterton had to divine, he has divined miraculously.'[26] He also had a dig at Chesterton's errors of fact, a minor blemish considering the probing quality of Chesterton's 'divination' of the three Shaws he set up for consideration: the Irishman, the Progressive and the

Puritan. Shaw had digs at a good deal else in the book, protesting that Chesterton was madly wrong about him in all manner of ways. For once the Shavian smokescreen did not work: Chesterton's wizardry with the telling paradox frequently revealed more of Shaw than Shaw wanted the world to know.

Because they were unlike and alike Chesterton could see Shaw clearly; also, however, because they were unlike and alike he could not quite fathom Shaw in all his aspects. It is when discussing Shaw's 'Puritanism' that he seems least secure. The spirit of Puritanism, Chesterton says, which is to say the spirit that animated Shaw, 'was a refusal to contemplate God or goodness with anything lighter or milder than the most fierce concentration of the intellect ... You must praise God only with your brain; it is wicked to praise Him with your passions or your physical habits or your gesture or your instinct of beauty.'[27] The most obvious 'Puritan' answer to this is that to praise God without your brain is the real wickedness and to praise Him by means of your passions or physical habits or gesture or instinct of beauty without benefit of brain is insulting; moreover, that God has many aspects and praise by the most fierce concentration of the intellect would certainly earn Divine approval. The point is that the epicure (to call Chesterton that), for all his breadth and humaneness and geniality of vision, cannot really manage to see all the way round the ascetic (to call Shaw that) and cannot understand that what to the epicure may seem like denial is to the ascetic the celebration of a joy that is as valid, as genuine and capable of voluptuous consummation (ascetically speaking) as the epicure's. That was where Chesterton fell short in his reading of Shaw, but it was a brilliant failure and the book continues to delight and instruct.

In 1910, *Bernard Shaw* by the influential critic Julius Bab[28] announced that in Germany the subject was being treated with proper respect – not surprisingly, considering that 40 productions of Shaw's plays were seen in German-speaking Europe in 1909–10. Bab focuses on the philosophic content of the plays, which he discusses more expertly than anyone else at the time; as for the plays as plays (as distinct from their philosophic content), he sees them as comparing favourably, as achieved works of art, with those by Hauptmann. Bab's solemnity is a far cry from Shaw's vivacity but there is a good deal of solid Germanic substance in his commentary, and he may still be read with profit.

The seventh and last work of this period was Archibald

Henderson's first biography of Shaw (1911).[29] Henderson gives an account of how he became Shaw's 'authorized' biographer in (to cite the most accessible source) his preface to *Bernard Shaw: Man of the Century*. It is an entertaining tale; also a mystifying one, the mystery being why Shaw should have selected this stodgy professor of mathematics as his biographer. Henderson was not ever remotely Shaw's Boswell (which Shaw would have liked him to be), still less a Gibbon of the age (which Shaw said he wanted him to be). He lacked a vital quality: buoyancy. Everything he touched turned to dough. One may guess why Shaw was attracted to him. Here was a man, his intuition would have told him, whose lack of imaginative celerity and commensurate limitation as a writer was more than compensated for by a rare capacity for sustained, plodding work: a disciplined disciple who would put everything down the master told him to put down. Fortunately Henderson did not turn out quite this much of a drudge, and his three biographical studies – *Life and Works* (1911), *Playboy and Prophet* (1932) and *Man of the Century* (1956) – thanks largely to his academic independence of mind and scientific training were – and remain, mines of documented information, not all of it passed by Shaw's censoring pen. These biographies are monuments in a unique rather Gothic way, and the Edwardian one, rescuing the first 50 years of Shaw's life from oblivion, may be accounted the most impressive.

In sum, Shaw was not badly served by his major critics in these years. Although he would probably not have been satisfied with most of their findings, he would not have quarrelled with the implicit admission of their efforts, that he was an eminent contemporary, the embodiment of progressive, assertive, opinionated Edwardian man.

The same could not be said of the theatre critics of the daily and weekly press. To these gentlemen Shaw remained the embodiment of everything distasteful and uncomfortable. He was their punishment for being critics, their albatross, best shrugged off with the refrain that he was a garrulous bore lacking even a journeyman's skill with the finer demands of dramaturgy. This had been going on for twenty years; Shaw's resentment had been mounting for twenty years. Something had to be done about these critics and Shaw did something. He played his magnifying glass over the inert body of old England and discovered them – accretions of grit causing widespread inflammation. He wrote a play about those pieces of grit, the English theatre critics. They and the play they inspired are the subject of the Postscript.

# Postscript
## 1911: *Fanny's First Play*

I

How important is the critic? Enormously important and enormously contemptible, if the reactions of literary artists – of all artists, for that matter – are anything to go by. John Steinbeck's advice is a counsel of perfection: 'Unless the bastards have the courage to give you unqualified praise, I say ignore them.'[1] The problem is the bastards are impossible to ignore when they fail to give unqualified praise, which is always. Passing judgment on the children of one's brain as they are, their every word of adverse criticism is a gratuitous insult to one's offspring, like a whiplash across the face. Yet, masochistically, the author will return time and again to be whipped while hating the critic for what he deals out. Literature is strewn with exclamations of contempt, disgust, loathing and good old-fashioned curses, all directed at those who dared find fault. 'Critics are like brushers of noblemen's clothes,' said Francis Bacon, who knew precisely how very low in the order of being a brusher of noblemen's clothes had his niche.[2] Dryden was more direct: 'They who write ill, and they who ne'er durst write,/ Turn critics out of mere revenge or spite.'[3] (Shaw had much the same idea with his 'He who can does. He who cannot, teaches.'[4]) Pope reserved a good deal of his awesome store of invective for critics: 'Some have first for wits, then poets pass'd./ Turn'd critics next, and prov'd plain fools at last.'[5] The twentieth century has maintained this happy tradition and, turning to playwrights of the recent past, one is not surprised to find them disposed to regard the critic as a form of lowlife. 'Has anyone ever seen a drama critic in the daytime?' asks P. G. Wodehouse, no stranger to the playhouse. 'Of course not. They come out after dark, up to no good.'[6] Christopher Hampton is less polite: 'Asking a working writer what he thinks about critics is like asking a lamp-post what it thinks about dogs.'[7] The exchange in Beckett's *Waiting for Godot* where Estragon and Vladimir compete in abuse of each other culminates in Estragon's famous withering 'Crritic!' which said it all for all playwrights, for all time.

Shaw may be allowed an appropriate concluding flourish: 'A dramatic critic is a man who leaves no turn unstoned.'[8]

As the foregoing chapters have made abundantly clear, Shaw's stance *vis-à-vis* his critics was the classic one: he despised them and he depended on them. He attached great importance to what they said about his plays, and the burden of his complaint for twenty years was that, instead of trying to understand him, they were collectively trying to destroy him. It had been war between him and a – to him – by no means negligible foe from the beginning. By 1910 he seems tacitly to have acknowledged defeat at home, at least in that he sent his new plays, *Androcles and the Lion* (1912) and *Pygmalion* (1913), to Germany for their premières, thus by-passing the damning judgment of London. In his eyes the critics of that city would always be a dangerous lot.

Yet the situation was not as cut and dried as this. Shaw made considerable headway in the Edwardian years and, pointing to this, he would emphasize how much the critics had shifted their ground, moving from initial rejection to tolerance, even to grudging acceptance the third time round. This brought scant comfort. It was the initial rejection that set him back; this, the blinkered, mulish refusal to judge him on his terms the first time round, that rankled.

Hindsight affords another consideration, which is that what one sees of the major critics through their notices of Shaw's plays and of other productions at the Court is that they were quite a galaxy. As a group they excel any similar group London or New York could have mustered either before their time or since. William Archer of the *World* and then the *Tribune*, MacCarthy of the *Speaker*, Beerbohm of the *Saturday Review*, Grein of the *Sunday Times* and Walkley of *The Times* were men of integrity pursuing their calling to the best of their not inconsiderable ability.

One may particularize. At the conclusion of the first season at the Court, Archer wrote the monograph, *The Court Theatre: A Record and a Commentary*, and in 1907 MacCarthy produced *The Court Theatre, 1904–1907*, both cited in these pages, two books by two critics who showed themselves fully aware of the importance of the undertaking and praised the major role-players unstintingly. Archer could never identify himself with Shaw as a playwright, which is not to say that he ever failed to recognize him as a major voice of the time, in the theatre as much as elsewhere. As for MacCarthy, Shaw would always see him as one of his better critics. Beerbohm's notices were usually kindly disposed, even if they were not always sympathetic, and when *Major Barbara* was produced he penned as witty and graceful an 'apology' to Shaw as only he could manage. Grein was limited by his less than perfect command of English, but he made up for this by his ardent advocacy of the new drama, of the Shaw of the earlier plays in particular. Walkley emerged time and again as a major critic – his was certainly the authoritative voice, albeit a conservatively inclined one – whose aberrations of judgment were those of a man too civilized and comfortably set in his ways to estimate the importance of the revolution taking place in the theatre; but not even he – least of all this cultured impeccably stylish man – deserved Shaw's scorn.

Whether criticism can actually help a play to succeed or, conversely, 'kill' it is problematic. Shaw was convinced that it had this power, yet his years as a drama critic should have told him that this was not necessarily so, and when one comes to the critical responses at the Court during the Vedrenne-Barker years, one sees scant if any correlation between critical opinion and public response. Almost all the critics praised *Prunella*, yet it failed initially. They liked Hauptmann's *The Thieves' Comedy* – Walkley excepted – and it failed. Many of them, the *Morning Post* critic in particular, loathed *Major Barbara*, yet it succeeded. Harcourt's *A Question of Age* was not a good play and it deserved to be adversely criticized. And Masefield's *The Campden Wonder*, which the critics had shouted down to Shaw's profound disgust, is not nearly as good as he and Barker thought it, although on this occasion critical reaction was excessive. *Getting Married* earned itself a universal hiss of derision from the critics yet, as Shaw gleefully pointed out, audiences kept on returning to it. The chorus of denunciation that greeted *Misalliance* was followed by poor attendance, but here, least of all here, considering the advanced kind of play *Misalliance* is, there is again no necessary connection between critical reception and public response.

On balance, the critics mentioned above, plus a few others, were not unsympathetically inclined to the new drama as presented by Vedrenne and Barker at the Court, but, yes, to echo Shaw in his address at the Criterion Restaurant, they were often grudging of their praise, inclined to be petulant in their responses, and prone to disparage what they could not understand. It was not as though goodwill and fair dealing were in short supply, and one cannot cast the critics as villains in the Shavian melodrama. And yet, products of the nineteenth century as they were, their understanding of him fell short by a quarter-century at least. They wrote a good deal about him, much of it friendly, much of it unfriendly, filling their columns with discussion that failed conspicuously to come to grips with what the play was saying and how it was saying it. This was where they let Shaw down. They did not do what the exemplary critic should do: suspend judgment for the nonce and stand with the playwright at the vanguard of his work and interpret for its potential audience the aims, the playwriting method and the ideas of the piece on offer.

There is no mystery surrounding this failure. Archer, Beerbohm, MacCarthy and others were highly intelligent but ordinary men. Shaw was no ordinary man; he was ahead of them, ahead of his time, to such an extent that his professional contemporaries, born and bred in the mechanist tradition of nineteenth-century dramaturgy, found themselves confused and confounded by the new kind of play he was writing. If, in the plays of the 1890s in particular, he provided a recognizable plot derived from the stock-pot of popular melodrama and romance, he would regularly confound expectations by subverting the expected cliché step by calculated step. We may recall the complaint of the *Morning Post* critic in this regard, that Shaw was forever doing the unexpected thing and in effect yanking the carpet from under the critics' feet. And then, as though *Candida, Arms and the Man* and *Captain Brassbound's Conversion*, among others, were pandering to an outrageous lust for sensationalism, he seemed to abandon 'plot' entirely to become, as he declared, a 'dramatic poet' instead, where his 'action' was in the words, and the words were required to carry the play forward at dizzying speed. Thus the 'farragoes' and 'debates' of *John Bull's Other Island, Man and Superman, Major Barbara* and the rest; thus the 'plotless' situation comedies of *Getting Married* and *Misalliance*. Here one may recall Walkley's grand remonstrance of the new drama, published in *The Times* in 1910: 'Wandering attention, boredom, the irritation that comes from unsatisfied expectations and a sense of wasted material ...' Thus our Edwardian critic, balked of what he regards as a legitimate requirement.

So much for the new technical, or formal, conventions of the new Shavian drama and the bewilderment it left in its wake. There was also the shocking fact of Shaw's 'new-world' philosophy – the radical cast of mind that tore into everything Edwardian society held sacred and dear – which, the new message within the new medium, was patently calculated to challenge, confront, demolish the cornerstones of that society. Thus, inevitably, the 'immoralities', the lapses of 'taste', the 'profanities', the 'nastiness' and general 'indecency' of the Shavian play at the time.

No wonder even the better critics floundered.

The subtext of most of Shaw's diatribes against the critics shows his awareness of these difficulties. Those 'interviews' were not only publicity stunts. When he taunted the critics or gave warning that he planned to be revenged on them by writing such-and-such a play, he was as much as telling them to exert the sinews of their minds somewhat more than was their lethargic wont, to extend their horizon beyond those reached by the Pineros, the Joneses and the Sutros of the Edwardian theatre and to accept the 'aesthetic distance' he had created as a new road to be taken, a new 'horizon of expectations' to be explored and seen to be a 'culinary', which is to say a comprehensible, experience.[9]

By 1910 he was forced to admit that the critics had proved inadequate to the task; that he had not yet fulfilled his agenda set out for Ellen Terry's benefit 12 years before, to educate a new generation of playgoers (and critics) in the ways of Shavian dramaturgy. He was still ahead of his time; he had to realize that it was no good speaking to audiences (and critics) ten or twenty or fifty years hence; he had to speak to them in the present, at least in forms that satisfied certain basic expectations. He would have to shorten his horizons in certain respects. The critics had failed him; he could never forgive them for this. They had also defeated him; he would never forgive them for this.


II


In 1910 Lillah McCarthy and her husband Barker, who had taken over the lease of the Little Theatre in London, asked Shaw to write a play for them. Shaw agreed; and he set about writing *Fanny's First Play*. He decided to do three things to pre-empt the customary negative reception and so give the play the chance to be assessed on its merits.

First, he stipulated, his name had to be withheld from the playbill. Lillah McCarthy assented and *Fanny's First Play*, when produced, was advertised as by Mr \*\*\*\*\*\*\* \*\*\*\*.

Shavian critics do not take this attempt at anonymity seriously.

Dan Laurence says it was a 'whim',[10] and in the event it was an open secret among most of the critics. On the other hand, it seems that many members of the public thought the play was by some other writer than Shaw[11] and Shaw himself, two days after the opening night, referred to the 'duffers' – that is, the critics – 'who [were] mystified'.[12] When he came to write his short preface to the play before publication in 1914, he seemed in retrospect to take his subterfuge at least semi-seriously, remarking that concealment of authorship, to the extent that it was concealed, was a necessary part of the play and that:

> In so far as it was effectual, it operated as a measure of relief to those critics and playgoers who are so obsessed by my strained legendary reputation that they approach my plays in a condition which is really one of derangement ... If it were possible, I should put forward all my plays anonymously ...[13]

We may recall his remark to Gertrude Elliott after the disappointment of *Caesar and Cleopatra*: 'I am sorry now that it was not possible to produce the play anonymously ...' Here now, with *Fanny's First Play*, he was going to try to do just this and perhaps, just perhaps, it would help to stifle critical disparagement and public suspicion.

The second thing Shaw decided to do was write a play that would be 'culinary', that is to say a play that would be immediately understood and would fall largely within the horizons of experience of both critic and public. So he produced as his central play – Fanny's play – a short three-act domestic comedy, full of surprises and inversions, with parallel expositions and conflicts in Acts I and II brought together in Act III, where a series of reversals and revelations leads to the climax and resolution, all brought about with nice dramatic timing.

The plot depicts the upheaval in two middle-class households when the children (a son in one household, a daughter in the other, both of whom land up in goal for minor offences) bring moral chaos into the ordered respectability of their homes and insist on their right to live their own lives. This is the play Fanny writes and it was custom-built in all respects, in its characterization, its themes and conflicts, and structurally, for easy consumption by a moderately alert audience; or at all events an audience prepared to see and laugh at aspects of middle-class respectability for its stuffiness. Also, as even this gloss indicates, it was strongly Shavian in its themes and indeed may be seen as a sequel to *Misalliance* in its dissection of middle-class morality.

The third thing Shaw decided to do was to put a cross-section of contemporary critics on stage in an 'Induction' and an 'Epilogue' to form a kind of theatrical sandwich.[14] This came as an afterthought when he had already written Fanny's play, but afterthoughts can often be inspired and seen in retrospect as inevitable and necessary components of the organic whole. Certainly the introduction of critics into the play seems the natural culmination of a process that had been going on for nearly twenty years. The critics Shaw depicts are by now acquaintances of fairly long standing: Walkley of *The Times* is Trotter in Fanny's play, Baughan of the *Daily News* is Vaughan, Cannan, formerly of the *Star*, is Gunn. There are two other critics, each more generalized than this trio: Fanny's father, the Count O'Dowda, halted in an eighteenth-century time warp and a reverential disciple of 'beautiful realities', and Flawner Bannal, a composite creature representing the hacks who echoed the opinions of their superiors in the trade and pandered to public prejudice. These five present themselves in the Induction where the audience learns that they have been invited to see a private performance of a new play by their host's daughter, Fanny. However, the authorship of the play is kept a secret from them. Fanny's play follows. After this, the critics come together again and argue about the play and its still unknown author.

The idea is not new. But no one had ever done what Shaw does with his critics, which is first to create recognizable caricatures of at least three prominent members of that fraternity and then in effect to haul them out of the stalls onto the stage and present them for public and critical scrutiny. He does this not simply to hold them up to ridicule or to use their reactions as a mirror of what he had endured for so long. He also does it to manipulate reception in such a way as briefly to arrest its usual course, which is from performance to the critic and on to the reception of the critic's notice by the reading public. Shaw holds up the process on stage, while each critic in turn has his reception and the criteria on which he bases his reception scrutinized – by his fellows on stage and, of course, the critics and the audience in the theatre. This is done, it is important to remember, after the performance of a play which has proved a delightful entertainment and is so neatly packaged as to satisfy the demands of the most rigorous advocate of the well-made play. Some of the fun in all this would disappear after the first night, with the critics no longer in the stalls to see themselves not-so-solemnly making asses of themselves on stage, but the manipulation of reception and the alienation effect Shaw would have wanted to achieve would remain. The principle on which this was based, that of reviewing the aesthetic of reception, ranging from notions about dramatic form to notions about 'good taste', from different, contradictory and almost endlessly reflexive and amusing points of view would hold good for as long as the central point remained valid – that the critics were duffers when it came to judging a play by Shaw.

The five critics in Fanny's play are 'placed' very precisely regarding their ways of reacting to plays, and as three of them are exaggerated images of their counterparts in the stalls, they react as their counterparts react when reviewing a play by Shaw. A further refinement is that each complements the other, so that reception is given five faces, so to speak, taking in Count O'Dowda's rhapsodic adherence to 'Beauty', Trotter's elevated views on Aristotelian laws of dramaturgy and so on down to the fawning banalities of the comically unspeakable Flawner Bannal. Thumbnail sketches of each are given in the Induction: Trotter (Walkley of *The Times*) must not be chaffed about Aristotle; Vaughan (that is, Baughan of the *Daily News*) has no sense of humour; Gunn (that is, Cannan of the *Star*) is a fierce Intellectual; and Flawner Bannal is the man in the street whose word is law to the men and women in the street.[15]

It is also in the Induction, before Fanny's play has been performed, that Trotter-Walkley is given an opportunity to express himself on a certain unnamed playwright (Shaw, of course) who 'resorts to the dastardly subterfuge of calling [his stage presentations] conversation pieces, discussions, and so forth'. Trotter excitedly insists that they are not plays; he takes this seriously; it is a matter of principle with him.[16] Shaw pays Walkley the backhanded compliment at the end by allowing Trotter to guess that Fanny has written the play, which is right if we allow that the work is a fiction, but hopelessly wrong otherwise.

The other critics get their opportunity in the Epilogue, after the performance. Vaughan-Baughan's censorious tones have been heard when he dismissed *Getting Married* and *Misalliance*. He dismisses Fanny's play equally censoriously. It is intensely disagreeable, therefore not by Barrie, but, he says, 'Poor as this play is, theres the note of passion ... Now Ive repeatedly proved that Shaw is physiologically incapable of the note of passion.' Therefore, he concludes, the play must be by Pinero.[17] The 'advanced' critic

Cannan/Gunn, sees it as a 'rotten old-fashioned domestic melo-drama ... as old and stale as a fried fish shop on a winter morning.' The author's signature is in every line: Granville Barker, of course, says Gunn.[18] Bannal, lacking any ideas of his own, latches on to everything the others say, but ironically and to compound the joke, it is he who guesses that Shaw is the author, only to be shouted down by the others.[19] By the end, then, all the critical clichés about Shaw's plays are paraded, assessed and, in the context of Fanny's delightful play, shown to be absurd. The rapid and continuous interplay between fiction and reality that all this entails, between alienation on the one hand jostling against identification on the other, is as dazzling as it is amusing.

The play opened on 19 April 1911. Walkley helped with Trotter's make-up and the next morning helped a bit more by going along with the joke at his expense quite charmingly. He managed to get an Aristotelian dig in but admitted that whatever the qualities and defects of 'Mr X's' plays, 'There is much to be thankful for.' This, from Walkley, was saying a lot. He made a good deal of not having been able to recognize his stage image, Trotter.[20] Baughan, on the other hand, thought that Trotter was the most amusing of the critics; the others were 'very dull dogs'. He did not agree with Vaughan that Shaw was incapable of the note of passion, 'for the same kind of feeling which underlies this piece has been sounded before in *Major Barbara*, in *Getting Married*, and in *John Bull's Other Island*. I liked those plays because of their feeling, and I liked *Fanny First Play* because the same vein of seriousness runs through it.'[21] Perhaps critics have to cultivate short memories in order to live with themselves. Cannan, who had left the *Star*, did not write a critique either for that paper or, apparently, any other, but we may be sure that he came to know about Shaw's 'revenge' on him for that attack on *Misalliance*.

The other critics liked *Fanny's First Play*, except, oddly enough, Grein, who thought it offensive. It was also a critical success when taken to America in 1912, so much so that the *Bookman* published an amusing skit of the Epilogue, using American critics as the target.[22] Shaw dismissed the play as a 'potboiler' and it is a slight piece by Shavian standards. It is not, however, a trivial piece, and the more one looks at *Fanny* the more complex it becomes.

Did Shaw's manipulation of reception cause the critics to switch to a more amiable mode when writing their notices? Possibly. Fanny's play was well within the collective horizon of perception and the customary complaints could not be made; and perhaps it succeeded in making the point that dogmatically prescriptive criticism was inimical to the spirit and evolution of drama. The public, whether they knew who had written the play or not, reacted like the critics: *Fanny* was fun, and it became a box office hit, Shaw's first in London. It ran for 622 performances.

*Fanny* won the war for Shaw. This is not to say the critics stopped going for him, but they could not seriously question his preeminence any longer, not after he had put them so neatly and amusingly in their place. What about Shaw? Did the merciless panning he had received for *Getting Married* and *Misalliance* cause him to draw back from that kind of drama and acknowledge the Walkleyan demand for what was vital in the old dramatic modes, in particular the need to be a 'plot-monger', at least in sufficient measure to hold an audience's attention – to, in a word, satisfy a basic demand for a 'story'? Did *Fanny* signal his perception of this reality of his profession? One critic, a certain 'P.J.' writing for the *Saturday Review*, suggested, perhaps more acutely than he realized, that the play inaugurated a new mood in Shaw's career.[23] Hindsight seems to endorse this. Shaw himself would have denied any such change of tack. But the fact is that, if he did not abandon his aesthetic of a drama of ideas expressed in the interplay of words, he seems consciously to have shrunk his personal horizon the better to enable his near-sighted contemporaries to see what he was getting at. He gave them something of a 'plot' as an additive to his 'action-in-words'. A year after *Fanny* London had the benefit of a music-hall romp complete with a stage lion and a comical Roman Emperor; two years after that another 'potboiler', this one with a Cinderella plot, no less: *Pygmalion*. That – as far as this history is concerned – was the clincher.

# Notes

## INTRODUCTION: G.B.S. IN THE 1890s

1. One of the pieces in *Essays in Fabian Socialism*, 'The Common Sense of Municipal Trading', was published in 1904; all the others belong to the 1890s.
2. *Saturday Review* (London), 26 September 1896. *Our Theatres in the Nineties*, II, pp. 195–6.
3. Holbrook Jackson, *The Eighteen Nineties* (Harmondsworth: Pelican (Penguin), 1939, repr. 1950), p. 194.
4. *Bernard Shaw: Theatrics*, ed. Dan H. Laurence (Toronto: University of Toronto Press, 1995), p. 42.
5. *Star* (London), 10 December 1892; an unsigned notice but almost certainly by Walkley.
6. Appendix I: 'The Author to the Dramatic Critics', *Widowers' Houses* (London: Henry & Co., 1893), p. 102 *passim*.
7. *Athenaeum* (London), 28 April 1894.
8. *World* (London), 25 April 1894.
9. *Speaker* (London), 28 April 1894.
10. 5 November 1896. *Collected Letters, 1874–1897*, ed. Dan H. Laurence (London: Reinhardt, 1965), p. 695.
11. 8 November 1896. Ibid., p. 698.
12. *Critic* (New York), July–August 1898.
13. *The New York Times*, 3 October 1897.
14. *The New York Times Illustrated Magazine*, 10 October 1897.
15. 27 January 1900. *Bernard Shaw. Collected Letters, 1898–1910*, ed. Dan H. Laurence (London: Reinhardt, 1972), p. 143.


## CHAPTER 1 JANUARY–MAY 1901: A NATURAL-BORN MOUNTEBANK

1. *The Times* (London), 1 January 1901.
2. Kipling's 'Recessional' marked 1897, the year of the Queen's Diamond Jubilee; his 'The Young Queen' 1900, the year in which Australia became a Federation.
3. *The Times* (London), 23 January 1901. Austen's poem continues:

> Can it be
> That She who scarce but yesterday upheld
> The Dome of Empire, so the twain seemed one,
> Whose goodness shone and radiated round
> The circle of her still expanding Rule
> Whose Sceptre was self-sacrifice, whose Throne
> Only a loftier height from which to scan
> The purpose of her People, their desires
> Thoughts, hopes, fears, needs, joys, sorrows, sadnesses …

4. To the editor of the *Morning Leader*, undated, probably 27 January 1901. Parke's reply 28 January 1901. *Collected Letters, 1898–1910*, p. 216.

5. *Humane Review*, I (London), January 1901, pp. 298–315.

6. It has, however, been resuscitated after a lapse of ninety years and appeared in Shaw 10: *The Annual of Bernard Shaw Studies*, eds Stanley Weintraub and Fred D. Crawford (University Park: Pennsylvania State University Press, 1989).

7. *Three Plays for Puritans* was published by Grant Richards in London on 15 January 1901. The American edition (New York and Chicago: H. S. Stone) came out in February.

8. Preface to *Three Plays for Puritans*, pp. xxi–xxiv.

9. *Academy* (London), 9 February 1901.

10. Preface to *Three Plays for Puritans*, pp. xxxv–xxxvi.

11. *Daily Mail* (London), 7 February 1901.

12. Ibid., 2 April 1901.

13. *Candid Friend* (London), 11 and 18 May 1901.

14. *Shaw Gives Himself Away* (London: Gregynog, 1939).

15. *Sixteen Self Sketches* (London: Constable, 1949).

16. The bibliographies of 1899 and 1900, though not without their quota of entries, indicate a falling off of productivity, particularly regarding the publication of articles and larger works of general interest.

17. A portion of Archer's remarkable letter to Shaw is in *Collected Letters, 1898–1910*, pp. 356–7.

18. 'Epistle Dedicatory to Arthur Bingham Walkley' (Preface to *Man and Superman*), p.xxxi.

19. B. Ifor Evans, *A Short History of English Literature* (Harmondsworth: Penguin, 1961). p. 126.

## CHAPTER 2 1901–1902: PATHOLOGICAL EFFUSIONS

1. 4 August 1899. *Ellen Terry and Bernard Shaw. A Correspondence*, ed. Christopher St John (London: Reinhardt & Evans, 1949), p. 309.

2. 'The Sanity of Art', *Major Critical Essays*, p. 284.

3. 2 July 1894. *Collected Letters, 1874–1897*, p. 448.

4. 14 September 1901. *Collected Letters, 1898–1910*, p. 237.

5. In his letter to the *British Medical Journal* (London), 26 October 1901.

6. This letter is the only one of the controversy Shaw saw fit to include, slightly cut, in *Doctor's Delusions, Crude Criminology, and Sham Education*.

7. 22 February 1906. *Collected Letters, 1898–1910*, p. 607.

8. Ibid., p. 606.

9. 11 September 1905. Ibid., p. 558.

## CHAPTER 3 1903–1904: FABIAN SHAW

1. Edward R. Pease, *The History of the Fabian Society* (London: Cass, 1918, 3rd edn 1963), p. 284.

2. *The Diary of Beatrice Webb*, II, 1892–1905, 'All the Good Things of Life',

eds Norman and Jeanne MacKenzie (London: Virago and London School of Economics, 1983), p. 267.

3. Quoted by Steve Jones, 'No Further Room for Improvement', *Spectator* (London), 12 June 1993.
4. Patricia Pugh, *Educate, Agitate, Organise: One Hundred Years of Fabian Socialism* (London: Methuen, 1984; repr. Methuen University Paperback, 1987), p. 2.
5. Norman and Jeanne MacKenzie, *The Fabians* (New York: Simon & Schuster, 1977), p. 28.
6. John Palmer, 'Mr Bernard Shaw: An Epitaph', *Fortnightly Review* (London), XCVII, N.S., Jan.–Jun. 1915.
7. Pease, *The History of the Fabian Society*, p. 39.
8. 'Does Modern Education Ennoble?', *Great Thoughts* (London), 7 October 1905. *Doctor's Delusions, Crude Criminology and Sham Education*, p. 339.
9. 'An Educational Confession', *The Schoolmistress* (London), 17 November 1927. *Doctor's Delusions, Crude Criminology and Sham Education*, p. 355.
10. 'The Educated Working Man', *New Standards* (London), October 1923. *Doctor's Delusions, Crude Criminology and Sham Education*, pp. 334–5.
11. 'The Educated Working Man', p. 337.
12. 'Does Modern Education Ennoble?' *Doctor's Delusions, Crude Criminology and Sham Education*, p. 341.
13. Ibid.
14. 'Education and Electioneering', *Daily Mail* (London), 27 February 1904. *Doctor's Delusions, Crude Criminology and Sham Education*, p. 368.
15. 7 October 1903. *Collected Letters, 1898–1910*, p. 375.
16. 'The Fabian Society: What it has Done and How it has Done it', *Essays in Fabian Socialism*, p. 131.
17. See Pease, *The History of the Fabian Society*, pp. 81–2.
18. 30 June 1904. *Collected Letters, 1898–1910*, pp. 425–6.
19. Margaret Cole, *The Story of Fabian Socialism* (London: Heinemann, 1961), p. 95.
20. *Clarion* (London), 2 February 1906.
21. *The Diary of Beatrice Webb*, II, p. 287.
22. Dan H. Laurence, *Bernard Shaw: A Bibliography*, I (Oxford University Press, 1983), pp. 62–3.
23. Pease, *The History of the Fabian Society*, p. 160.
24. Norman and Jeanne Mackenzie, *The Fabians*, p. 302.
25. *Fabianism and the Fiscal Question* (London: Fabian Society, February 1904), p. 6.
26. Ibid., p. 22.
27. Ibid., p. 25.
28. See C. E. Hill, 'Shaw and Local Government', *Shaw and Politics*, ed. T. F. Evans. Shaw 11: *The Annual of Bernard Shaw Studies* (University Park: Pennsylvania State University Press, 1991), pp. 132–4.
29. 25 February 1904. *Collected Letters, 1898–1910*, p. 408.
30. 12 March 1904.

31. 3 March 1904. *The Diary of Beatrice Webb*, II, pp. 315–16.
32. *St James's Gazette* (London), 5 March 1904.
33. 7 March 1904. *The Diary of Beatrice Webb*, II, p. 318.
34. *New Age* (London), 4 April 1908.
35. Marion Barton, in a letter to *The New York Times*, 19 April 1933.

CHAPTER 4  1903–1905: INTERNATIONAL SHAW

1.  12 January 1903. *Collected Letters, 1898–1910*, pp. 300–1. Archer's article, 'The Two Georges' (*Morning Leader* of 10 January 1903) was in response to George Brandes' 'Bernard Shaw's Teater' (*Politikken* (Copenhagen) of 29 December 1902).
2.  7 November 1902. Ibid., p. 285.
3.  Assigned to 17 February 1903. Ibid., pp. 310–11.
4.  3 May 1903. Ibid., pp. 320–2.
5.  Ibid., p. 332.
6.  Ibid., p. 335.
7.  F. A. Mumby and Ian Norrie, *Publishing and Booksellers* (London: Cape, 1930, 5th edn 1974), p. 345.
8.  *Collected Letters, 1898–1910*, p. 332.
9.  19 June 1903. Ibid., pp. 332–4.
10. 13 July 1903. Ibid., p. 337.
11. *Daily News* (London), 22 August 1903.
12. *Saturday Review* (London), 12 September 1903.
13. 16 January 1903. *The Diary of Beatrice Webb*, II, p. 267.
14. 15 September 1903. *Collected Letters, 1898–1910*, pp. 372–3.
15. 21 September 1903. Add. Ms. 50529, Bernard Shaw Papers, British Library.
16. Add. Ms 50542, Bernard Shaw Papers, British Library.
17. Undated. Aylmer Maude, *The Life of Tolstoy: Later Years* (London: Oxford University Press, 1920), pp. 461–2.
18. Add. Ms. 50528, Bernard Shaw Papers, British Library.
19. 2 September 1903. *Collected Letters, 1898–1910*, p. 357.
20. Siegfried Trebitsch, *Chronicle of a Life*, trans. Eithne Wilkens and Ernst Kaiser (London: Heinemann, 1953), pp. 95–6.
21. Ibid., p. 96.
22. Preface to *Jitta's Atonement, Translations and Tomfooleries*, pp. 3–4.
23. 10 December 1902. *Collected Letters, 1898–1910*, p. 293.
24. 26 December 1902. Ibid., p. 297.
25. 15 January 1903. Ibid., p. 304.
26. 18 December 1902. Ibid., p. 294.
27. 11 August 1906. Ibid., p. 640.
28. 20 January 1908. Ibid., p. 753.
29. 4 April 1906. Ibid., p. 615.
30. 28 July 1908. *Bernard Shaw: Theatrics*, p. 89.
31. This figure comes from *Collected Letters, 1898–1910*, p. 382; Henderson gives $350. *George Bernard Shaw: Man of the Century* (New York: Appleton-Century-Crofts, 1956), p. 476. Henderson's figure may be a trifle low, even for Daly.

32.  Henderson, *George Bernard Shaw: Man of the Century*, p. 476.
33.  4 January 1904. *Collected Letters, 1898–1910*, p. 395.
34.  *The New York Times*, 9 December 1903.
35.  Both Laurence and Henderson give 5 January as the opening date, but newspaper reviews make it clear that the opening was on Monday, 9 January 1905.
36.  *The New York Times*, 10 January 1905.
37.  This memorandum is discussed in a later chapter, '1904–1905: Shavian Farragoes'.
38.  *Collected Letters, 1898–1910*, p. 567.
39.  *The New York Times*, 11 October 1905.
40.  24 December 1905. *Collected Letters, 1898–1910*, p. 587.
41.  Assigned to 4 January 1904. *Collected Letters, 1898–1910*, pp. 398–9.
42.  Unless otherwise indicated, all references pertaining to the controversy are from *The New York Times*, 25 October 1905 – 2 November 1905.
43.  22–23 September 1905. *Collected Letters, 1898–1910*, p. 559.
44.  Ibid.
45.  *Critic* (New York), XLVII, November 1905, p. 388.
46.  December 1907. *Collected Letters, 1898–1910*, p. 739.
47.  Ibid., p. 740.

CHAPTER 5  1901-1910: TRANSFORMATION

1.  'The Sanity of Art', *Major Critical Essays*, p. 283.
2.  *The Times* (London), 25 March 1903.
3.  Ibid., 31 May 1904.
4.  23 July 1903. *The Diary of Beatrice Webb*, II, p. 289.
5.  *The Times* (London), 9 September 1904.
6.  Neville Cardus, *Second Innings* (London: Collins, 1950), p. 110.
7.  *Manchester Guardian*, 23 October 1905.
8.  *Blackwood's Edinburgh Magazine*, April 1910.
9.  *Daily Express* (London), 4 October 1907.
10.  'Man and Bannerman', *Punch* (London), 17 March 1906.
11.  'Dress and the Writer: A Talk with Mr George Bernard Shaw', *World of Dress* (London), March 1905.
12.  A. W. Pinero, *Mid-Channel* (London: Heinemann, 1922), p. 44.
13.  William Archer Papers, Add. Ms. 45296, British Library. Published 22 February 1906, the newspaper not indicated.
14.  14 October 1905. *The Diary of Beatrice Webb*, II, p. 355–6.

CHAPTER 6  1890–1904: PRIVATE VENTURE, PUBLIC ENTERPRISE

1.  Michael Orme, *J. T. Grein: the Story of a Pioneer, 1862–1935* (London: Murray, 1936), p. 76.
2.  Ibid., p. 102.
3.  Ibid., p. 78.
4.  14 March 1891. *Collected Letters, 1874–1897*, p. 285.
5.  *Sunday Times* (London), 27 February 1910.

6. *Saturday Review* (London), 26 January 1895. *Our Theatres in the Nineties,* I, p. 19.
7. Ibid.
8. *Bernard Shaw's Letters to Granville Barker,* ed. C. B. Purdom (London: Phoenix House, 1956), p. 2.
9. Ibid., p. 4.
10. 'Granville-Barker: Some Particulars by Shaw', *Drama* (London), Winter 1946, p. 7.
11. Max Beerbohm, 'Mr Shaw's Position', *Saturday Review* (London), 9 December 1905.
12. 2 January 1901. *Bernard Shaw's Letters to Granville-Barker,* p. 8.
13. *Mrs Warren's Profession* (London: Grant Richards, 1902.)
14. 20 June 1902. *Collected Letters, 1898–1910,* p. 276.
15. Allan Wade, 'Shaw and the Stage Society', *Drama* (London), Spring 1951.
16. See R. Mander and J. Mitchenson, 'The Royal Court Theatre', *The Theatres of London* (London: Hart-Davis, 1961), p. 154.
17. 'Granville-Barker: Some Particulars by Shaw'.
18. 21 April 1903. *Granville Barker and His Correspondents,* ed. Eric Salmon (Detroit, Mich.: Wayne State University Press, 1986), p. 41.
19. 27 September 1903. *Bernard Shaw's Letters to Granville-Barker,* p. 20.
20. *Morning Post* (London), during the controversy following the première of *Major Barbara,* 29 November–5 December 1905.
21. Irene Vanbrugh, *To Tell My Story* (London: Hutchinson, 1948, repr. Dec. 1950), p. 72.
22. 16 March [1904?]. *Granville Barker and His Correspondents,* p. 44.
23. *The Times Literary Supplement* (London), 7 September 1946.
24. 25 November 1905. *Ellen Terry and Bernard Shaw: A Correspondence,* p. 389.

CHAPTER 7 1904–1907: THE TWENTY-NINE PERCENTERS

1. H. G. Wells, *Experiment in Autobiography* (London: Gollancz & Cresset, 1966), pp. 621–2.
2. 16 February–6 October 1905. *The Collected Letters of Joseph Conrad,* III, eds Frederick R. Karl and Laurence Davis (Cambridge University Press, 1988).
3. 17 January 1909. *Collected Letters, 1898–1910,* pp. 827–8.
4. Duncan Wilson, *Gilbert Murray O.M., 1866–1957* (Oxford University Press, 1987), p. 94.
5. 23 March 1902. Quoted by Isobel Henderson, 'The Teacher of Greek', in Murray, *An Unfinished Autobiography,* eds Jean Smith and Arnold Toynbee (London: Allen & Unwin, 1960), p. 135.
6. Wilson, *Gilbert Murray O.M., 1866–1957,* p. 94.
7. Ibid., p. 105.
8. From Murray's first Presidential address to the Classical Association. Quoted by E. R. Dodds in Introduction: Murray, *An Unfinished Autobiography,* p. 15.
9. 'On Translating Greek Tragedy', *Essays in Honour of Gilbert Murray,*

eds J. A. K. Thomson and A. J. Toynbee (London: Allen & Unwin, 1936), p. 245.

10. Ibid., p. 243.
11. Monday, January 1905. *Granville Barker and His Correspondents*, p. 209.
12. 5 March 1905. *Collected Letters, 1898–1910*, p. 519.
13. *World* (London), 25 October 1904.
14. 23 October 1904.
15. Wilson, *Gilbert Murray O.M., 1866–1957*, p. 105.
16. Purdom, *Harley Granville Barker* (London: Rockliff, 1955), p. 35.
17. Ibid.
18. Ibid.
19. *The Times Literary Supplement* (London), 14 April 1905.
20. Fn., Sybil Thorndike and Lewis Casson, 'The Theatre and Gilbert Murray', in Murray, *An Unfinished Autobiography*, p. 154.
21. 'Euripides in London', *Nineteenth Century and After* (London), LIX, January–June 1906.
22. *Fortnightly Review* (London), LXXXI, January–June 1907.
23. *Sunday Times* (London), 1 October 1905.
24. *The Times Literary Supplement* (London), 29 September 1905.
25. *Saturday Review* (London), 7 October 1905.
26. *World* (London), 3 October 1905.
27. 26 February 1907. Cited by permission of the Trustees of the Theatre Museum (Victoria and Albert Museum), London.
28. From the *Tribune, The Times Literary Supplement* and the *Observer* in the week following the opening.
29. To A. W. Pinero, 17 March 1910. *Collected Letters, 1898–1910*, p. 912.
30. 18 June 1909. *Collected Letters, 1898–1910*, pp. 847–8.
31. Purdom, *Harley Granville Barker*, p. 15.
32. *The Times* (London), 28 January 1902.
33. 8 April 1922. *Granville Barker and His Correspondents*, p. 158.
34. *The Old Drama and the New: An Essay in Re-valuation* (London: Heinemann, 1923), pp. 357–64.
35. *Saturday Review* (London), 11 November 1905.
36. *The Times Literary Supplement* (London), 12 November 1905.
37. *World* (London), 14 November 1905.
38. 11 August 1905. *Granville Barker and His Correspondents*, p. 158.
39. To McNulty, 27 June 1908. *Collected Letters, 1898–1910*, p. 790.
40. Circa 20–24 May 1907. *Collected Letters, 1898–1910*, p. 686.
41. Purdom, *Harley Granville Barker*, pp. 102–3.
42. 13 July 1905. *Letters from John Galsworthy 1900–1932*, ed. Edward Garnett (London: Cape, 1934), p. 96.
43. 25 January 1907. Ibid., p. 131.
44. *Daily Telegraph* (London), 14 February 1932.
45. 10 March 1906. *Letters from John Galsworthy*, p. 116.
46. H. W. Marrott: *The Life and Letters of John Galsworthy* (London: Heinemann, 1936), p. 137.
47. 'Some Platitudes Concerning Drama', *Fortnightly Review* (London), December 1909.
48. Thursday, September 1906. *Letters from John Galsworthy*, p. 121.

49. *The Life and Letters of John Galsworthy*, p. 196.
50. Purdom, *Harley Granville Barker*, p. 59.
51. These notices followed the opening on 25 September 1906.
52. 21 April 1907. *Bernard Shaw's Letters to Granville Barker*, p. 81.
53. 7 July 1908. Desmond MacCarthy, *The Court Theatre 1904–1907. A Commentary and Criticism* (originally published London: Bullen, 1907; edition used Coral Gables, Fla.: University of Miami, 1966, ed. Stanley Weintraub), p. 171.
54. Theodore Stier, *With Pavlova Round the World* (London: Hurst & Blackett, 1929), pp. 264–5.
55. These notices followed the opening on 8 January 1907.
56. 22 January 1907. Cited by permission of the Trustees of the Theatre Museum (Victoria and Albert Museum), London.
57. MacCarthy, *The Court Theatre, 1904–1907*, p. 172.
58. 10 July 1907. Bernard Shaw Papers, British Museum.
59. Laurence Housman, *The Unexpected Years* (London: Cape, 1937), pp. 218–19.
60. 9 July 1904. *Granville Barker and His Correspondents*, pp. 203–4.
61. 29 December 1904. Ibid., p. 208.
62. Purdom, *Harley Granville Barker*, pp. 32–3.
63. *Saturday Review (London)*, 11 May 1907.
64. Housman, *The Unexpected Years*, p. 219. Housman's first play, *Bethlehem*, was refused a licence by the Lord Chamberlain.
65. These notices followed the opening on 9 April 1907.

CHAPTER 8 1904–1905: SHAVIAN FARRAGOES

1. 12 March 1900. *The Letters of W. B. Yeats*, ed. Allan Wade (London: Hart-Davis, 1954), p. 335.
2. Preface to *John Bull's Other Island*, p. 13.
3. 5 October 1904. Bernard Shaw Papers, British Library. Published in part in *Collected Letters, 1898–1910*, pp. 452–3.
4. 7 November 1904. *The Letters of W. B. Yeats*, p. 42.
5. 12 June 1904. *Ellen Terry and Bernard Shaw: A Correspondence*, p. 372.
6. 4 August 1904. *Bernard Shaw's Letters to Granville Barker*, p. 22.
7. 25 August 1904. *Collected Letters, 1898–1910*, p. 445.
8. *Daily Mail* (London), 30 August 1904.
9. Unless otherwise indicated, quotations relating to *John Bull's Other Island* are from *Bernard Shaw's Letters to Granville Barker*, August–December 1904, pp. 22–45.
10. Add. Ms. 50615, Bernard Shaw Papers, British Library.
11. All notices cited here followed the opening on 1 November 1904.
12. *Tatler* (London), 16 November 1904.
13. 6 November 1904.
14. 15 February 1905.
15. *The Diary of Beatrice Webb*, II, p. 351.
16. 7 May 1905.
17. 26 November 1904. *Collected Letters, 1898–1910*, p. 468.
18. Purdom, *Harley Granville Barker*, p. 30.

19.  Purdom, *A Guide to the Plays of Bernard Shaw* (London: Methuen University Paperback, 1964), p. 168.
20.  14 March 1905. *Collected Letters, 1898–1910*, p. 522.
21.  Purdom, *Harley Granville Barker*, p. 33.
22.  5 July 1896. *Ellen Terry and Bernard Shaw: A Correspondence*, p. 29.
23.  8 September 1896. Ibid., p. 52.
24.  Ibid., p. 178.
25.  27 January 1900. *Collected Letters, 1898–1910*, p. 140.
26.  4 May 1900.
27.  6 December 1904. *Collected Letters, 1898–1910*, p. 471–2.
28.  See Alan Andrews, 'From the Page to the Stage: The Theatrical Realization of *Man and Superman*', *Bernard Shaw on Stage*, eds E. W. Conolly and Ellen Pearson (Guelph: University of Guelph, 1991.)
29.  See *Collected Letters, 1898–1910*, p. 529.
30.  *The Times Literary Supplement* (London), 26 May 1905.
31.  *World* (London), 30 May 1905.
32.  25 May 1905.
33.  Archer, *The Vedrenne–Barker Season, 1904–1905 (Royal Court Theatre, Sloane Square, S.W.)* (London: D. Allen & Son, 1905), p. 10.

## CHAPTER 9  1905–1906: SHAVIAN PROFANITIES

1.  2 October 1905. *Collected Letters, 1898–1910*, p. 565.
2.  24 December 1905. Ibid., p. 589.
3.  29 November 1905. Ibid., p. 585.
4.  *Daily Telegraph* (London), 19 October 1905.
5.  8 December 1905.
6.  29 November 1905. *Collected Letters, 1898–1910*, p. 585.
7.  *Our Partnership*, eds Barbara Drake and Margaret J. Cole (London: Longmans, Green & Co., 1948), p. 314.
8.  4 December 1905. *The Letters of Sidney and Beatrice Webb: Partnership*, II, 1892–1912, ed. Norman Mackenzie (Cambridge: University Press and London School of Economics and Political Science, 1978), p. 216.
9.  The quotations that follow are from the *Morning Post* (London), 29 November 1905 – 5 December 1905.
10.  *World* (London), 3 December 1905.
11.  1 January 1906. *Collected Letters, 1898–1910*, p. 599.
12.  *The Times* (London), 29 November 1905.
13.  28 November 1905; 2 December 1905.
14.  27 August 1905. *Ellen Terry and Bernard Shaw: A Correspondence*, p. 382.
15.  25 November 1905. *Collected Letters, 1898–1910*, p. 581.
16.  14 March 1906. Ibid., p. 607.
17.  5 May 1906. *Ellen Terry and Bernard Shaw: A Correspondence*, p. 394.
18.  27 May 1906. *Collected Letters, 1898–1910*, pp. 623–4.
19.  16 May 1906. Cited by permission of the Trustees of the Theatre Museum (Victoria and Albert Museum), London.
20.  *Circa* July 1897. *Ellen Terry and Bernard Shaw: A Correspondence*, p. 202.
21.  *The Court Theatre, 1904–1907: A Commentary and Criticism*, p. 80.
22.  19 July 1906. *Bernard Shaw's Letters to Granville Barker*, p. 65.

## CHAPTER 10 1906–JULY 1907: SHAVIAN BAD TASTE

1. *Tribune* (London), 14 July 1906.
2. 21 August 1906. *Bernard Shaw's Letters to Granville Barker*, p. 69.
3. 3 September 1906.
4. 4 December 1906. *Collected Letters, 1898–1910*, p. 664.
5. 28 August 1906. *Bernard Shaw's Letters to Granville Barker*, p. 70.
6. 'Granville-Barker: Some Particulars by Shaw', *Drama* (London), Winter 1946, p. 9.
7. 17 October 1906. Cited by permission of the Trustees of the Theatre Museum (Victoria and Albert Museum), London.
8. *Bernard Shaw: Theatrics*, pp. 75–6.
9. *Tribune* (London), 21 November 1906.
10. *Morning Post* (London), 22 November 1906.
11. *Collected Letters, 1898–1910*, pp. 136.
12. Ibid., p. 242.
13. *Bernard Shaw's Letters to Granville Barker*, p. 74.
14. 28 August 1896. *Bernard Shaw and Ellen Terry: A Correspondence*, p. 38.
15. 8 June 1903. *Collected Letters, 1898–1910*, p. 328.
16. Ibid., p. 376.
17. 28 December 1906. *Bernard Shaw's Letters to Granville Barker*, p. 73.
18. *The Times Literary Supplement* (London), 8 February 1907.
19. 26 February 1907. To Vedrenne; cited by permission of the Trustees of the Theatre Museum (Victoria and Albert Museum), London.
20. 27 December 1905. *Collected Letters, 1898–1910*, p. 590.
21. 24 May 1907. Ibid., p. 690.
22. *The Times Literary Supplement* (London), 7 June 1907.
23. Henderson, *George Bernard Shaw: Man of the Century*, p. 580.
24. *Bernard Shaw's Letters to Granville Barker*, p. 89.
25. 24 May 1907. *Collected Letters, 1898–1910*, p. 691.
26. 28 November 1895. *Ellen Terry and Bernard Shaw: A Correspondence*, p. 18.
27. This 'Souvenir' pamphlet was subsequently reprinted in the *Shaw Review* of May 1959 and as an Appendix in MacCarthy's *The Court Theatre, 1904–1907*, ed. Stanley Weintraub.

## CHAPTER 11 1904–1907: PRICE AND VALUE

1. *The Green Room Book*, ed. John Parker (London: Seaby Clark, 1907), p. 480.
2. In replying to the proposal, 'Health of the Guests of the Evening', at the testimonial dinner, Criterion Restaurant, 7 July 1907. In MacCarthy, The *Court Theatre, 1904–1907*, ed. Stanley Weintraub, p. 163.
3. Purdom, *Harley Granville Barker*, p. 65.
4. William Archer Papers, Add. Ms. 45,296, pp. 212–21, British Library. The context is a plea for money for the endowment of a National Theatre. The document, dated 4 March 1909, is a draft memorandum (a 'Letter to Millionaires'), written by Shaw for Archer and Dame

Edith Lyttleton. It does not appear to have been used.
5.  Archer, *The Old Drama and the New*, p. 340.
6.  In replying to the toast, 'The Authors of the Court Theatre', at the testimonial dinner, Criterion Restaurant, 7 July 1907.
7.  This is Bernard F. Dukore's *Bernard Shaw, Director* (London: Allen & Unwin, 1971).
8.  In a letter to Archer, 21 April 1903. *Granville Barker and His Contemporaries*, p. 42.
9.  H. Granville Barker, *The Exemplary Theatre* (London: Chatto & Windus, 1922), pp. 222–4.
10. Ibid., pp. 225–6.
11. Casson, 'G.B.S. and the Court Theatre', *Listener* (London), 12 July 1951.
12. McCarthy, *Myself and My Friends* (London: Butterworth, 1933), p. 59.
13. Casson, 'G.B.S. at Rehearsal', *Drama*, Spring 1951.
14. Hardwicke, *A Victorian in Orbit* (London: Methuen, 1961), p. 133.
15. 'G.B.S. at Rehearsal'.
16. 'Thanks to Bernard Shaw', *Theatrical Companion to Shaw* (London: Rockliff, 1954), p. 14.
17. 'G.B.S. at Rehearsal'.
18. 23 November 1904. Bernard Shaw Papers, British Library.
19. 2 November 1904. Ibid.
20. Personal interview, 1969.
21. *Theatre Arts* (New York), September 1949.
22. 'Notes on Directing Shaw', *Shaw and Other Playwrights*, ed. John A. Bertolini, Shaw 13, *The Annual of Bernard Shaw Studies* (University Park: Pennsylvania State University Press, 1993), p. 136.
23. 7 July 1907, Criterion Restaurant.
24. *Saturday Review* (London), 11 November 1905.
25. *The Court Theatre, 1904–1907*, pp. 12–17.

### CHAPTER 12  1907–1908: STORMING THE CITADEL

1.  Dan H. Laurence Collection, Archival Collections, University of Guelph Library.
2.  To Vedrenne, 27 July 1907. *Collected Letters, 1898–1910*, p. 703.
3.  1 July 1907. Dan H. Laurence Collection, Archival Collections, University of Guelph Library.
4.  10 October 1907. *Collected Letters, 1898–1910*, p. 715.
5.  *The New York Times*, 31 October 1906.
6.  'Bernard Shaw and the Heroic Actor', *Play Pictorial*, X, October 1907.
7.  *Yorkshire Post* (Leeds), 17 September 1907.
8.  *The Times* (London), 26 November 1907. Other notices cited here appeared on the same date.
9.  *Bernard Shaw's Letters to Granville Barker*, p. 112.
10. 4 December 1907. *Collected Letters, 1898–1910*, pp. 737–8.
11. Undated, December 1907. *Collected Letters, 1898–1910*, p. 740.
12. Dan H. Laurence Collection, Archival Collections, University of Guelph Library.

13. 19 August 1908. *Collected Letters, 1898–1910*, p. 809.
14. 1 March 1911. *Bernard Shaw's Letters to Granville Barker*, p. 171.
15. 3 April 1908. Ibid., p. 120.
16. These comments taken in turn from the *Daily Mail*, 13 May 1908; *Daily Telegraph*, 13 May 1908; Baughan in the *Daily News*, 13 May 1908; Walkley – a relatively mild-minded Walkley, to whom Shaw had given the text of *Getting Married* two or three days before the performance – in *The Times* of 13 May 1907.
17. See *Bernard Shaw and Alfred Douglas. A Correspondence*, ed. Mary Hyde (London: Murray, 1982), p. xxxi.
18. Anonymous, 'Chronicle and Comment', *Bookman* (New York), August 1908.
19. 4 July 1931. *Bernard Shaw and Alfred Douglas. A Correspondence*, p. 12.
20. 6 July 1931. Ibid., p. 13.
21. *Daily Mail* (London), 14 May 1908.
22. 22–23 May 1908. *Collected Letters, 1898–1910*, p. 786.
23. 29 June 1908. Ibid., p. 792.

CHAPTER 13  1908–1909: DOWN WITH THE CENSOR!

1. *The Times* (London), 6 August 1909.
2. Samuel Hynes, *The Edwardian Turn of Mind* (London: Oxford University Press, 1968), p. 222.
3. *The Times* (London), 30 July 1909.
4. 4 November 1907. *Collected Letters, 1898–1910*, p. 718.
5. 10 October 1907. Ibid., p. 715.
6. No date, probably 24 and 25 February 1908. Purdom, *Harley Granville Barker*, p. 78.
7. *Star* (London), 18 October 1889. *London Music in 1888–89*, p. 231.
8. 'The Late Censor', *Our Theatres in the Nineties*, I, pp. 48–55.
9. 1 March 1895. *Collected Letters, 1874–1897*, p. 489.
10. 'The Late Censor', p. 54.
11. 19 August 1897. *Collected Letters, 1874–1897*, pp. 796–7.
12. 12 March 1898. *Collected Letters, 1898–1910*, p. 13.
13. 14 March 1898. Quoted by Laurence, Ibid., p. 14.
14. *Our Theatres in the Nineties*, III, pp. 350–1.
15. In 'The Solution of the Censorship Problem', *Academy* (London), 29 June 1907.
16. *Sketch* (London), 26 July 1905.
17. *Observer* (London), 23 May 1909.
18. Ibid.
19. *The Times* (London), 29 May 1909.
20. Ibid., 4 June 1909.
21. Ibid., 7 June 1909.
22. Ibid., 26 June 1909.
23. See '*Punch*: J. M. Barrie's Gentle Swipe at "Supershaw"', ed. Leon H. Hugo, *The Annual of Bernard Shaw Studies*, 10, eds Stanley Weintraub and Fred D. Crawford (University Park: Pennsylvania State University Press, 1990).

24. See 'Shakespear v. Shaw', by J. B. Fagan, ed. Leon H. Hugo, *Shaw Review* XIII, 3, ed. Stanley Weintraub (University Park), September 1970.
25. *The Times* (London), 30 July 1909. Unless otherwise indicated, references to the hearings of the Joint Select Committee are derived from *The Times* of 30 July 1909 to 3 November 1909. Many papers reported in some detail on the proceedings, but none more meticulously than *The Times*, through whose accounts the interested reader could keep abreast of the proceedings week by week. Shaw himself would find occasion to congratulate *The Times* on the excellence of its reporting.
26. 28 July 1909. *Collected Letters, 1898–1910*, p. 852.
27. 31 July 1909. Ibid., p. 854.
28. Ibid.
29. Ibid., p. 748.
30. 17 July 1909. Ibid., p. 850. The 'Milton' referred to is his *Areopagitica*, published in 1640; it is to be doubted whether Shaw's statement 'supersedes' the earlier, rather more amply and nobly expressed objection to the censorship.
31. 31 July 1909. Ibid., pp. 853–4.
32. Shaw's evidence is on pp. 46–53 of the Minutes of Evidence of the *Report from the Joint Select Committee of the House of Lords and the House of Commons on the Stage Plays (Censorship) together with the Proceedings of the Committee, Minutes of Evidence, and Appendices* (London: H.M. Stationery Office, 11 November 1909). Paragraph numbers (879–965) have been omitted.
33. 31 July 1909. *Collected Letters, 1898–1910*, p. 854.
34. Hynes, *The Edwardian Turn of Mind*, p. 234.
35. See the Preface to *The Shewing-Up of Blanco Posnet*, pp. 408–25.

## CHAPTER 14  1910: SHAVIAN NASTINESS

1. 'The Rejected Statement', Preface to *The Shewing-Up of Blanco Posnet*, p. 374.
2. 29 November 1909. *Collected Letters, 1898–1910*, p. 887.
3. October 1909. Ibid., p. 882.
4. 4 May 1909. Ibid, p. 842.
5. 3 October 1909. Ibid., p. 871.
6. *The Diary of Beatrice Webb*, III, 1905–24, 'The Power to Alter Things', eds Norman and Jeanne MacKenzie (London: Virago and London School of Economics, 1984), p. 331.
7. Their notices appeared on 24 February 1910.
8. *Saturday Review* (London), 26 February 1910.
9. 27 February 1910.
10. *Sunday Times* (London), 27 February 1910.
11. *Observer* (London), 12 June 1910.
12. 17 September 1929. *Bernard Shaw: Theatrics*, p. 185.
13. This was an address by Walkley at a dinner in aid of the Royal General Theatrical Fund, held on 12 June and reported in *The Times* on 13 June 1910. Dan H. Laurence attributes 'Leaving Aristotle Out'

to Walkley, by inference, then, also 'Got and the New Dramaturgy'. *Bernard Shaw: A Bibliography* II, p. 641.

14. *The Times* (London), 12 May 1910.

## CHAPTER 15 1910: EDWARDIAN SHAW

1. 29 June 1908. *Collected Letters, 1898–1910*, p. 791.
2. To Beulah Jay, 17 November 1917. *Bernard Shaw: Theatrics*, p. 142.
3. 31 December 1909. *Collected Letters, 1898–1910*, p. 823.
4. 'Mainly About Myself,' Preface to *Plays Unpleasant*, p. xix.
5. Preface to *Widowers' Houses* (1893), *Prefaces by Bernard Shaw* (London: Constable, 1934), p. 671.
6. Preface to *Plays Pleasant*, p. vii.
7. 8 August 1899. *Ellen Terry and Bernard Shaw: A Correspondence*, pp. 312–13.
8. 6 April 1896. Ibid., p. 26.
9. Dryden's translator's licence here – 'Alban' is of course the ancient term for England – suggests that he, like Shaw two hundred years later, was not averse to adapting the words of classical antiquity to suit contemporary national sentiment.
10. *G. B. Shaw: An Annotated Bibliography of Writings About Him*, I: 1871–1930, compiled and edited by J. P. Wearing (Dekalb, Northern Illinois University Press: 1986). The years scrutinized, 1901–1910, are on pp. 13–112.
11. *Cornhill Magazine* (London), April 1905.
12. G. K. Chesterton, *Heretics* (London and New York: John Lane, 1905).
13. Anonymous, 'Yellow Dramatist', *Outlook* (New York), 25 November 1905.
14. *Current Literature* (New York), December 1905.
15. *Fortnightly Review* (London), May 1906.
16. 3 June 1907. William Archer Papers, Add. Ms. 45296, p. 185, British Library.
17. *Independent* (New York), March 1908.
18. 19 April 1917. *Bernard Shaw: Theatrics*, p. 136.
19. Henry L. Mencken, *George Bernard Shaw: His Plays* (Boston: John Luce, 1905).
20. Gunnar Castron, *George Bernard Shaw* (Helsinki: Forlagsaktiebolaget Helios, 1906).
21. Holbrook Jackson, *Bernard Shaw* (London: Grant Richards, 1907).
22. C. J. A. van Bruggen, *George Bernard Shaw* (Haerlem: H. D. Tjeenk Willink and Zoon, 1908), in the series *Mannen en Vrouwen van Beteekenis in Onze Dagen*, gen. ed. J. Kalff Jr.
23. G. K. Chesterton, *George Bernard Shaw* (London: Lane, 1906).
24. G. K. Chesterton, *Autobiography* (London: Hutchinson, 1936, repr. 1949), p. 224.
25. Belloc and Chesterton, *New Age* (London), 15 February 1908.
26. 'Chesterton on Shaw', Nation (London), 25 August 1909. *Pen Portraits and Reviews*, pp. 81–9.
27. Chesterton, *George Bernard Shaw* (London: Bodley Head, 1949), p. 21.

28. Julius Bab, *Bernard Shaw* (Berlin: S. Fisher, 1910).
29. Archibald Henderson, *George Bernard Shaw: His Life and Works* (London: Hurst & Blackett; Cincinatti: Stewart & Kidd, 1911).

POSTSCRIPT 1911: *FANNY'S FIRST PLAY*

1. J. K. Galbraith, *A Life in Our Times* (1981).
2. Francis Bacon, *Apophthegms* (1625).
3. John Dryden, *The Conquest of Granada* (1670).
4. 'Maxims for Revolutionists', *Man and Superman*, p. 213.
5. Alexander Pope, *An Essay on Criticism* (1711).
6. P. G. Wodehouse, *New York Mirror*, 27 May 1955.
7. Christopher Hampton, *Sunday Times* (London), 1977.
8. *The New York Times*, 5 November 1950.
9. These terms, 'horizon of expectations', 'aesthetic distance' and 'culinary' are derived from the Theory of Reception Aesthetics of Hans-Robert Jauss.
10. *Collected Letters, 1911–1925*, p. 146.
11. Purdom, *A Guide to the Plays of Bernard Shaw*, pp. 238–9.
12. *Pall Mall Gazette* (London), 21 April 1911.
13. Preface to *Fanny's First Play*, p. 248.
14. See Charles A. Carpenter Jr, 'Shaw's Cross-Section of Anti-Shavian Opinion', *Shaw Review* (University Park), VII, 3 (September 1964) for a revealing analysis of Shaw's schematic representation of critical opinion.
15. *Fanny's First Play*, Induction, pp. 255–6.
16. Ibid., p. 261.
17. Ibid., Epilogue, pp. 322–4.
18. Ibid., pp. 321–2.
19. Ibid., p. 323.
20. *The Times* (London), 20 April 1911.
21. *Daily News* (London), 20 April 1911.
22. 'Fanny's Second Play', *Bookman* (New York), November 1912.
23. *Saturday Review* (London), 22 April 1911.

# Index